Marriage Breakdown and Divorce Law Reform in Contemporary Society

Marriage Breakdown and Divorce Law Reform in Contemporary Society

S. JAFFER HUSSAIN

Foreword by

V.R. Krishna Iyer

CONCEPT PUBLISHING COMPANY (P) Ltd.,
NEW DELHI-110 059

The Indian Council of Social Science Research gave the financial support towards the publication of this work. However, the responsibility for the contents of the book—facts, opinions, conclusions, etc.—is entirely that of the author and not of the ICSSR

2010

Published and Printed by

Concept
Since 1974

Conçept Publishing Company (P) Ltd.

Regd. Office:

A/15-16, Commercial Block, Mohan Garden
New Delhi-110059 (India)

Editorial Office:

H-13, Bali Nagar, New Delhi-110 015, India.

Phones : 25351460, 25351794, *Fax* : 091-11-25357109

Email : publishing@conceptpub.com,
Website: www.conceptpub.com

FOREWORD

THERE are two types of law books—some are written with passion for reforms, others with accent on information, although both are geared to instruction. Dr. Jaffer Hussain's comparative study of divorce laws and reforms in America and in India belong to the latter category which unobtrusively blends advocacy of a cause with accurate and adequate erudition. I prefer warm argument based on cold facts to cold neutrality charged with mere learning; and so it is that I write this brief foreword, appreciating the author's purposive presentation. A developing country like India with much leeway to be made up in its lawways, cannot but take sides when progressive trends are resisted by orthodox forces in sensitive areas like family laws. Dr. Hussain's contribution, marked by well-arranged case-law, well-planned structure and well-argued thesis, is a welcome addition to the not-so-plentiful literature on comparative matrimonial law.

Indian humanity is not an island but part of the continent of homosapiens. And so, in this inter-acting world, life and law, individual and institutional, must be viewed in collective perspective. History and geography abolish social insularity, and trans-national glimpses of legal development have a special value in understanding our own legal system. From this angle Dr. Hussain's comparative study of a vital branch of family law in India and America, both of which have been through different aspects of colonial rule, is interesting and edifying. The soils are different, the skins are different, the heritages are different and the religions and social conditions are different but the basic impulses which project the institution of marriage are the same. Likewise, the social milieu, conditioned by myriad variables, has compelled the fabrication of divorce as complementary to marriage in both countries, despite stubborn resistance by some religions. The zigzag course, the mosaic of forms and the impact on ancient currents of modern winds, make for a rich harvest in the field of socio-legal investigation. And here, judges, legislators and leaders of reformist movements are the major actors. Naturally, enactments and decided cases supersede Manu, Moses and Mahommad, sometimes by interpretative operations, sometimes by legislative departures. *Vox populi vox dei* and judges and parliamentarians represent, in some measure, the *zeitgeist*. Activist judges, a perusal of Dr. Hussain's book will prove, are mysteriously veiled legislators, at once conservative and liberal and even radical, and maintaining a progressive continuity between the past, the present and the future. More plainly, the legislators also react to the pushes and pressures of popular wishes pro and con, and the conflict between the thesis and antithesis gives rise to a new legislated synthesis. Thus the march of society's legal life keeps pace with contemporary hopes and fears. These broad generalities are mirrored in the well-documented dissertation of Dr. Hussain which now re-incarnates as a book on Divorce with primary focus on India fortified by Anglo-American sidelights.

A nation's integrity depends largely on the cohesive strength of its units. So long as the family is the unit, it was not, in several communities in the past, and is not, in some countries of the West and East now—the institution of marriage commands people's attention and its solemnity or looseness, its rigidity or flexibility, its unbreakability or easy dissolution deserves careful legal engineering. India—and other countries too—has another perplexity injected into the issue—the plurality of "totalitarian" religions claiming to channel personal laws relating to secular matters like marriage and succession and even gifts, along sacred courses. The demand for a common civil code, constitutionally sanctified in Article 44 has a bearing on national solidarity. One citizenship, one system of law. But the processes of legal manipulation of sensitive topics like marriage and divorce, when these are rooted in history, sentiment and religion, demand statesmanship more than logic, realism more than ideology. Nevertheless, the national streams must flow forward towards the goal since stagnation is petrifaction. Dr. Hussain's study provides inter-continental raw material for social scientists to advance the cause of secular family law and strikes a forward-looking note.

Law is evolutionary, but jurists with a creative bent may mould its course in the desired direction. This process is discernible in the handling by Dr. Hussain of "breakdown" and "no fault" *vis-a-vis* divorce. There is no conscious propagandist effort but the compelling logic of the argument, reinforced by Anglo-American developments, is more powerful than pamphleteering.

Indians, despite independencc, have continued under British and American influence, in the field of law and technology; and our intellectuals are generally under their ideological spell. Therefore, the best way to sell a reformist idea is to point to these trans-Atlantic nations. That is the value of Dr. Hussain's comparative study.

I have cursorily paged through the book—not thoroughly though—and am impressed with the manner of marshalling the chapters, the force of the presentation and the thrust of his submission. A comparative study widens our vision and deepens our learning. Our scholars and sociologists must know what the developments in this area of law are in other countries which affect our thoughtways. Dr. Hussain has dealt adequately, though not tediously, with divorce law in America. The historical background, the judicial approach, the statutory changes, the fortunes of grounds like breakdown, incompatibility and desertion, a social audit of the progress in the various States—these are all covered selectively and carefully, without encumbering the pages with profusion of details.

A similar statement and appraisal of the English law on the subject has been made together with a welcome study of the Divorce Reforms Act, 1969. The guidelines there are signposts here, with necessary adaptations, of course. This extensive analysis is a fitting introductory to the major essay of the author, which, as I see it, is Divorce Law Reform in India—for all Indians. Here we find a challenge to jurists and social scientists, statesmen and opinion-makers. In the last chapter the author raises and answers seminal divorce questions of deep import to all communities in our country. The tangled web of archaic divorce laws, further complicated by the touch-me-not cry of "religion in danger", is what we confront in India. Article 44 of the Constitution sets our sights high. Article 14, with accent on equality of the sexes before the law, and Article 15, showing special concern for women and children, set the new tone. Progressive law-makers and legal scholars, however, cannot wish the ferocious realities of fanatical opposition away, and must imaginatively evolve strategies which will not end in heroic disaster but will weld the nation's family code slowly but surely. Law is not logic but experience. It is the pragmatic art of the possible, woven out of given social reactions, not an "ivory tower" adventure in social engineering.

Dr. Hussain's final contribution is illuminating and constructive. He asks the right questions and hints at correct tactics. He surveys Anglo-American legal experience and highlights likely hurdles and hopeful solutions.

What there are the provisional issues of today, if tomorrow, law is to fulfil national aspirations ?

1. Do we need a common civil code as contemplated in Article 44 of the Constitution, or is it a non-negotiable issue? If we do desiderate a uniform Civil Code for the citizens of India, are customary variations or denominational deviations and other regional or religious diversities to be stamped out in the name of "one citizenship, one law"? Thus, should pluralism become a fatal enemy of nationalism?

2. If the demand is merely that the secular affairs of the members of a society should be settled by secular laws and not by religious directives, is it not possible, pragmatically speaking, to detach personal laws from religious tenets ?

3. Assuming that a uniform family law is a paramount objective what are the strategies to be adopted to achieve the goal?

4. Could we reform portions of the Muslim Law and make them uniform for all Mussalmans, as a first step? Likewise, for Christian Family Law, etc.? (In Kerala, the Christian Law of inheritance differs between Malabar and Cochin and Travancore, I guess.)

5. Could we progressively blend legislation and judicial interpretation, both geared to a unification of the Personal Law of the Muslims regulating marriage and divorce?

6. Could we stimulate the progressive forces from within the Muslim community to demand change and uniformity? (A few

years ago, when I visited Lakshadweep and met the islanders, a large body of youngmen, all Muslims, demanded a uniform Civil Code and liberation from obscurantist religious leadership in matters of Family Law).

7. Should we think in terms of a facultative legislation which may be taken advantage of by members of any religious persuasion and by popular movements, encouraging more and more people to resort to the benefits of such legislation?

8. Can a majority, by using its status as a majority, force upon a sensitive minority a Family Law, or will such a tactic provoke more resistance merely because it is likely to be regarded as tyranny by the majority?

9. Should the country wait solicitously till the last fanatic is converted or can the Legislature enact if a substantial number has offered support? When the world outlook on matrimonial law, in its evolutionary stages, develops new concepts, should we allow the ethos or national laws to be moulded by these winds of change?

10. What is the role of activist judges in fulfilling this branch of Part IV? Interpretatively erode obscurantism and ensure modernism or let the politicians spoil the cause by push and pressure?

These are some of the questions which agitate the minds of many jurists in the country currently. A forced step may well be a false step and one hasty step forward, two unhappy steps back. The resistance generated was so furious that even Nehru in his best days had to retreat, as happened in the case of the Hindu Code. Wisdom dictates caution, but there is a distinction between caution and stagnation. In tackling this sensitive subject we derive considerable assistance from the broad thesis of Dr. Hussain whose own unobtrusive yet purposeful treatment is a better weapon than crude blows which may recoil. Dr. Tahir Mahmood's works are an example. Jurists have a silent yet pursuant role to play in generating benign change.

The project has been undertaken in timely fashion and well executed. But a futurologist will address himself to more fundamental problems of legal integration, facultative legislator, secular appetizers and faster legal locomotiar. Which means more dynamic follow-up, jurist cadres, and west judges and informed sociological researchers. The journey is long but the secular pilgrimage must be pushed by supportive legislature. Dr. Hussain has placed us in debt of enlightened learning.

The goal is a viable common family code. Legal experiments must be geared to this goal. And we must remember, that the legal cosmos comprises non-English-speaking homosapiens and the Socialist sector of the earth has made advances in matrimonial legislation which deserve study. Way back in 1970 while on the Kerala Bench, I had occasion to observe, in *Yusuf Rowthan* v. *Sowramma*:*

I am impressed with the reasoning of Tyabji, C.J., which, in my humble view, accords with the holy Islamic texts and the ethos of the Muslim community which together serve as a backdrop for the proper understanding of the provisions of Act 8 of 1939.

I may also point out with satisfaction that this secular and pragmatic approach of the Muslim law of divorce happily harmonises with contemporary concepts in advanced countries. For instance, in the Family Code of the German Democratic Republic, recently enacted, the provisions on the dissolution of marriage have been explained in an official legal publication, thus :

> Their most characteristic feature is the doing away with the guilt principle of the erstwhile German civil family law. According to that principle a partner of a petition for divorce had to prove that the other partner had in a culpable manner violated marital duties. According to the principle which now prevails in the German Democratic Republic the only valid yardstick for the dissolution of a marriage are its objective conditions. If a marriage—as formulated in the draft—has lost its significance for the married partners, for the children and thereby for society, if it has become merely an empty shell, it must be dissolved, independently whether one of the married partners or which of the two bears the blame for its disintegration. In view of the most personal and variegated relations within married life and the fact that conflicts which lead to divorce, have frequently been simmering for

*1970 KLT 477.

> years, and might have their deepest roots in an ill-considered marriage, it may be, as a result, hardly possible to declare either of the spouses guilty for the disintegration of the marital partnership. (Law and Legislation in the G.D.R. 2/65, p. 32.)

One of the serious apprehensions judges have voiced, if the view accepted in AIR 1950 Sind 8 were to be adopted, is that the women may be tempted to claim divorce by their own delinquency and family ties may become tenuous and snap. Such a fear is misplaced has been neatly expressed by Bertrand Russell in his *Marriage and Morals*:

> One of the most curious things about divorce is the difference which has often existed between law and custom. The easiest divorce laws by no means always produce the greatest number of divorces. I think this distinction between law and custom is important, for a while I favour a somewhat lenient law on the subject, there are to my mind, so long as the biparental family persists as the norm, strong reasons why custom should be against divorce, except in somewhat extreme cases. I take this view because I regard marriage not primarily as a sexual partnership, but above all as an undertaking a co-operate in procreation and rearing of children.
>
> The law of the Marumakkathayees provides a large licence for divorce but actual experience allays the alarm. The law has to provide for possibilities, social opinion regulates the probabilities. For all these reasons, I hold that a Muslim woman, under Sec. 2(ii) of the Act, can sue for dissolution on the score that she has not as a fact been maintained even if there is good cause for it—the voice of the law, echoing public policy is often that of the realist, not of the moralist.

The G.D.R. Family Code is modern, equitable and abolishes sex discrimination and in many respects, including divorce and consequential property division, repays scrutiny. So also the Soviet Code.

Another obscure point. The Malabar Marumak kathayee

has been governed by legislation permitting divorce without fault and yet no matrimonial chaos has marred the life of the Malayalee. Indeed, in Rowthan I held it up as a paradigm and as in accord with Bertrand Russell:

For 45 years the Madras Marriage Act has held the field (until replaced recently) and a research study into its working may fortify Dr. Hussain's plea to abandon the theory of matrimonial wrong and to introduce the "breakdown-cum-no fault" ground.

Judge,
Supreme Court of India
NEW DELHI

V.R. KRISHNA IYER

July 1978

CONTENTS

ABBREVIATIONS

A.	: Atlantic Reporter
A.B.A.	: American Bar Association
A.B.A.J.	: American Bar Association Journal
A.C.	: Appeal Cases
A.I.R.	: All India Reporter
A.L.R.	: American Law Reporter
All.	: Allahabad
Am. Jur.	: American Jurisprudence
Andh. Pra.	: Andhra Pradesh
Ariz. Rev. Stat. Ann.	: Arizona Revised Statutes Annotated
Ark. Stat. Ann.	: Arkansas Statute Annotated
Bom.	: Bombay
Bom. L.R.	: Bombay Law Reports
Bom. L.R. Jl.	: Bombay Law Reports Journal Section
Boston U.L. Rev.	: Boston University Law Review
C.A.	: Court of Appeal
C.L.P.	: Current Legal Problem
C.W.N.	: Calcutta Weekly Notes
Cal.	: Calcutta
Cal. Reptr.	: California Reporter
Can. B. Rev.	: Canadian Bar Review
Cmnd.	: Command Papers
Colo. Rev. Stat. Ann.	: Colorado Revised Statute Annotated
Conn. B.J.	: Connecticut Bar Journal
Cumb. Sam. L. Rev.	: Cumberland Sam Law Review
Del. Code Ann.	: Deleware Code Annotated
Dic. L. Rev.	: Dickenson Law Review
Drake L. Rev.	: Drake Law Review
E.R.	: English Reports (Reprint)
E.R.A.	: English Report Annotated
F.B.	: Full Bench
Fam. L.Q.	: Family Law Quarterly
F.L.R.	: Family Law Reporter

Fla. Stat. Ann.	: Florida Statute Annotated
Hist. Dh. S.	: History of Dharma Sastras
H.L.	: House of Lords
Harv. L. Rev.	: Harvard Law Review
I.A.	: Indian Appeals
I.C.	: Indian Cases
I.L.R.	: Indian Law Reports
Ind. L.J.	: Indiana Law Journal
Ind. Legal Forum	: Indiana Legal Forum
Int. Comp. L.Q.	: International and Comparative Law Quarterly
J. Am. Jud. Soc'ty.	: Journal of American Judicature Society
J. Fam. L.	: Journal of Family Law
J.I.L.I.	: Journal of the Indian Law Institute
J. & K.	: Jammu & Kashmir
K.B.	: King's Bench Division
Ker.	: Kerala
Ky. Rev. Stat. Ann.	: Kentucky Revised Statute Annotated
Los Angeles B. Bull.	: Los Angeles Bar Bulletin
L.Q.R.	: Law Quarterly Review
L.T.	: Law Times
Law & Comtp. Prob.	: Law and Contemporary Problems
M.I.A.	: Moore's Indian Appeals
M.L.J.	: Madras Law Journal
M.L.R.	: Modern Law Review
Mad.	: Madras
Madh. Pra.	: Madhya Pradesh
Mass. Ann. Laws	: Massachusetts Annotated Laws
Md. Code Ann.	: Maryland Code Annotated
Mich.	: Michigan
Mich. L. Rev.	: Michigan Law Review
Mich. S.B.J.	: Michigan State Bar Journal
Minn. Stat. Ann.	: Minnesota Statute Annotated
Miss. Code Ann.	: Mississippi Code Annotated
Mo. B.J.	: Missouri Bar Journal
Mys.	: Mysore
N.D.	: North Dakota
N.D. Cent. Code.	: North Dakota Century Code
N.H. Rev. Stat.	: New Hampshire Revised Statutes

N.W.	: North Western Reporter
N.Y. Dom. Rel. Law	: New York Domestic Relation Law
N.Y.L.F.	: New York Law Forum
N.Y. Rev.	: New York Review
N.Y.S.	: New York Supplement
Nag.	: Nagpur
Nev. Rev. Stat.	: Nevada Statute Annotated
Ore.	: Oregon
Ore. L. Rev.	: Oregon Law Review
P.	: Pacific Reporter
P.C.	: Privy Council
P. & H.	: Punjab and Haryana
Pac. L.J.	: Pacific Law Journal
Pat.	: Patna
Punj.	: Punjab
R.I. Gen. Laws Ann.	: Rhode Island General Laws Annotated
Raj.	: Rajasthan
Salk.	: Salkeld's Reports
S.C.	: Supreme Court
S.C.L. Rev.	: South Carolina Law Review
S.C.R.	: Supremc Court Report
S.D.L. Rev.	: South Dakota Law Review
S.E.	: South Eastern Reporter
S.P.C.K.	: Society for Promoting Christian Knowledge
S.W.	: South Western Reporter
Sw. U.L. Rev.	: South Western University Law Review
Sol. Jl.	: Solicitor Journal
Stanf. L. Rev.	: Stanford Law Review
Suffolk U.L. Rev.	: Suffolk University Law Review
Tul. L. Rev.	: Tulane Law Review
U.C.L.A.L. Rev.	: University of California Los Angeles Law Review
U. Ill. L.F.	: University of Illinois Law Forum
U. Kansas L. Rev.	: University of Kansas Law Review
U.L.A.	: Uniform Laws Annotated
V.I.	: Virgin Islands
Va. Code	: Virginia Code

Va. L. Rev.	: Virginia Law Review
Vand L. Rev.	: Vanderbilt Law Review
Wash.	: Washington
Wash. Rev. Code	: Washington Revised Code
Wis. L. Rev.	: Wisconsin Law Review
Wyom. L.J.	: Wyoming Law Journal

ACKNOWLEDGEMENTS

I SHOULD like to record my grateful thanks to the Chairman and the members of the Committee on Graduate Studies, Harvard Law School, Cambridge, Mass. U.S.A. whose generous grant of a scholarship made this study possible.

I owe a special debt of gratitude to Professor Von Mehren, whose interest, encouragement and kindness sustained me throughout my stay at Harvard. I wish to express my deepest sense of indebtedness to my teacher and supervisor, Professor Frank Sander under whose inspiring guidance this project was pursued.

I am highly grateful to Mr. David N. Smith, Assistant Dean Harvard Law School who helped me in ways too numerous to recount here. My thanks are also due to Dr. Rahmatuallah Khan, Professor, J.N.U. Delhi and Mr. Muzaffer Baig, Advocate, Kashmir for their valuable assistance.

Publication of this work has been made possible by a grant from the Indian Council of Social Science Research, New Delhi. I wish to express my thanks to the Council.

Mr. Justice V.R. Krishna Iyer, one of the greatest judges ever to adorn the bench of the Supreme Court of India has very kindly contributed the Foreword to this book. I deem it a special honour done to me. My most sincere gratitude to him.

Finally, I must thank the Concept Publishing Company, New Delhi who have done a competent job.

S. JAFFER HUSSAIN

Law Faculty
Delhi University
University Campus
DELHI-110007.

PREFACE

MOST societies seek to regulate divorce through the instrumentality of law. The laws and grounds of divorce of course vary. Divorce reforms in the United States are generally premised upon the theory of breakdown of marriage. The Indian law, on the other hand, follows a different philosophy and is conditioned by the religion of the spouses and the laws that govern them. Both the American and the Indian laws have imbibed common law traditions in every sphere of legal life. It is, therefore, no wonder that the law of divorce in its major emphasis and bias is common to peoples in the United States, India and the United Kingdom.

Divorce has been subjected to study and analysis in America, India and England primarily from the perspectives of a single legal system, except for the notable study of Rheinstein on *Marriage Stability, Divorce and the Law*. Rheinstein has demonstrated the potentialities of the comparative approach to the study of divorce. The parameters of divorce, we believe, are best studied in the matrix of comparative law. For, divorce is a social phenomenon that cuts across national boundaries.

This study is not merely diagnostic. Besides finding out the causes for the failure of marriage, it considers a variety of changes that must be effected in the substantive and procedural laws of divorce, especially in India. The focus of the study is on reforms in the law of divorce, with emphasis on the concept of "breakdown" of marriage rather than on the notions of "fault". Insofar as the latter serves as a backdrop to the transformation of divorce law from the state of "matrimonial wrong" to "marital failure", it receives our attention, study and analysis.

Contemporary developments in English law have altered the principal basis of divorce by substituting "irretrievable breakdown" in place of the fault-oriented grounds. Several states in the United States have followed suit. The question arises whether the time and context are ripe for India to import the breakdown theory into its divorce law. With this end in view, the Indian law of divorce is examined against the background of judicial decisions unfolding the artificiality and inadequacy of the statutory law. Of course, no attempt is made herein to study the conditions in Indian society either facilitating or hindering the adoption of the breakdown theory. Such an approach would have gone beyond the confines of what we consider a legal study. However, we believe on the basis of a judicious examination of law and practice, that the Indian law should gravitate in favour of the theory of breakdown of marriage.

As indicated above, this is a legal and not a sociological study. Materials bearing upon the development of legal norms are consulted. Statutory law, judicial decisions, reports of governmental bodies and a spate of legal periodicals are consulted and relied upon. No data are collected from questionnaires, interviews and discussions or persons interested in the reforms of divorce. In other words, this study is based upon the traditional legal sources.

This work is substantially based upon my doctoral thesis "Divorce Laws and Reforms : A Study in Comparative Law" submitted in 1975 to Harvard Law School, Harvard University, U.S.A. It is satisfying indeed that some of the changes suggested in 1975 in regard to the reforms of Hindu law find a place in judicial decisions and in the enactment of the Marriage Laws Amendment Act of 1976. The Law Commission too in its recent report has recommended the adoption of "breakdown of marriage," as a ground for divorce.

S. Jaffer Hussain

INTRODUCTION

THE history of the divorce laws and their reforms in the Anglo-American complex as well as in the Western world is the history of the forces of conservatism and liberalism operating against each other.[1] Modernistic legislation in some places has threatened to pierce the heart of the social fabric of unity—the family. Courts have sought to counterbalance the claims of sanctity of marriage on the one hand and individual liberty on the other. It is in this clash that the divorce laws have manifested themselves into a novel form.

The emergence of the industrial era, the assertions of individualism, the passion for freedom and liberty, the change in the cultural and social climate, not to speak of the women's liberation movement, have all contributed in moulding the attitudes of Western society towards divorce. The revolution that has taken place in the recent past in this branch of the law is a striking example of how the law is keeping pace with the needs and aspirations of modern society.

In a majority of the American states divorce law is based on the concept of "fault" or "guilt" pronouncing the breakdown of matrimony. In the remainder, however, divorce can be obtained without proof of "fault" by one of the parties after a requisite period of separation. In some jurisdictions incompatibility—a non-fault ground—exists alongside the conventional "fault" grounds. Some jurisdictions such as Iowa, Kentucky, Oregon and Michigan, in fact, have recently substituted a completely non-fault breakdown of marriage standard as the sole ground for divorce. The Uniform Marriage and Divorce Act of 1970 drafted by the National Conference of Commissioners on Uniform State Laws also displaced the fault system completely and substituted in its place "irretrievable breakdown" as the sole ground for the dissolution of marriage. The State of New York had until 1966 adultery as the only ground for divorce. It could not resist the rising demands for liberal divorce laws for long. In 1967 it reformed its law by recognizing separation, cruelty and insanity, in addition to adultery, as grounds for divorce.[2]

The wide variations in state laws on marriage and divorce have been described picturesquely by Richard H. Wels thus :[3]

> The citizens of twentieth century America live in an age in which distances have been telescoped, and in which political boundaries exist only to be crossed. Ease and speed of transportation and communication have made it almost as possible to be married in New York and divorced in Nevada as it is to have breakfast in New York and dinner in California.

The bewildering diversity in the United States divorce law provides an unique opportunity for a student of comparative law to study these developments and the impact they have had upon the institution of marriage, as such, and to compare them with those of other societies. The legal systems obtaining in India have been chosen for such comparison.

In India there are different laws governing different communities. Here also great diversity exists in the divorce laws—not only in the matter of grounds but also in the manner in which marriage could be dissolved. Until 1955, divorce was not allowed to a vast section of the Hindu community. It was permitted among certain castes based on custom. In some states like Madras, Bombay and Baroda, however, the remedy of divorce was made available by legislative enactments during the British rule. The Hindu Marriage Act enacted in 1955 revolutionized the law of that community. This Act entitled all Hindus to obtain divorce on specific grounds such as adultery, insanity, or incurable leprosy. The enactment drew heavily from the Matrimonial Causes Act, 1950 of England, and, as such, borrowed the concept of "fault".

Muslims who are the largest minority in India are governed by their own religious laws in the matter of divorce. The traditional Islamic law as applied to Muslims allows a husband to dissolve the marriage by pronouncing what is called a *talaq* upon his wife; whereas the similar right was denied to the wife. In order to rectify this inequity, the Indian legislature, during

British rule, enacted the Dissolution of Muslim Marriages Act, 1939, which entitled the wife to obtain divorce on certain grounds which included the conventional grounds.

The Christians are governed by the Indian Divorce Act of 1869—an Act now more than a century old. This Act, as was the case in New York until 1966, recognizes adultery as the only ground for divorce.[4] In 1969 the Law Commission[5] recommended the incorporation of additional grounds. Nothing has been done so far in this regard.

For persons professing different religious faiths, provision is made to contract a civil form of marriage under the Special Marriage Act, 1954. Persons whose marriages are solemnized under this Act are governed by the Act and not according to their personal laws. The Act is modelled on the basis of the English Matrimonial Causes Act, 1950. The grounds of divorce are based on the "fault" concept. Apart from the specific grounds on which either party to a marriage can obtain divorce, provision is made under the Act to dissolve the marriage by mutual consent.[6] All that the parties need do is to present a petition to the court stating that they have been living separately for a period of one year or more and that they have mutually agreed to dissolve the marriage.

This study intends to survey the divorce laws and reforms in some selective jurisdictions in the United States of America and to compare corresponding developments in the Indian law. The application of the Anglo-American experience to Indian conditions will also be examined as the divorce law in India is essentially based on the common law of England.

Although generally divorce law is an index of individual freedom and liberty, it has also a hidden dark side inasmuch as respect for the matrimonial bond is vastly diminished.[7] The ideal of a healthy family—knit by all that is good in life—is slowly eroded. More than a century ago Lord Westbury observed:[8]

> Marriage is the foundation of civil society, and no part of the laws and institutions of a country can be of more vital importance to its subjects than those which regulate the manner and conditions of forming, and, if necessary, of dissolving the marriage contract.

While it is difficult to disagree with Lord Westbury, it must be stated that the state's interference in terminating a marriage which has failed to achieve its objects will be justified for the same reason. As stated by Cheshire:[9]

> Divorce, since it disintegrates the family unity, is, of course, a social evil in itself, but it is a necessary evil. It is better to wreck the unity of the family than to wreck the future happiness of the parties by binding them to a companionship that has become odious.

NOTES AND REFERENCES

1. O' Neill says : "The failure of divorce to justify either the expectations of liberals or the fears of conservatives is, therefore, part of the whole process by which their system of attitudes and ideas has been replaced by our own. What was once a moral issue has become increasingly a clinical problem". See William L. O' Neill, *Divorce in the Progressive Era* 273 (1967). In the opinion of Rheinstein "Liberalism seems to be about to achieve a breakthrough or has perhaps achieved it already. Conservatism seems to have lost much of its former influence". See Max Rheinstein, *Marriage Stability, Divorce and the Law* 313 (1972). See further his observation where he says "Officially or unofficially, liberalism has come to dominate the American practice of divorce". Ibid. at pp. 29-30.
2. N.Y. Dom. Rel. Law Sec. 170 (McKinney, 1970).
3. Wels, *New York : The Poor Man's Reno*, 35 Cornell L.Q. 303 at 303 (1950). The reference to New York and Nevada made by the author was due to the fact that New York had strict divorce law, whereas Nevada afforded an easy divorce to the couples at that time.
4. The Indian Divorce Act, 1869, Sec. 10.
5. The Law Commission of India, *Law Relating to Marriage and Divorce amongst Christians in India* (15th Report 1960).
6. Special Marriage Act, 1954, Sec. 28.
7. See generally Robert J. Moskin, *Morality in America* 268-90 (1966).
8. *Shaw* v. *Gould*, [1868] 1 E.R.A. 454 at 467; [1868] L.R. 3 H.L. 55 at 82.
9. Cheshire, *The International Validity of Divorces*, 61 L.Q. Rev. 352 at 352 (1945).

Divorce in Anglo-American Law 1

HISTORICAL BACKGROUND

IN ENGLAND the church had for a long time exclusive jurisdiction over matrimonial affairs.[1] The ecclesiastical courts used to administer and apply the canon law in matters relating to marriage and divorce. But in America the divorce laws took a different course.

At the time the settlers founded the American colonies, matrimonial causes were, in their own country, under the jurisdiction of the church. Being themselves Protestants, having no church or ecclesiastical courts, canon law could not be applied.[2] The settlers brought with them the common law. As stated by Howard "while the colonists carried with them the English law, they did not bring likewise the English courts".[3] The common law courts had no inherent jurisdiction over matrimonial causes. So the remedy of divorce was to be provided either by the legislatures or by the Governors in councils. From the earliest time divorce was granted only by the Governors in councils before the legislatures took their place to grant divorces by private statutes.[4]

The Governors in councils, particularly in New England, did not recognize divorce *a mensa et thoro*—a remedy which was purely of ecclesiastical origin. In fact Governor Hutchinson is reported to have said:[5]

> In matters of divorce they left the rules of canon law out of the question; with respect to some of them, prudently enough. I never heard of a separation, under the first Charter, *a mensa et thoro.*

According to Keezer the canon law was never adopted and the

ecclesiastical court system never recognised in the United States.[6]

When the colonies became independent after the revolution, there were at least two courses left open for them to adopt. First, they could clothe the local courts with jurisdiction over matrimonial matters. Secondly, they could provide for legislative divorce. The latter course was adopted for a considerable time before jurisdiction was given to the courts. Even during the British administration of the colonies, legislative divorce was in vogue. The procedure consisted of petitioning the parliament by the party seeking divorce and an act would be passed granting divorce to the party. The usual causes on which such a type of divorce was granted were adultery, desertion and cruelty. As stated by Bishop[7], "legislative divorce being part of the legal course of things which our forefathers brought from England and practiced here a divorce of this sort should be deemed *prima facie* good. . ." The only difference between the legislative divorce in America and that of England is that in the latter a decree of separation was to be obtained in the ecclesiastical court and thereafter an absolute divorce could be granted only by passing an Act to dissolve the marriage.[8]

The question before the independent American legislatures was as to the grounds on which divorce could be granted. Some legislatures adopted the law as developed by the ecclesiastical courts as part of the common law and others rejected it, so much so that a great diversity came into existence in the grounds among the various states. Further, the difference in social, moral and religious faiths of different areas contributed a great deal to the variations which are still witnessed in the divorce law. According to Keezer[9] "such a situation of diversified laws was the inevitable result of the application of confused and divergent religious and social philosophies to a problem which presented many new aspects in America". He further states[10] that "each state, impregnated as it was with its own peculiar religious faith and social philosophies, made laws believed by its legislatures to be necessary to promote permanency of family relations and protect the social fabric".

Divorce by private statute (a legislative procedure) continued in practice for more than half a century in the majority of the states legislatures.[11] Gradually, however, the grounds for divorce began to be defined by the legislatures. In the middle of the nineteenth century, a majority of the states abolished this kind of legislative procedure respecting divorce and gave jurisdiction to the courts. Later, all the states abolished this practice completely.

DIVORCE IN AMERICA: GENERAL

It is proposed here to portray an overall picture of divorce in various jurisdictions with some emphasis on the conventional grounds such as adultery, cruelty and desertion.

Except for recent reforms, the law of divorce in America has been the same as obtained in England at the time of reformation.[12] In England, after reformation, the concept of divorce was based upon "material fault" which was a compromise between the Roman privilege of repudiation and the Catholic dogma as to the indissolubility of a valid marriage. Therefore, in America all the three conventional grounds, namely, adultery, cruelty and desertion found a place as a natural consequence of the impact of the British administration of justice in the early period. During the nineteenth century, the fault-oriented framework of divorce was retained and it still continues in the majority of the jurisdictions, though there has been an expansion of the grounds both by the legislature and by judicial relaxation. In the twentieth century, particularly in the recent past, there have been some significant developments in this branch of the law. In some jurisdictions the fault-based grounds have been abolished and breakdown of marriage substituted in its place.

Adultery

Adultery[13] as a matrimonial fault giving rise to a remedy of divorce, has been recognized in all the states[14] excepting those which have abolished the fault-oriented grounds. The offense consists of a breach by either party to the marriage which gives a right to the innocent party to obtain a divorce. A single act of sexual intercourse by a married person with a third party will constitute adultery for the purpose of divorce. It may be mentioned in passing that under the Indian law as applied earlier to Hindus, a single act of sexual intercourse will not give rise to an action for divorce but to an action for judicial separation.[15] In order to obtain divorce the petitioner has to prove that the respondent "is living in adultery".[16] Thus the Indian law differs to a great extent from the American law on this point.

Until 1967, adultery was the only ground for divorce in New York.[17] It was because of the difficulty of proving adultery and as no other ground was available to the spouses who wanted to escape from the bonds of matrimony, that they resorted to migratory divorce.[18] Some spouses used to obtain divorce by committing a fraud upon law by faking adultery. The extent to which this practice was resorted to has been mentioned by Blake.[19] He points out that a divorce lawyer used to arrange his lady stenographer to accompany his client to a hotel and remove a few outer garments. The hired witnesses, generally the private detectives would crash into the hotel room and collect the evidence for a good divorce case. In uncontested divorce cases and where the husbands were cooperative, obtaining of a divorce was a matter of routine. With the expansion of the grounds in New York and particularly the adoption of separation ground with a short period, the problem of migratory divorce seemed to have been solved to a very great extent. As respects other jurisdictions, reforms in divorce law and the reduction in the residential period before a divorce could be obtained have contributed a good deal in solving the migratory divorce practices.[20] According to Jacobson three per cent of the American divorces were on the ground of adultery.[21]

Cruelty

Cruelty is a cause for divorce in all the states except North Carolina, Maryland and Virginia. It is also not recognized in the district of Columbia.[22] Statutes employ varying language to describe cruelty. For instance, the New York divorce statute[23] provides "cruel and inhuman treatment". Under the Minnesota statute[24] also it was earlier described as "cruel and inhuman treatment". The majority of the statutes use the words "extreme cruelty".[25]

It has been recognized that no exact definition of "legal cruelty" can be given and the courts have made no attempt to define it precisely. The concept of cruelty has been developed by judicial decisions.[26] It has been changing from time to time. The generally accepted principle laid down by the courts is that when the legislature made "cruelty" a ground of divorce without further defining the term, it must be understood by reference to the law as enunciated by the ecclesiastical courts. Cruelty was designated by such courts as "Saevitia" for the grant of a decree of judicial separation.[27]

The law relating to cruelty in United States has travelled on the same lines on which it has been developed by the English courts. The legal standard of cruelty there was laid down in the leading case of *Russell* v. *Russell*.[28] It was held in that case that conduct must be of such a character as to cause injury to body, health or mind or which raises a reasonable apprehension of such injury to body or health. This has been the general standard which also found favor in American jurisprudence. As observed by Lord Penzance:[29]

> The essential features of cruelty are familiar. There must be actual violence of such a character as to endanger personal health or safety or there must be reasonable apprehension of it. The court, as Lord Stowell once said, has never been driven off this ground.

The extent or limits of cruelty as laid down in *Evans* v. *Evans*[30] have been approved and followed by the American courts. It was observed in that case:[31]

> Mere austerity of temper, petulance of manner, rudeness of language, a want of civil attention and accommodation, even occasional sallies of passion, if they do not threaten bodily harm, do not amount to legal cruelty: they are high moral offences in the marriage-state undoubtedly, not innocent surely in any state of life, but still they are not that cruelty against which the law can relieve.

In theory, American law too does not consider mere incompatibility of temperament or trivial causes or even marital wrongdoings which make life of the spouses unhappy as constituting cruelty. Religious, social, racial or political differences which fall below the standard of "legal cruelty" are not recognized as causes for separation.[32] Various theories were developed by English courts such as the "aiming at" theory, the "protection" theory and the rule of "wear and tear" of conjugal life,[33] to limit the concept of cruelty or contain it within legal bounds. All these theories have been engrafted without reluctance in the American law of divorce.

Changes in the concept of cruelty were bound to occur with the exigencies of time. What could not have been, a hundred years ago, regarded as cruelty might be regarded as cruelty in the present day. Social changes, the growth of equality of sexes have to a large extent expanded the concept of legal cruelty. A cursory glance over the law reports would reveal the extent to which the concept has undergone radical change. From refusal to speak to the other spouse to a threat to commit suicide, and from denial of sexual intercourse to refusal to have sexual intercourse without contraceptive have been held to amount to cruelty.[34] In fact as Clark states:[35]

> One further influence in the direction of expanding cruelty comes from a change in the underlying policy. A few courts today explicitly recognize that the purpose to be served by making cruelty a ground for divorce is not to protect the plaintiff, but to enable the court to dissolve the marriages which have so far deteriorated that they no longer serve the interest of the parties or of society.

Since cruelty or mental cruelty[36] covers a wide range of matrimonial misconduct or wrongdoings, this ground seems to have become most popular. Further there is much scope for the parties to obtain consensual divorce by alleging cruelty.

Desertion

Desertion[37] for a specified period ranging from one year to several years is a ground for divorce in almost every state except of course those states which have, of late, adopted the "no-fault" divorce statutes. While describing the offense of desertion many statutes use adjectives such as "willful"[38], "utter and continued"[39] or "obstinate". Though the statutory language qualifies desertion with these adjectives the meaning and the concept of desertion remains the same.

Desertion is a voluntary separation of one of the spouse from the other or voluntary refusal to renew a suspended cohabitation without justification either in consent or the wrongful conduct of the second party.[40] The separation by one spouse from the other must be without the latter's consent and with the intention to bringing cohabitation permanently to an end. The essential elements of desertion are the *factum* of separation and the *animus deserandi* of the deserting party and it must continue for the whole statutory period. The fact of separation and the intention to desert must coincide in point of time and continue for the statutory period. It may be that a party has separated in the first instance without the necessary *animus* to bring termination of cohabitation for ever to an end, but later on he or she may develop the required intention. It is from this moment that desertion will commence.[41]

In order to constitute desertion it is not necessary that the parties should separate physically. Desertion is not a withdrawal from a place but from state of things. Thus the parties may live together under the same roof and yet one may be guilty of desertion. Resumption of cohabitation puts an end to desertion even though the parties separate after a short period of cohabitation. There is a conflict of opinion among various jurisdictions on the point whether the period necessary to establish desertion could be interrupted by a single act or isolated acts of sexual intercourse. One view is that such conduct will not break the continuity of desertion when it could be found that the deserting party did not intend to resume marital relations on a permanent basis. The other view is that single or isolated acts of cohabitation will break the continuity of the statutory period. However, if cohabitation has taken place by fraud and not with a genuine desire to reconcile, then such acts will not have the effect of breaking the continuity for the purpose of the statutory period.[42]

Since the essence of desertion is the withdrawal from a state of things and not a withdrawal from a place, the party who leaves the matrimonial home is not necessarily the deserting party. Where one spouse's conduct is such as to force the other to leave the home, then the former and not the latter will be guilty of what is known as "constructive desertion".[43] In order to justify the leaving of the home by the spouse, the conduct must be grave and weighty. Here again there is a cleavage of juristic opinion between the states as to whether the conduct which will justify a spouse in leaving the home should be a ground for which divorce could be granted. In some states it has been held that the misconduct must be one which constitutes a ground for divorce whether limited or absolute. Other jurisdictions have taken a contrary view. According to them the misconduct which will justify a spouse to leave the home need not be one which will be a ground for divorce.[44]

Thus, in American divorce law, or for that matter, in any legal system of civilized countries, adultery, cruelty and desertion are the universally recognized grounds for divorce. In fact as Turner says:[45]

> The classic trilogy of matrimonial offenses represents a practical compendium of that inexcusable conduct which most civilized societies at most times have found serious enough generally to destroy marital solidarity. They are as it were, the *actus rei* of matrimonial guilt.

The above observation will apply only to those jurisdictions which have retained the fault-based grounds in the United States. The "inexcusable conduct" referred to by Turner, "serious enough generally to destroy marital solidarity" has been subsumed under the term "breakdown" in some of the jurisdictions.[46] Apart from these conventional grounds a majority of the states have insanity, habitual drunkenness, imprisonment and impotency as grounds for divorce. Some have "indignities"[47] as ground for divorce. The most significant ground is that of "living separate and apart". About half of the states have recognized separation as a ground for divorce. New York, too, in 1967 added this ground when its law was reformed by the Divorce Reform Law.[48] The statutes had prescribed longer periods and the trend has been to reduce the period of time of separation. It is anything between two years to six months now. Separation and living apart as a ground for divorce is discussed in detail in the ensuing pages.

Realistic and pragmatic approach to divorce led to the frank recognition of incompatibility as an "honest ground" for divorce. Several jurisdictions list incompatibility along with other traditional grounds. The law relating to incompatibility and how it has worked in practice is also dealt with at the appropriate place.[49] We are told that this ground is most frequently used in the jurisdiction in which it is recognized.[50]

By far the most significant and drastic reforms in the divorce law that have been made in the recent past are those seen in some of the states like California, Florida, Kentucky, Oregon, Colorado and Iowa.[51] They have completely abolished the traditional grounds and replaced the divorce law with "breakdown" of marriage as the ground for divorce. Some jurisdictions like Alabama[52], and New Hampshire[53] have merely added breakdown of marriage as an additional ground to their statutes containing fault grounds.

In the year 1970 the National Conference of Commissioners on Uniform State Laws proposed the Uniform Marriage and Divorce Act which provides "irretrievable breakdown" of marriage as the sole ground for divorce.[54] Many states which have now the fault-oriented grounds may perhaps adopt in the foreseable future the Uniform Marriage and Divorce Act. Recently, the Family Law Committee of the Connecticut Bar Association proposed a draft statute[55] on the lines suggested by the National Conference of Commissioners as a result of which the divorce law of this state was reformed in 1973.[56] The new law establishes the two no-fault grounds for divorce, namely, (1) irretrievable breakdown of marriage and (2) living apart for a continuous period of at least eighteen months by reason of incompatibility. But these new grounds have been engrafted to the existing traditional grounds for divorce. We also hear some voices from lawyers and legal writers stating that time has come to reform the law on a more realistic and rational basis.[57]

NOTES AND REFERENCES

1. See Ch. IV on History of Divorce in England.
2. See B. Kitchin, *A History of Divorce*, 211 (1912).
3. 2 G.E. Howard, *History of Matrimonial Institutions*, 366 (1904).
4. Ibid. at 328. A detailed account of divorce in the various American colonies will be found in N. Blake, *Road to Reno* 34 et seq. (1962).
5. Governor Hutchinson as quoted in Howard, supra note 12 at 330.
6. See Frank Keezer, *Marriage and Divorce*, pp. 269-99, Sec. 240 (1946).
7. J.P. Bishop, *Marriage, Divorce and Separation* 602, Sec. 1450 (1891).
8. See Ch. IV at 117.
9. See Keezer, supra note 6, at 298.
10. Ibid. at 298.
11. Paul H. Jacobson, *American Marriage and Divorce* 89 (1959).
12. Kitchin states that the divorce laws of America are generally those of the Reformation as extended by judicial interpretation. See B. Kitchin, *A History of Divorce* 215 (1952).
13. Encyclopaedia of law defines adultery as "the sin of incontinence between two married persons, or it may be when only one of them is married". See 1 *American and English Encyclopaedia of Law* 747 (1968). See further Ann. 15 ALR 2d 680, Sec. 7 (1951).
14. See 24 Am. Jur. 2d Sec. 24 (1966); H. Clark, *Law of Domestic Relations*, 327, Sec. 12.2 (1968).
15. Sec. 10(1)(f) of the Hindu Marriage Act, 1955.
16. Sec. 13(1)(i) of the Hindu Marriage Act, 1955.
17. See N.Y. Dom. Rel. Law Sec. 170 (McKinney Supp. 1974) adding cruelty, abandonment and other grounds.
18. Articles abound in the law journals on the problem of migratory divorces. See for example, Swanson, *Migratory Divorce : The Sherrer case and the Future—A Prophecy*, 40 A.B.A.J. 672 (1954); Comment, *Divorce Jurisdiction by consent of the parties—Development since "Sherrer v. Sherrer"*, 26 Ind. L.J. 380 (1951); Paulsen, *Migratory Divorce : Chapters III and IV*, 24 Ind. L.J. 25 (1948); Ingram and Ballard, *The Business of Migratory Divorce in Nevada*, 2 Law & Contem. Prob. 302 (1935); Rosenau, *Those "Quickie" Alabama Divorces*, 18 Ala. Lawyer, 37 (1957); Note, *Migratory Divorce : The Alabama Experience*, 75 Harv. L. Rev. 568 (1962), see further N. Blake, *The Road to Reno* (Ch. 11 entitled "Divorce and the Tourists Trade") at 152 (1962).
19. See Blake, supra note 18, at 193.
20. For example, in Nevada the divorce petitions declined by 2,000 from 10,951 in 1959 to 9,138 in 1970. The California no-fault divorce law seems to have contributed towards the decline in divorce petitions. See Goddard, *A Report on California's New Divorce Law : Progress and Problems*, 6 Fam. L.Q. 405 at 410 (1972).
21. Paul H. Jacobson, *American Marriage and Divorce* 124 (1959).

22. See Clark supra note 14, Sec. 12.4 at 341.
23. N.Y. Dom. Rel. Law Sec. 170 (McKinney Supp. 1974).
24. Minn. Stat. Ann. Sec. 518.06 West (1969) as amended Minn. Stat. Ann. Sec. 518.06 (West Supp. 1974).
25. See for example Mont. Rev. Code Ann. Sec. 21-106 (1967); Kan. Stat. Ann. Sec. 60-1601 (Vernon 1963).
26. See 24 Am. Jur. 2d Sec. 32 (1966).
27. Ibid. at 203.
28. *Russell* v. *Russell*, (1897) A.C. 395. See further Biggs, *The Concept of Matrimonial Cruelty* (1962).
29. *Milford* v. *Milford*, (1866) L.R. 1 P & D 295 at 299.
30. *Evans* v. *Evans*, 161 E.R. 466.
31. Ibid. at 467.
32. Am. Jur. supra note 26, Sec. 45 at pp. 215-16.
33. An excellent account of the development of these theories will be founded in Goodhart, *Cruelty, Desertion and Insanity in Matrimonial Law*, 79 L.Q. Rev. 98 (1963); Neville Brown, *Cruelty without Culpability and Divorce without Fault*, 26 M.L. Rev. 625 (1963); Hall, *Matrimonial Cruelty and Mens Rea*, 104 Cambridge, L.J. 104 (1963); For the development of the law relating to cruelty in the United States see Levine, *Marital Cruelty : New Wine in Old Bottles*, 2 Fam. L.Q. 296 (1968). See also Note, *A Survey of Mental Cruelty as a Ground for Divorce*, 15 DePaul L. Rev. 159 (1965).
34. See Clark, supra note 14, Sec. 12.4 at 346.
35. Ibid. at 344.
36. See note, *A Survey of Mental Cruelty as a ground for Divorce*, 15 DePaul L. Rev. 159 (1965).
37. See Clark, supra note 14, Sec. 12.3 at 331.
38. See for example Ga. Code Ann. tit. 30, Sec. 30-102 (1969); Miss. Code Ann. Sec. 93-5-1 (Supp. 1973).
39. M.G.L.A. c. 208, Sec. I (Supp. 1975).
40. *Walker* v. *Walker*, 125 Md. 649, 94 A, 346 (1915); *Buckner* v. *Buckner*, 118 Md. 101, 84 A, 156 (1912).
41. See Clark, supra note 14, Sec. 12.3 at 331.
42. See Am. Jur. supra note 26, Sec. 112 at 273.
43. Ibid. at 273.
44. Ibid. Sec. 116 at 276.
45. Turner, *Retreat from Fault—An English Lawyer's View*, 46 Neb. L. Rev. 64 at 77 (1967).
46. Example, California, Florida, Michigan and Kentucky.
47. Pennsylvania and Tennessee may be mentioned as examples.
48. N.Y. Dom. Rel. Law Sec. 170(6) (McKinney Supp. 1974).
49. See Ch. II Section B.
50. See Clark supra note 14, Sec. 12.5 at 349.
51. See Ch. 111, Section C at 88.
52. Ala. Code Ann. tit. 34, Sec. 20 (Supp. 1974).
53. N.H. Rev. Stat. Sec. 458. 7 A (Supp. 1971).

54. Uniform Marriage and Divorce Act Sec. 302 (1973 Version).
55. See the proposed draft of the statute in 44 Conn. B.J. 411 (1970); For the critical comments on this proposed draft see Cohen, *Divorce Reform—Another Point of View*, 47 Conn. B.J. 88 (1973); Hefferhan, *Finding Fault with No-Fault Divorce—The Proposed Connecticut Divorce Statute*, 47 Conn. B.J. 99 (1973).
56. C.G.S.A. Ch. 811, Sec. 46-32 (Supp. 1975). For the legislative history and comment on the new law see McAnerney and Schoonmaker, *Connecticut's New Approach to Marriage Dissolution*, 47 Conn. B.J. 375 (1973).
57. See note, *No Fault Divorce : A Time for Change* : 7 Suffolk U.L. Rev. 86 (1972). It has been pointed out there that the archaic laws of divorce in the state of Massachusetts have promoted adultery and marriage instability. Therefore, a more realistic and sensible approach to divorce problem should be adopted by recognizing breakdown of marriage as the basis for dissolution. See also Comment, *Arizona Divorce Law : Time for a Better System*, Law & Social Order, 620 (1970). But Arizona has since adopted a no-fault divorce law : Ariz. Rev. Stat. Sec. 25-312 (Supp. 1973). Doppler vehemently advocates for the abolition of the present system of divorce law based on the theory of matrimonial wrong. See Doppler, *America Needs Total Divorce Reform Now* (First ed. 1973). Lasch says that Americans should reform not divorce but the "myth of domesticity". See Lasch, *Divorce American Style*, N.Y. Rev. 3 at 4 (1966).

Reforms in the United States Divorce Law 2

DATING from the middle of the nineteenth century to the present time, the major reforms in divorce in the United States have been on three lines. They are, first, adding the separation and living apart ground to the existing statutory grounds. Secondly, incorporating a new non-fault ground of incompatibility to the statutes containing conventional grounds and thirdly, replacing completely the fault-oriented ground and substituting breakdown of marriage as the sole basis for divorce. We shall now deal with these reforms in detail.

SEPARATION AND LIVING APART AS A GROUND FOR DIVORCE

Separation as a ground for divorce is not of a recent origin. More than a century ago Kentucky[1], Wisconsin[2] and later Rhode Island[3] had provided separation and living apart as causes for which divorce could be granted. Soon other states followed suit. Today one-half of the states have on their statute books separation as a ground for divorce. The period of separation required, before an action for divorce could be brought, vary from jurisdiction to jursdiction. The statutes had prescribed longer periods; sometimes seven years or even ten years. But at the present time almost every state has reduced the period of time.

The policy behind the recognition of "separate and living apart" as a ground is based on the assumption that when married persons have not lived together for a considerably long time without any inclination to resume cohabitation, it is a sufficient proof, though not a conclusive one, that the marriage has ceased to function. Under these circumstances if the parties desire a divorce it ought to be given. Further, the best interest of the society as well as the parties would be served by giving a speedy burial to a union which has become odious. This spirit is echoed in the ruling of *Parks* v. *Parks*[4] wherein the court held that the purpose of the 1935 Amendment to the D.C. Code, providing for absolute divorce for voluntary separation, was "... to permit termination in law of certain marriages which have ceased to exist in fact".[4a]

The most important question before the legislature is to determine the length of time sufficient to justify that the marriage is no more viable and that a divorce could be pronounced. As stated by McCurdy[5] "the period should be sufficiently long to indicate no likelihood of a resumption of cohabitation and not so long as to encourage the formation of meretricious relationships".

The first proposition that arises in the context is, what constitutes "separation" and what is meant by the expression "living apart".[6] Under the statutes, a physical separation of the parties with the intent to sever marital relations is generally necessary. Some states expressly provide that separation must be beyond reasonable expectation of reconciliation. If the parties do not live under the same roof but have cohabited from time to time divorce cannot be granted. For the same reason, where the statute provides the ground as "living separate and apart" the fact that they have lived under the same house but with strained relations will not entitle them to divorce.[7] However, the fact that the parties have lived under the same roof does not preclude a finding that they have voluntarily separated. It was said in *Boyce* v. *Boyce*[8] that the essential thing was not "separate roofs but separate lives". This decision is noteworthy because the court did not insist that there should necessarily be a physical separation. The concept of "living separate and apart" was thus expanded by the court to meet all such situations in married life when it could be said that the spouses were not living together as man and wife. Physical separation only aids the court in arriving at the conclusion that the marriage is dead and that a divorce can be pronounced if separation has lasted for the prescribed period.

Broadly speaking the separation statutes can be grouped under two heads[9]: (i) the living apart statutes and (ii) the conversion type statutes. Under the first category the statutes require that the separation continue without interruption for a prescribed minimum period before an action for divorce can be instituted. In the second type, a judicial decree or a formal separation agreement can be converted after the stipulated period into an absolute divorce.

The living apart statutes can be further divided into three categories :

(1) Voluntary living apart statutes;
(2) Statutes which allow divorce to the party who is not at fault; and
(3) Statutes which allow divorce regardless of whether the parties agreed to separate or even though the fault of one of the spouses may have contributed to the separation.

Voluntary separation statutes

This apparently simple ground for which divorce can be granted has raised many legal problems. For example, to what extent should the living apart be voluntary, should it be voluntary at the outset or should it be the result of the husband's misconduct; should it continue to be voluntary for the entire statutory period? We shall examine all these propositions.

The Delaware[10], Maryland[11] and Wisconsin[12] statutes expressly require that living apart must be voluntary. Since separation under these statutes has been qualified to be "voluntary" it must be alleged and proved by the party seeking divorce. No formal written agreement is necessary. The fact can be proved by oral testimony or by proof of a written document if there is any. The Supreme Court of Delaware in *Maloney* v. *Maloney*[13] took a broad view of voluntariness. The wife in this case petitioned for divorce. The husband did not contest nor tried for reconciliation. It was held that silence and inaction of the husband constituted a tacit consent in a voluntary separation. Since there was no reasonable prospect of reconciliation, the court granted the decree of divorce to the wife. It may be pointed out that the Delaware statute not only does speak of living apart and separate for the period of eighteen months but also states that separation must be "beyond any reasonable expectation of reconciliation". The view adopted in several states is that it is sufficient if the separation is voluntary as to one party and that it need not be by the consent of both parties.[14] The other view holds that when the statute requires that separation be voluntary, it must be "mutually voluntary".[15] The position in Wisconsin as to voluntary separation can be summarized as follows:[16]

(1) Plaintiff cannot get a divorce on grounds of voluntary separation if the defendant proves that the separation was caused by the plaintiff's own misconduct. Such a separation is not voluntary on the part of the defendant and plaintiff's complaint will be dismissed.[17]

(2) A plaintiff cannot get a divorce on ground of voluntary separation if the defendant proves that he or she has made a good faith attempt at reconciliation. The defendant's attempted reconciliation means that separation is not voltuntary on his part and plaintiff's complaint will be dismissed.[18]

(3) When fault is not proved, the court will try to determine the true intention of the parties. If the defendant seems sincere in his desire to continue the marital relationship, separation is not voluntary on his part.[19] If the court does not believe he has any such intention, then separation is voluntary on his part in spite of his claims to the contrary.[20]

As respects the question whether voluntary separation should last for the whole statutory period, it has been held that it must be so. The Court of Appeals in the District of Columbia[21] did not grant a divorce to the husband on the ground that separation did not remain voluntary on the part of the wife as he had made repeated efforts towards reconciliation. The Maryland[22] court also ruled that separation must be voluntary in its inception and that it should remain so for the entire statutory period.

Statutes which allow divorce only when the party seeking divorce is not at fault

The Wyoming divorce statute[23] is the only one which specifically requires that fault be considered. Under the statute, a divorce can be had if there is a separation for two years without cohabitation and without material fault on the part of the plaintiff. Of course, the fault or conduct need not be one on which divorce could be granted. Even if the conduct of the plaintiff seeking divorce does not fall within the conventional grounds, the courts have refused decree to the plaintiff. Thus there is much scope for the exercise of judicial discretion in granting or refusing divorce.

Statutes which allow divorce regardless of whether parties are at fault

A good number of states like Idaho, New York, Rhode Island, Texas, Virginia, Washington and North Carolina provide that either spouse may file a petition for divorce on the ground of separation.[24] Under these provisions separation need not have been voluntary. If there has been continuous separation for the prescribed statutory period, then either party is entitled to get divorce. The traditional fault defenses are inapplicable. The Nevada[25] and the Rhode Island[26] statutes expressly provide the courts with a discretion in the matter of awarding divorce decrees based on separation. In North Corolina, a non-discretionary non-fault statute has been interpreted in such a way as to include fault notions and divorce was refused to a husband who had abandoned his wife. Again in *O'Brien* v. *O'Brien*[27] divorce was refused on the ground that there was no mutual consent between the parties at the time of separation.

The conversion type statutes

A good number of states have statutes which authorize divorce once a decree of separation has been obtained and the period prescribed has been observed. A few examples are Alabama[28], Connecticut[29], District of Columbia[30], Utah[31], Virginia[32] and Minnesota.[33] Under these statutes either party may get an absolute divorce irrespective of the fact whether the petitioner was a plaintiff or the defendant in a suit for legal separation initially. In some states such as North Dakota[34], the court has a discretion. In New York[35] the petitioner who wants to convert the decree of separation into an absolute divorce has to prove that he has substantially complied with all the terms of the separation decree or agreement.

An interesting question came up for decision in *Gleason* v. *Gleason*[36] in the state of New York. Until 1966, the only ground on which a spouse could obtain divorce was adultery. In that year the Divorce Reform Law was passed in New York which extended the grounds for divorce. The new section 170 of the Domestic Relations Law provides two "non-fault" grounds in addition to the other extended grounds. They are (1) living apart pursuant to a decree or judgment of separation for two years (one year after September 1, 1972) and (2) living apart pursuant to a written separation agreement for two years (again reduced to one year after September 1972). The husband in the *Gleason* case brought action in October 1968 for divorce. He alleged that he and his wife had been living apart for more than two years, pursuant to a separation decree obtained in June 1954. He further alleged that he had complied with all the terms of the separation decree which was one of the conditions before he could be granted divorce under the existing law. The wife contended first, that section 170(5) was prospective in operation and if applied "retroactively" it would be unconstitutional. Secondly, she had not the warning that the separation decree granted to her might be used in the future by the husband—a guilty party—to deprive her of valuable rights such as pension rights, inheritance and social benefits without notice. We are concerned here more about the second contention raised by the wife leaving aside the constitutional wranglings and the problem of statutory retroactivity. However, on both counts the court negatived the plea of the wife. As respect the granting of a decree to the "guilty party" the court said:[37]

> Since, as is apparent, the legislative design was to render this a basis for divorce, it follows that it makes no difference whether it is the "innocent" or "guilty" party who seeks to convert the judicial separation into a final divorce. . . In a word, if there is no longer a viable marriage, the question of fault, of "guilt" or "innocence" is irrelevant.

When the law was reformed in 1967 *Gershenson*[38] hailed it by saying "a giant step has been taken in Divorce Law to bring New York into twentieth century". Foster[39] regards the decision of *Gleason* as a "landmark". The Appellate Court of New York has certainly given a progressive interpretation to the provisions relating to separation. However, the importance of the decision lies not so much in its disregard of the traditional doctrine, to wit, he who comes to equity court must come with clean hands, as in its acknowledgement of the concept of "breakdown of marriage". Writing in 1937, Bradway suggested that "... the rule of the innocent spouse has long since outlived its social usefulness, if in fact it ever had any, and that the time is at hand to substitute for this outmoded rule and its accompanying procedure a more efficient and satisfactory system of control of familial relations".[40] At the same time, the court has declared the public policy to terminate in law certain marriages which had ceased to exist in fact.

The relative merits or otherwise of the separation statutes

We have examined the various types of separation statutes and how they work in practice. We must now be able to point out the relative merits and defects of these statutes which authorize a divorce on the ground of separation.

The voluntary separation statutes can be regarded as incorporating a non-fault ground in two ways. First, the parties may mutually agree to a divorce and live apart for the requisite period of time in order to terminate the marital relationship. Secondly, since they have voluntarily agreed to separate, whatever the cause of separation be, the consideration of fault becomes irrelevant. Where the statutes have provided for voluntary separation, mutual agreement or consent has been insisted upon by the courts. If one of the parties has not willingly agreed to separate then the other party cannot obtain a divorce. Further, as we have noticed, the courts have looked to the conduct of the plaintiff. If the plaintiff was at fault, then divorce was denied, which may give rise to an anomaly in some cases. The defendant can withhold consent to separate thus preventing the other party from obtaining the divorce. Such is the case under the English Divorce Reform Act, 1969. According to the provisions of that Act[41], if the parties have lived apart for a period of two years or more, divorce can beg ranted provided the respondent consents to a decree being given. Therefore, if there has been no consent, a divorce cannot be obtained. But under the English law, there is a wayout. That is, if the parties have lived apart for a period of five or more years immediately preceding the presentation of the petition, irrespective of the fact whether one of the parties objects to the grant of the decree, a divorce can be given.[42] But this remedy has the effect of dragging out the separation for an inordinately long period of five or more years. Better results could perhaps be obtained by joining the separation issue to the fact of discord than to the quest of guilt.

We have also examined the effect of misconduct of one of the parties when a divorce action is based on separation. It varies considerably from state to state. In some jurisdictions fault considerations are expressly excluded. There is no difficulty with these types of statutes as a clear directive is given just not to consider fault while granting divorce. Some statutes are silent as to fault and the courts have rightly interpreted that fault notions need not be pressed into service in respect of separation ground.

Under some jurisdictions a discretion is given to the courts expressly. In such cases, the courts have tended to look to the conduct of the plaintiff at the time of separation. Where the plaintiff was at fault, a decree was denied. In other words, when the statute has rested the discretion with the court, it has taken shelter under the umbrella of fault. At least the Wyoming statute is straightforward and perhaps honest in the sense that it provides that fault must be considered.

In some jurisdictions, a decree of separation is necessary before it can be converted into an absolute divorce after the prescribed period. Under these types of statutes, there are two steps instead of one, thus prolonging the adversary process. This may be a burden on a party who can ill afford the expense.[43] As the authors of a more popular book on family have observed in respect of New York that "by adding a 'ground' of voluntary separation for a given period . . . the New York law appears likely to perpetuate the 'two class' situation which has plagued that state for so long. Those with sufficient means avail themselves of migratory divorces in the easier climes of Nevada and Mexico. Those less well-off are remitted to the law at home". In their view "one law obtains for the rich and another for the poor".

Another difficulty that will be encountered under the separation statutes is in cases where the parties attempt a reconciliation for a short period of time and separate again. Under the voluntary separation statutes, the separation is temporarily terminated and under the statutes which merely require the parties to live apart for a prescribed period, the continuity of their separation will be interrupted. Under these circumstances, naturally, the parties will have to wait for a fresh period. Thus under these circumstances, as pointed out by Wadlington[44], the principal problem becomes one of proof of time when the breakdown occurred. In order to overcome the problem of proof, the statutes can provide that a short period of time during which the parties live together with a view to effect reconciliation shall not interrupt the prescribed statutory period. We can take inspiration from the English law. Under the Divorce Reform Act, 1969[45], it is provided that while considering whether the statutory period of two years in case of desertion or where parties have lived apart for the specified period, no account shall be taken of any one period not exceeding six months in all during which the parties resumed cohabitation, but no period during which the parties lived each other will count as part of the period of desertion or of the period for which the parties have lived apart as the case may be. It is submitted that the reformers in the United States should seriously consider following English law in their divorce practices.

Before we pass on to the next non-fault ground, just one more problem attendant upon the separation ground must be emphasized. It is not always the fact that parties to a marriage live separate and apart due to mutual aversion, dislike or discord. Separation may result due to military service, requirement of employment or business, hospitalization or incarceration. The question becomes all the more important in view of the fact that, of late, many jurisdictions have provided for shorter periods of separation. Reformers must guard against the abuse of such a provision which might lead to unjust and dangerous results in which the whole institution of marriage would be imperilled. We have not yet known what mischief this shorter period of time of separation has done to matrimonial relations. No statistics are available in the knowledge of the present writer. And, in the absence of any statistics it is premature to draw conclusions upon the merits or otherwise of the separation ground with shorter periods.

Be that as it may, the legislature must spell out clearly the policy behind recognition of separation as a ground for divorce. It may even provide that "living apart" shall not be made applicable to cases of hospitalization, incarceration, military service or necessities of employment or business. In cases of separation which may have resulted due to mental illness and insanity, a separate ground for divorce may be provided. This has been done in some jurisdictions: Vermont, Maryland, Puerto Rico, Utah, Washington and Virginia where insanity is made an independent ground alongside with separation. As respects the jurisdiction which have done away with the fault grounds, insanity is made a separate ground alongside with the breakdown of marriage as a ground of divorce: California and Florida may be mentioned as examples.

INCOMPATIBILITY AS A CAUSE FOR DIVORCE

More than a century ago, when legislative divorce was available, some of the states had "omnibus clauses" in their divorce statutes broad enough to include incompatibility of temperament.[46] Earlier, the Illinois statute provided divorce for causes not prescribed for by any law of the state. The Iowa statute recognized granting of divorce if the court was satisfied that the spouses could not "live in peace and happiness".[47] The Minnesota divorce law as it stood in 1885 had a similar provision. A Washington statute effective until 1921 provided that a divorce may be granted upon application of either party for "any other cause deemed by the court sufficient, and the court shall be satisfied that the parties can no longer live together".[48] It must be pointed out that none of these statutes used the expression "incompatibility" but some courts interpreted them as authorizing a grant of divorce on personal indignities, disharmony or temperamental incompatibility.[49] All such statutes which allowed absolute divorce have ceased to exist. These statutes now provide for specific grounds on which divorce could be obtained.

Several states recognize incompatibility as a ground for divorce They are: Alabama[50], Alaska[51], Delaware[52], Idaho[53], Nevada[54], Oklahoma[55], North Dakota[56], Texas[57], New Mexico[58] and Virgin Islands.[59] Virgin Islands was the first to recognize incompatibility as a legal basis for dissolution of marriage.

New Mexico and Alaska followed suit in 1933 and in 1935 respectively. The recent "convert" to incompatibility are Texas and Alabama. Delaware added this ground in 1968.

Ever since the appearance of "incompatibility" or "incompatibility of temperament" as a ground for divorce on the statute books of the above jurisdictions, the courts are burdened with the unenviable task of administering the remedy to the disgruntled spouses. This seemingly simple remedy has brought in its train complex legal problems both for lawyers and judges. As pointed out by Clark[60] "incompatibility is of interest in American law not because of its practical importance but as an illustration of the complexities which may lurk in an ostensibly simple legal proposition".

The concept has been borrowed from the Prussian Code which used "insuperable aversion".[61] The Prussian Code in turn had received the idea from Montesquieu who, a century ago, had advocated that it was due to incompatibility that marriage might end in failure and require the remedy of divorce.[62]

Definition and judicial interpretation

Except for the statute of Delaware which defines incompatibility as reciprocal conflicts of personalities which destroy the matrimonial relations, none of the statutes define this term. Earlier the New Mexico court declined to define incompatibility.[63] The guidelines were laid down in the leading case of *Burch* v. *Burch*.[64] Judge Maris observed:[65]

> ... incompatibility of temperament ... does not refer to those petty quarrels and minor bickerings which are but the evidence of that frailty which all humanity is heir to, it unquestionably does refer to conflicts in personalities and dispositions so deep as to be irreconcilable and to render it impossible for the parties to continue a normal marital relationship with each other.

The same court on another occasion said:[66]

> ... in determining whether a married pair are so incompatible as to justify a divorce on that ground the inquiry is not as to the fault of either or both but rather as to

> whether their marital barque has so far floundered upon the rocks of disharmony and discord as to be beyond the possibility of salvage. It is to the question whether the marriage is in fact ended because of the basic unsuitability of the spouses for each other, . . . rather than causes of the state in which they find themselves, that the court must direct its inquiry in determining whether incompatibility of temperament exists.

The above guidelines have been approved and followed by other states. For example, in *Wegener* v. *Wegener*[67], the Oklahoma court held that actionable incompatibility exist when such a conflict of personalities comes about as to destroy the legitimate ends of matrimony and possibilities of reconciliation. Incompatibility has been found in "inability to get along" the "drifting apart" excessive drinking of whisky, extraordinary pangs of jealousy and disparity in age.[68] A few cases may be mentioned by way of illustration to know how this remedy has worked in practice.

In *Kirkland* v. *Kirkland*[39] the wife became an ardent lover of Christian dogma and ethics. She completely devoted her time studying the Bible which resulted in a loss of social companionship. The court on evidence found actionable incompatibility. In another interesting case[70] the husband complained that his wife refused to serve meals on exact schedule and that she had temper fits. He alleged that being a physician with a rigid schedule it was important that he got his meals at the appointed time. The lower court did not find incompatibility to such a degree as would give rise to an action for divorce. On appeal the Supreme Court of Delaware reversed the decision of the lower court and said, ". . . we are of the opinion that facts lead clearly to the conclusion that the trouble in this marriage is far more than 'trivial'. . . ".[71]

In contrast to the above rulings we have decisions wherein divorce was denied. In *Sachs* v. *Sachs*[72], the husband alleged that he had a right to maintain the relationship with his mistress. It was held that there was not sufficient evidence to establish incompatibility. The Oklahoma court in *Vincent* v. *Vincent*[73] confronted with similar facts came to the same conclusion. It was found in this case that there was no irreconcilable differences between the parties which enabled the court to dissolve the marriage. Without multiplying illustrations it may be said that the courts in deciding what constitutes incompatibility have tried to harmonize seemingly irreconcilable factors, like happiness and stability in marriage and the rival claims of the parties.

A close scrutiny of the cases on the subject reveals two dominant principles. First, the legitimate objects of matrimony must have been destoryed, secondly, there should be no reasonable prospects for reconciliation in the future. This theme runs throughout the judicial interpretation of incompatibility. As stated in *Shearer* v. *Shearer*[74] "there is no disagreement on the definition and meaning of incompatibility laid down in *Burch.* v. *Burch*. . . It exists where the conflict in the personalities of the parties is so deep as to be irreconcilable and this condition has existed sufficiently long to justify the conclusion that it is irremediable. *The real question is in the application of that definition to the evidence*".

Thus some courts may find or have in fact found incompatibility in situations which could have been overlooked as "wear and tear" of conjugal life. Others have applied stricter standards. All that can be said is that it is a question of degree or intensity of incompatibility or the kind of irreconcilable differences that would authorize a court to untie the conjugal knot. A heavy responsibility no doubt rests upon the court. It should go into the whole history of the marriage, extract full evidence of facts, weigh the probability of reconciliation and examine the extent to which the objects of matrimony have been frustrated. At the same time courts are not driven ". . . to make a simple case of incompatibility of temperament a contest between psychiatric experts plumbing the depths of the unconscious qualities of the parties".[75]

Mutuality in incompatibility

The concept of mutuality has been introduced by judicial legislation in cases on incompatibility. A question arose whether incompatibility should be unilateral or bilateral. In other words, should both parties feel incompatibility or is it sufficient that only one does, while the other does not desire a divorce? There is a conflict of decisions among the various state courts. The Oklahoma court[76] in an earlier case insisted on mutual incompatibility. The Supreme Court of the state revised the stand taken by the court earlier.[77] It was held in *Kennedy* v. *Kennedy*[78] and other cases[79] that it was not necessary that there should be mutual incompatibility. In *Wegener* v. *Wegener*[80] the Supreme Court laid down broad propositions relating to incompatibility. They were as follows :

(1) Actionable incompatibility exists when such a conflict of personality develops that the legitimate ends of matrimony and possibility of reconciliation are destroyed;
(2) Such a state may exist although the situation is considered serious by one spouse and less so by the other;
(3) Where incompatibility exists as a result of the misconduct of the complaining spouse, the court is vested with broad discretion in weighing the possibilities of reconciliation and the restoration of a normal marital status against granting divorce;
(4) If, in the opinion of the court, the evidence establishes the bilateral incompatibility of the parties, then the grounds for divorce are proven regardless of the degree that each of the parties contributed to such incompatibility.

In Delaware[81], courts had generally not insisted on mutuality. In fact they had avoided the problem by saying that if conflicting personalities produce a rift and discord, it was by its nature reciprocal or bilateral.[82] However, in *Doran* v. *Doran*[83] it was held that actionable incompatibility must be mutual. Commenting upon the Delaware cases on incompatibility, Gallagher[84] points out that when the courts spoke about fault most domestic relations lawyers thought that the courts should not be talking about fault, which had always been equated with aggression, but about "no-fault" and inquiring whether there had been marriage failure within the terms of the statute. He says that in practical effect that was the result.

Doctrine of recrimination : Whether applicable to incompatibility cases

While deciding cases on the ground of incompatibility courts have had to grapple with the proposition whether recrimination could be invoked to bar a suit for divorce. The difficuly has arisen due to the fact that incompatibility is basically a "non-fault" ground. The problem had arisen even earlier when incompatibility was not a statutory ground but nevertheless, as we have seen, covered by "omnibus clauses" in some of the jurisdictions. Even at that time the courts of Iowa and Washington had in their discretion rejected the doctrine.[85] Recriminationwas held not to be an absolute bar to a divorce action.

The same proposition cropped up when incompatibility became a statutory ground for divorce. Under the Virgin Islands statute, divorce for incompatibility may be obtained "at the instance of the injured party". A question has arisen as to who is an injured party. The Court of Appeals in *Burch* v. *Burch*[86] was confronted with the issue. The facts of this case, briefly stated, were as follows :

The husband sued the wife for divorce on the ground of incompatibility. The wife countered the petition on the ground of her husband's cruel treatment. The jury gave a verdict in favour of the husband. The wife appealed. The court was called upon to construe the statutory phrase "injured party". The question was whether the injured party meant only one who was injured by the grounds allowed for divorce, or one who was innocent of any conduct which would afford his or her spouse grounds for divorce. It was held that incompatibility injures both parties. The court said:[87]

> ... the evidence in this case supports a finding of incompatibility of temperament between the parties. Since the cruelty of the plaintiff to the defendant does not under the Virgin Islands law bar the granting of a divorce to the plaintiff on the ground of incompatibility and, in our judgment, was not such as to call for the discretionary denial of the divorce he seeks, it appears that the plaintiff was entitled to a divorce.

Thus the husband was granted a divorce despite his cruelty towards the wife. On the other hand, under similar circumtances in *Schlesinger* v. *Schlesinger*[88], Kalodner, denounced the granting of divorce to the husband who was found to be at fault. He forcefully stated:[89]

> To award a divorce, under the prevailing circumstances, to an unfaithful husband on the ground that the righteous wrath of his betrayed wife has made them incompatible would be to reward him for marital infidelity. The Virgin Islands divorce statute cannot be construed to sanction such an ironic result.

The statute of New Mexico does not expressly mention that divorce be obtained at the instance of the injured party nor do the statutes of other jurisdictions. The New Mexico decisions on the point have been fluctuating. In *Pavletich* v. *Pavletich*[90], it was held that recrimination was not a bar in incompatibility cases. But, four years later the same court in *Clark* v. *Clark*[91] took a contrary view. It was stated that the court could deny a divorce under circumstances which "shock the conscience". It must be pointed out that the decision in the *Clark* case did not overrule the earlier decision of *Pavletich*. What it did lay down was simply that recrimination could be a bar to an action on incompatibility but that a discretion should rest with the court granting or withholding the remedy of divorce. This is clear when the court said:[92]

> If the chancellor believes the parties are reconcilable, he will, no doubt, endeavor to bring about a reconciliation. But where the parties are irreconcilable we believe that the public policy of this state as expressed by the legislature, is against denying a divorce on the doctrine of recrimination.

This is the position so far as New Mexico is concerned. In other jurisdictions recrimination does not bar a suit for divorce.[93] According to Clark[94] the defense of recrimination has no place in divorce actions for incompatibility. But in the opinion of Orfield[95] recrimination should not be a bar "nevertheless a remnant of discretion should be retained by the court as to certain cases where the applicant is overwhelmingly at fault and the other spouse is relatively innocent, or where children are concerned." In this respect Orfield subscribes to the view taken in the *Clark* case in New Mexico. It may be mentioned in passing that Judge Schulman,[96] in a recent article, has advocated the adoption of incompatibility as a ground for divorce. In his view, since the Supreme Court in Kansas has liberally construed "extreme cruelty" and "gross neglect"—reminiscent of that found in incompatibility—Kansas should not have any difficulty in integrating incompatibility into its present divorce practice.[97]

Recrimination is still a valid defense to a divorce action in many jurisdictions generally and particularly when divorce is sought on the ground of adultery. Some statutes explicitly mention[98] it as a bar and others do not.[99] Where it is explicitly incorporated in a statute the courts have had to raise their hands in despair and apply recrimination as a defense to a divorce action grounded on adultery, cruelty or desertion. As an illustration, the case of *Kucera* v. *Kucera*[100] may be mentioned. Until 1963, the North Dakota divorce statute had provided that recrimination should bar a divorce. In the instant case the wife filed a suit for divorce against her husband alleging cruelty. It was found that she was also guilty of cruelty and desertion. The court was convinced that the marriage had utterly broken down, yet was compelled by the mandatory provision of the statute in invoking recrimination to deny a divorce decree to the wife. In the year 1966, that is after the decision of *Kucera*, North Dakota revised the statute[101] and deleted recrimination as a bar though it retained other defenses of collusion, condonation and connivance to prevent the granting of the decree of divorce. In jurisdictions where recrimination is not a statutory bar, courts have used their discretion and in most cases the trend has been not to follow the doctrine mechanically.[102] As many as five jurisdictions[103] in the recent past have abolished recrimination as a bar.

Many writers[104] have criticized and advocated that the doctrine be abolished in the interest of promoting social good and on reasons of public policy. It may be mentioned that in jurisdictions where "breakdown" of marriage has been made the sole ground for divorce, recrimination and comparative rectitude have been completely discarded. For instance, in California, a "non-fault" divorce state, the Supreme Court in *McKim* v. *McKim*[105] had no hesitation to lay down that recrimination and comparative rectitude under the Family Law Act, 1970 cannot be applied as a bar to a divorce. Justice Mosk referred *De Burgh* v. *De Burgh* an earlier decision which abandoned the doctrine and declared:[106]

> With that decision the defense of recrimination, for all practical purposes, became moribund, and a faint ray of rationality illumined the field of domestic relations.

In Iowa, another "non-fault" divorce state, in *In Re Marriage of Williams*[107], the Supreme Court was emphatic in stating that the Dissolution Act eliminated the "guilty party" concept. We may recall that under the jurisdictions which have fault-oriented grounds as well as separation ground alongside, the defense of "unclean hands" was rejected.

Judging from the trends in judicial decisions as well as legislatively revised statutes we have referred to, it may safely be concluded that the role of this doctrine is dwindling day by day. It is heartening to note that the courts in majority of the decisions on the subject have rightly rejected the doctrine of recrimination—an outdated remnant of ecclesiastical vestige. When more and more states adopt the "breakdown" concept, as it seems likely that they would, this doctrine would be burried under the debris of Anglo-American divorce law. At least Moore[108] expressed a hope that "the doctrine will eventually go the way of the dinosaur".

A pertinent question may be asked at this juncture : where was the need, what was the reason for the inclusion of incompatibility in the already long list of grounds for divorce ? In other words, could it not have been covered by the grounds such as "mental cruelty" and personal indignities, particularly when the courts have broadened the concepts while construing these grounds liberally ? The writer was intrigued when he had the chance to look into the divorce statutes of various states. To employ a hyperbole, almost every ground that exists on earth has been recognized—from impotency to insanity, from incarceration to attempt to poison the other spouse, from habitual drinking to gross neglect, not to mention the conventional grounds. New York had been a solitary exception in this respect. It had listed only one ground, adultery (an offence *par excellance*). It held the banner of ecclesiastical law till 1966 at a time when wife swapping was gaining ground as a lively sport. North Carolina surpassed even New York. It stuck, till late, religiously to the Biblical command : "What God hath joined together, let no man put as under".

Reverting to the question raised, it may be stated that in a majority of jurisdictions which have recognized "mental cruelty" and "personal indignities", it is necessary to prove misconduct of a very serious nature.[109] The legal concepts that had developed require in such cases proof of physical harm or injury to health or a reasonable apprehension of it. Further, the rule of "innocent" and "injured party" or the doctrine of "clean hands" is always applicable to these remedies. Incompatibility is rid of all these drawbacks. The rationale behind the remedies of mental cruelty and indignities is to protect the victim and give her or him a right to dissolve the marriage. The philosophy of incompatibility is to bury a dead marriage which has failed to achieve its object without allocating any fault on the part of either spouses. Further, incompatibility encompasses[110] all those serious types of matrimonial wranglings which go to the very root of marriage making it appear an empty shell. And, when there are no prospects of reconciliation between the parties, it becomes necessary to separate them rather than allow to continue the marital relations which may have become odious. It is then that the state should take upon itself the responsibility to terminate the marriage. Recognition of incompatibility as a basis for the dissolution of marriage is indicative of the shift in the very concept of marriage. Its adoption is nothing more and nothing less than the anxiety on the part of the legislatures to narrow the distance between law and social needs.

NOTES AND REFERENCES

1. Kentucky has now only one ground for the dissolution of marriage: Irretrievable breakdown. See Key. Rev. Stat. Ann. Sec. 403, 140 (Supp. 1974).
2. Wisconsin now provides for one year separation. See Wis. Stat. Ann. 247.07 (b) (Supp. 1974).

3. Rhode Island now provides for 5 years separation. See R.I. Gren. Laws Sec. 15-5-3 (1970).
4. *Parks* v. *Parks*, 116 F. 2d 556 (D.C. 1940).
4a. Ibid. at 557.
5. McCurdy, *Divorce—A Suggested Approach with Particular Reference to Dissolution for Living Separate and Apart*, 9 Vand. L. Rev. 685 at 702 (1956).
6. See generally 24 Am. Jur. 2d Sec. 148-149 (1966); 35 A.L.R. 3d 1238 (1971); See further Wadlington, *Divorce Without Fault Without Perjury*, 52 Va. L. Rev. 32 (1966).
7. *Richardson* v. *Richardson*, 257 N.C. 705, 127 S.E. 2d 525 (1962).
8. *Boyce* v. *Boyce*, 153 F. 2d 229, 230 (D.C. Cir. 1946).
9. See Ploscowe, Foster and Freed, *Family Law Cases and Materials* 353-57 (2nd ed. 1972) (hereinafter cited as Foster).
10. Del. Rev. Code. Ann. tit. 13, Sec. 1522 (11) (1975).
11. Md. Ann. Code Sec. 24 (1973).
12. Wis. Stat. Ann. 247.07 (b) (Supp. 1974).
13. *Maloney* v. *Maloney*, 54 Del. 578, 183 A. 2d 172 (1962).
14. See H. Clark, *Law of Domestic Relations*, Sec. 12.6, at 351-356.
15. 24 Am. Jur. 2d Sec. 152 at 309 (1966).
16. See note, *Voluntary Separation as Grounds for Divorce in Wisconsin* 1972. Wis. L. Rev. 1215 at 1220-1221.
17. *Powless* v. *Powless*, 269 Wis. 552, 69 N.W. 2d 753 (1955); *Jakubke* v. *Jakubke*, 125 Wis. 635, 104 N.W. 704 (1905).
18. *Kranse* v. *Kranse*, 177 Wis. 165, 187 N.W. 1019 (1922).
19. *Sanders* v. *Sanders*, 135 Wis. 613, 116 N.W. 176 (1908).
20. *Salinko* v. *Salinko*, 177 Wis. 475 188, N.W. 606 (1922).
21. *Martin* v. *Martin*, 160 F. 2d 20 (D.C. Cir. 1947).
22. *Stumpf* v. *Stumpf*, 228 Md. 350, 179 A. 2d 893 (1962).
23. Wyo. Stat. Ann. Sec. 20-47 (Supp. 1971).
24. Foster, Supra note 9, at 356.
25. Nev. Rev. Stat. Sec. 125.010 (2) (1973).
26. R.I. Gen. Laws. Ann. Sec. 15-5-3 (Supp. 1974).
27. *O'Brien* v. *O'Brien*, 266 N.C. 502, 146 S.E. 2d 500 (1966).
28. Ala. Code Ann. tit. 36, Sec. 22 (1) (Supp. 1974).
29. C.G.S. Ann. Sec. 46-13 (Supp. 1971). But see the new law enacted in 1973. cf. C.G.S.A. Ch. 811, Sec. 46-32 (Supp. 1975).
30. D.C. Code. Ann. Sec. 16-904 (b) (1973).
31. Utah Code Ann. Sec. 30-3-1 (8) (1969).
32. Va. Code. Sec. 20-121 (Supp. 1972).
33. Minn. Stat. Ann. Sec. 518.06 (West. Supp. 1971).
    Minnesota is now a non-fault divorce state. See Minn. Stat. Ann. Sec. 518.06 (Supp. 1975).
34. N.D. Cent. Code. Sec. 14-06-05 (Supp. 1973).
35. N.Y. Dom. Rel. Law Sec. 170 (5) (McKinney 1974).
36. *Gleason* v. *Gleason*, 26 N.Y. 2d 28, 256 N.E. 2d 513 (1970).
37. Ibid./26 N.Y. 2d 28 at 35, 256 N.E. 2d 513 at 516.

38. Gershenson, *The Divorce Reform Law*, N.Y.L.J. July 2nd, 1967 at 3 col. 4.
39. Foster and Freed, *The Divorce Reform Law* 54 (1970).
40. Bradway, *The Myth of the Innocent Spouse*, 11 Tulane L. Rev. 377 at 398 (1937).
41. Divorce Reform Act, 1969, Sec. 2 (1) d.
42. Ibid. Sec. 2(1) e.
43. See Foote, Levy and Sander, *Cases and Materials on Family Law* 142 (Supp. 1971).
44. See Wadlington, supra note 6 at 70.
45. Sec. 3(5) of the Divorce Reform Act, 1969.
46. 2 Vernier, *American Family Laws* 65 (1932).
47. For a good discussion on the subject and the earlier use of incompatibility as a cause for absolute divorce, see Orfield, *Divorce for Temperamental Incompatibility*, 52 Mich. L. Rev. 659 (1954). Iowa, Washington and Minnesota have recently adopted a no-fault divorce law. The new law relating to these jurisdictions has been discussed and commented upon in Ch. 111.
48. See Orfield, ibid. at 660.
49. See for example, *Clyburn* v. *Clyburn*, 175 Ark. 330, 299 S.W. 38 (1927); *Haller* v. *Haller*, 149 Wash. 277, 270, p. 822 (1928).
50. Ala. Code tit. 34, Sec. 20(7) (Supp. 1973).
51. Alas. STAT. ANN. tit. 9, Sec. 09.55 110 (5) (c) (1973).
52. Del. Rev. Code ANN. tit. 13, Sec. 1522 (12) (1974).
53 Idaho. Code. Sec. 32-603 (8) (Supp. 1972).
54. Nev. Rev. STAT. ANN. Sec. 125.010 (10) (1969).
55. Okla. STAT. ANN. tit. 12, Sec. 1271 (7) (1961).
56. N.D. Cent. Codes, Sec. 41-05-09.1 (Supp. 1971).
57. Tex. Fam. Code ANN. Sec. 3.01 (1969).
58. N.M. STAT. ANN. Sec. 22-7-1.A (Supp. 1971).
59. V.I. Code ANN. tit. 16, Sec. 104 (a) 8 (1964). Now Virgin Islands has a no-fault divorce law. See V.I. Code ANN. tit. 16, Sec. 104 (Supp. 1974).
60. H. Clark, *Law of Domestic Relations* 349 Sec. 12.5 (1968).
61. *Burch* v. *Burch*, 195 F. 2d 799 (3rd. Cir. 1952).
62. See Max Rheinstein, *Marriage Stability, Divorce and the Law* 206 (1972).
63. *Poteet* v. *Poteet*, 45 N.M. 214, 114 P. 2d 91 (1941).
64. *Burch* v. *Burch* supra note 61.
65. *Burch* v. *Burch*, 195 F. 2d 799 at 806-807 (3rd Cir. 1952).
66. *Del Peschio* v. *Del Peschio*, 356 F. 2d 402 at 406 (1966).
67. *Wegener* v. *Wegener*, 365 P. 2d 728 (Okla. 1961).
68. For a good discussion of such cases see Comment, *Incompatibility of Temperament and Irretrievable breakdown—What they will mean in Alabama*? 3 Cum. Sam. L. Rev. 434 (1972).
69. *Kirkland* v. *Kirkland*, 488 P. 2d 1222 (Okla. 1971).
70. *Husband* v. *Wife*, 280 A. 2d 705 (Del. 1971).
71. Ibid. at 707.

72. *Sachs* v. *Sachs*, 155 F. Supp. 860 (D.C.V.I. 1957).
73. *Vincent* v. *Vincent*, 257 P. 2d 512 (Okla. 1953).
74. *Shearer* v. *Shearer*, 356 F. 2d 391 at 395 (Emphasis added).
75. See the observation of Freedman, J., ibid. at 398.
76. *Hughes* v. *Hughes*, 363 P. 2d 155 (Okla. 1961); *Rakestraw* v. *Rakestraw*, 345 P. 2d 888 (Okla. 1959).
77. See *Wegener* case supra note 67.
78. *Kennedy* v. *Kennedy*, 461 P. 2d 614 (Okla. 1969).
79. *Waller* v. *Waller*, 439 P. 2d (Okla. 1968); *Stuart* v. *Stuart*, 433 P. 2d 951 (Okla. 1967); *Bessinger* v. *Bessinger*, 372 P. 2d 870 (Okla. 1962).
80. *Wegener* v. *Wegener*, supra note 67, at 730.
81. See for example, *J.A.D.* v. *P.L.D.*, 259 A.2d 381 (Del. 1969).
82. Ibid.
83. *Doran* v. *Doran*, 245 A. 2d 434 (Supr. ct. 1968).
84. See Gallagher, *No-Fault Divorce in Delaware*, 59 A.B.A.J. 874 (1973).
85. See Orfield, supra note 47 at 666. He cites the following cases: *Inskeep* v. *Inskeep*, 5 Iowa 204 (1857); *Schirmer* v. *Schirmer*, 84 Wash. 1, 145 P. 981 (1915).
86. *Burch* v. *Burch*, supra note 61.
87. Ibid. at 810.
88. *Schlesinger* v. *Schlesinger*, 6 V. 1.671, 399 F. 2d 7 (3rd. Cir. 1968).
89. Ibid. 6 V. 1. 671 at 679, 399 F. 2d 7 at 10.
90. *Pavletich* v. *Pavletich*, 50 N.M. 224, 174, P. 2d 826 (1946).
91. *Clark* v. *Clark*, 54 N.M. 364, 225 P. 2d 147 (1950).
92. *Pavletich* v. *Pavletich*, 50 N.M. 226 at 233, 174 P. 2d 826 at 832.
93. See for example *De Burgh* v. *De Burgh*, 39 Cal. 2d 858, 250 P. 2d 598 (1952); *Hughes* v. *Hughes*, supra note 76. For a good discussion on the point see *Wells* v. *Wells*, 79 N.J. 388, 191 A. 2d 763 (1963).
94. See Clark, supra note 60 at 351.
95. See Orfield, supra note 47, at 680.
96. Schulman, *Incompatibility: A New Approach to the Dissolution of Marriage*, 20 U. Kansas. L. Rev. 227 (1972).
97. Ibid. at 236-37.
98. For example Nevada, Colorado, Washington and Oklahoma.
99. Recrimination has been abolished in the jurisdictions which have no-fault divorce laws. As examples of these California, Iowa, Florida, Oregon, Michigan may be mentioned. In Arkansas, the doctrine of recrimination is not applied when divorce is sought under the "living apart" ground. It is abolished in Texas in respect to the ground of insupportability. In Mississippi the court has a discretion either to apply recrimination as a defense or reject it.
100. *Kucera* v. *Kucera*, 117 N.W. 2d 810 (N.D. 1962).
101. N.D. Cent. Code Sec. 14-05-10 (1971).
102. See *Burgh* and *Wells*, supra note 93.
103. Colo. Rev. STAT. Sec. 46-1-4 (3) (1964); Nev. Rev. STAT. ANN. Sec. 125.120 (1973); N. D. Cent. Code Sec. 14-05-10 (1971); Okla. STAT. ANN. tit. 12, Sec. 1275 (1961); RCWA Sec. 26.08 150 (1961).

104. See Ruskin and Katz, *The Dying Doctrine of Recrimination in the United States of America*, 35 Can. B. Rev. 1046 (1957); Beamer, *The Doctrine of Recrimination in Divorce Proceedings*, 10 Kansas (city), L. Rev. 213 (1942); Comment. *O'Connor* v. *O'Connor : Recrimination in Retreat*. 3 Ind. Legal Forum. 538 (1970); Comment, *Recrimination for the Past*, 15 S.D.L. Rev. 366 (1970); Moore, *A Critique of the Recrimination Doctrine*, 68 Dic. L. Rev. 157 (1964).
105. *McKim* v. *McKim*, 6 Cal. 3d 673, 100 Cal. Reptr. 140 (West 1972).
106. Ibid. at 6 Cal. 3d at 683, 100 Cal. Reptr. at 147.
107. *In Re Marriage of Williams*, 199 N.W. 2d 339, 345 (Iowa, 1972).
108. Moore, *An Examination of the Recrimination Doctrine*, 20 S.C.L. Rev. 685 (1968).
109. See Moran, *Divorce for Incompatibility of Temperament*, 9 Duke B.A.J. 49 (1941); Note, *Indignities as Grounds for Divorce*, 1 Wyom. L.J. 187 (1946).
110. It may be mentioned that racial, political or religious differences are not causes on which divorce has been granted in American law. Incompatibility may cover such cases.

Breakdown 3

GATHERING STORM

If the stoic philosophers and orthodox Christians who frowned upon sexual freedom and abhorred divorce introduced matrimonial guilt as the basis and justification for separation during the middle ages, the social scientists and reformers recognized "breakdown of marriage" as a cause for divorce. Academic lawyers[1] and judges did not lag behind; they gave impetus to the liberalization and reforms in divorce law. The search for a more rational divorce law keeping in tune with the demands of society has always occupied their minds.[2] There was a general dissatisfaction about the grounds of divorce based on the concept of matrimonial guilt. The state's refusal to grant a divorce without a showing of fault did little to solve the marital problems. In fact the adversary process added to the tension and bitterness among the spouses. A few opinions which, in no uncertain terms, denounced the "fault" system and highlighted the evils of the adversary procedure in a divorce proceedings may be mentioned in order to appreciate the deplorable conditions under which divorce law operates.

Roger Traynor, the Chief Justice of California Supreme Court as he then was observed:[3]

> Perhaps in no other area has the discrepancy between law in dogmatic theory and law in action, evading dogma by fiction and subterfuge, become so marked as in divorce law. The withered dogma that divorce can be granted only for matrimonial fault, variously and eccentrically defined from state to state, is rendered still more irrational by the widespread rule that recrimination is an absolute defense. The

> result has been triumph, not for the dogma, but for hypocrisy. Rules insensitive to reality have been cynically circumvented by litigants and attorneys with the tacit sanction of the courts.

Paul W. Alexander, judge of the Family court centre, Toledo lamented:[4]

> No one is more painfully conscious than the legal profession of the utter imbecility of our present divorce procedure and the pernicious and almost wicked philosophy upon which it is based. Every honest lawyer is ashamed of the atmosphere of hypocrisy and lies in which he usually must handle a divorce case, ...

Paul Sayre commented:[5]

> This scheming of the parties themselves in an atmosphere of falsehood, as well as the fraud on our courts, works a degrading influence on the quality of our civilization and brings our whole system of justice into disrepute.

Max Rheinstein pointed out:[6]

> This discrepancy between law of the books and law in action, which we find in so many states, has, through its tolerance or promotion of collusive practices and perjury, developed into a serious threat to the morals of the bar and the respect for law among the public.

And, George Squire commenting upon the evils of adversary procedure declared:[7]

> The adversary principle is the Gibraltar of Anglo-American procedure. Embedded in it are standards of judicial function, such as the rules of evidence, which uncompromisingly block any major change in divorce or other civil litigation.

In short, the mounting objection to retention of "fault" grounds, the hypocrisy involved in divorce procedure, the widespread perjury percolating into the courts, the irksome formalities and the cumbersome processes attending the adversary system and to top it all the wounds that the unhappy spouses have to lick after having won or lost the legal battle left no one in doubt that a more realistic divorce law was necessary. The solution was found in the concept of "marital breakdown".[8]

The National Conference of Commissioners on Uniform State laws drafted in 1970 an Act which provided "irretrievable breakdown" as a sole ground for the dissolution of marriage.[9] Some states have incorporated the "breakdown" concept in their existing divorce statutes: either adding "breakdown" as an additional ground alongside the fault-oriented grounds or substituting it in place of conventional grounds.[10]

At the same time, other states are perhaps watching with growing interest and concern how these new statutes will work in practice. Some states may, sooner or later, follow suit. At least the present writer clearly sees the seeds being sown in some judicial decisions of some states. For instance, in three of the recent decisions handed down by the New York State Court the "breakdown" theory was accepted in principle. In *Jay* v. *Jay*[11], the court said:

> This appears to be one of those unfortunate situations where the marriage of this young couple must be dissolved and where the determination of the same is not a result of any particular "fault" of either party but rather a result of the "condition" existing between the parties.

The same trend appears in *Berlin* v. *Berlin*.[12] The court in this case granted a divorce at the instance of the wife on the ground of mental cruelty stating that the husband's conduct created a "dead marital relationship". Yet in another notable decision of *Gleason*, the New York Court of Appeal eliminated the concept of "innocent" and "guilty" party. This case is discussed in the previous pages.[12a]

We shall now deal with the jurisdictions wherein dissolution of marriage is allowed not because of any specific matrimonial misconduct but because there has been a marital failure.

CALIFORNIA

We have mentioned earlier that some states like California, Iowa, Florida, Oregon, Michigan, Colorado and Kentucky have completely revamped their laws by eliminating "fault-oriented" grounds and substituting breakdown of marriage as a ground for divorce. These reforms have been effected during the past five years. It is proposed to comment upon the new divorce statutes in light of the few cases that are available.

We will commence with California's divorce law. It was the first state which completely abolished the fault-oriented grounds and substituted irremediable breakdown of marriage as the basis for divorce. Its provisions have been commented upon and criticized by some writers.[13] The provisions have come under heavy fire at the hands of Rheinstein.[14] Some of the anomalies and flaws pointed out by Rheinstein are real. The issues raised are pertinent as well as colorful. The present writer's own reaction to the issues raised by the learned writer will be recorded in the course of the discussion on the California divorce statute which follows hereafter.

The relevant provisions of the Family Law Act, 1969, which became effective from January 1, 1970 completely displaced any requirement of a showing of fault of the respondent before a divorce can be obtained by the plaintiff. They read as follows:

Section 4506. (I) Irreconcilable differences, which have caused the irremediable breakdown of the marriage.

Section 4507. Irreconcilable differences are those grounds which are determined by the court to be substantial reasons for not continuing the marriage and which make it appear that the marriage should be dissolved.

A host of questions can be raised over this provision. For example, what are irreconcilable differences ? Under what circumstances can these differences be said to have caused the irremediable breakdown of marriage ? When can marriage be said to have broken down ? Can either party go to a law court and ask divorce by simply stating that his or her marriage has broken down ? What is the standard or test of irreconcilability ? Is it an objective test or a subjective one ? Is the issue of breakdown of marriage triable at all ?

Some of these questions have been answered in the few cases that have come up before the California courts. Section 4506(I) describes irreconcilable differences as those which have caused the irremediable breakdown of marriage. After the words "irreconcilable differences" the phrase "which have caused the irremediable breakdown of marriage" was added not as an imposition of a second standard to that of irreconcilable differences.[15] The phrase was meant to describe the relevant kinds of matrimonial differences.[16] As stated in *In Re Marriage of Walton*[17], the primary purpose of the statute was to indicate that the determination of the existence of irreconcilable differences specified in the section as a ground for dissolution of marriage, is to be made by the court and the second purpose was to make it clear that irreconcilable differences sufficient to justify dissolution of marriage must be substantial as opposed to trivial or minor.

Rheinstein[18] has pertinently asked : "What facts are substantial reasons for not continuing the marriage ?" It is submitted that the answer is found in the abovementioned case. While interpreting section 4506(I) the court référred to the existence of the marital problems which have so impaired the marriage relationship that the legitimate objects of matrimony have been destroyed in such a way that there was no possibility of elimination, correction or resolution.[19] Seen in the light of these observations, the "substantial reasons for not continuing the marriage" referred to in section 4507 must also mean the reasons which have destroyed the legitimate objects of marriage. The next question is : What are the legitimate objects of matrimony ? It is submitted that it does not need a master mind to understand what those legitimate objects are in the context of conjugal life. Common sense tells us that the legitimate objects of matrimony are, a happy home, love and affection, mutual trust and respect, sex, society *et al.*

We shall now pass on to the question whether the test of marital breakdown is subjective or an objective one; in other words, should the parties feel themselves that differences are irreconcilable or it is for the courts to determine that there are irreconcilable differences which have caused the irremediable breakdown of marriage.[20] In *McKim* v. *McKim*[21], the court ruled that it was for the court and not for the parties to say that the differences are irreconcilable. It was held:[22]

> Under the Family Law Act the court, not the parties, must decide whether the evidence adduced supports findings that irreconcilable differences do exist and that the marriage had broken down irremediably and should be dissolved.

Irreconcilable differences should be pleaded generally and the "court should sit as an overseeing participant to do its utmost to effect a healing of the marital wounds".[23] The facts in the *McKim* case, briefly stated, were as follows:

The wife filed for divorce on the ground of extreme cruelty in 1968. Her husband did not contest the petition and his default was entered in December 1968. Subsequently, the matter came on for hearing in 1970 under the new Family Law Act which permitted dissolution of marriage on the ground of irreconcilable differences. The wife did not appear at the hearing to testify the fact of irreconcilable differences upon which the relief was sought. The counsel on behalf of the wife introduced the testimony of the husband as to the irreconcilable differences. The trial court denied dissolution on the ground that the wife was required to appear personally at the hearing of the petition for dissolution of the marriage. It was further held that the ground of divorce, namely, irreconcilable difference causing irremediable breakdown of marriage could not be proved by the husband whose default had been entered.

The wife appealed against the decision and contended, *inter alia*, that the trial court was required to dissolve the marriage because the uncontradicted testimony of the husband was sufficient to establish irreconcilable differences. The Supreme Court of California by a majority opinion ruled that the personal appearance and the testimony of the petitioner were necessary in order to obtain proof of irreconcilable differences. However, the court was of the opinion that in exceptional circumstances, where the petitioner's absence could be explained to the satisfaction of the court, the requisite proof could be made by affidavit.

Mosk, J., did not agree with the majority opinion. In an eloquent dissent he observed:[24]

> The California Legislature took a giant leap forward in the field of domestic relations with adoption of the Family Law Act, operative as on January 1, 1970. Regrettably my colleagues in the majority take a step backward as they judicially legislate potentially burdensome requirements not contained in the statute.

Justice Mosk went further and said:[25]

> There is not a scintilla of authority contained either explicitly or implicitly within the Family Law Act for the fiat that, in the absence of "exceptional circumstances", the trial courts of this state "must require the petitioner to appear personally and testify at the hearing".

However, Justice Mosk laid down some propositions which are highly instructive. They are : assuming that in each of the following factual illustrations the petitioner was the wife and the respondent was the husband:[26]

1. The wife appears and testifies. The court is satisfied from her testimony that there are irreconcilable differences and that the marriage should be dissolved. No problem appears and the decree should be granted.
2. The wife appears and testifies. The court is not satisfied from her testimony that there are irreconcilable differences. The court may then require further testimony from the wife, from the defaulting husband after issuing a subpoena for his appearance, or from other witnesses, in whatever manner it deems appropriate.
3. The wife does not appear at the hearing. The defaulting husband appears and testifies. The court is satisfied from his testimony that there are irreconcilable differences. In such cicrumstances the court may properly grant the decree.
4. The wife does not appear. The defaulting husband appears and testifies. The court is not satisfied for his testimony that there are irreconcilable differences. The court reaches

that conclusion, however, not because of a predetermined policy of arbitrarily denying a decree in the absence of the petitioner, but solely because the proof in this instance is inadequate. The court may then require further evidence from the wife or from other witnesses.

5. Neither the wife nor the husband appears. Other competent percipient witnesses appear and testify, e.g., adult children, parents, close relatives. If the court is satisfied from the nature and extent of the testimony that there are irreconcilable differences, the court may grant the decree. If the court is not satisfied, it may require further evidence.
6. Neither the wife nor the husband appears personally at the hearing, and the matter is submitted solely on affidavits. In that event the court should require some additional personal testimony in order to reach a considered conclusion that a dissolution of the marriage is proper. On the other hand, if the trial court makes a finding of unusual circumstances, e.g., the wife is confined to a hospital, the husband is in custody, it may waive proof ordinarily "taken before the court" and grant a dissolution predicated on adequate affidavits.

We shall now deal with another problem that California's divorce statute has created. This relates to the evidence of misconduct in order to prove irreconcilable differences. Section 4509 provides :

> . . . [E]vidence of specific acts of misconduct shall be improper and inadmissible, except where child custody is in issue and such evidence is relevant to that issue, or at the hearing where it is determined by the court to be necessary to establish the existence of irreconcilable differences.

This section is obviously an exception to the general rule that fault consideration need not be brought into play. The question that we are confronted with is as to how to reconcile this section with the spirit and purpose of the Act which completely eliminates fault considerations. As pointed out by Reppy[27] the evidence of misconduct necessary to prove irreconcilable differences should be used sparingly and under certain special circumstances. For instance, in uncontested cases where the petitioner asserts that the marriage has broken down, it should not be necessary to insist that fault evidence be presented. In cases where the respondent contests denying that there are irreconcilable differences, fault evidence should be received only to avoid a futile referral to conciliation : in cases where it would be either unjust or needless to insist on a conciliation period.[28] An illustration may perhaps make matters clear. W petitions for dissolution on the ground of irreconcilable differences. H, her husband, asks that the case be referred for conciliation. Under this situation W should be entitled to present fault evidence in order to convince the court that reconciliation is not possible. It is by this way that the exception can be allowed to come into play; otherwise there will be a danger that the trial courts will tend to bring in the fault consideration in most of the cases. As pointed out by Reppy[29] "if the no-fault basis of the new law is to have teeth, the court cannot simply invoke section 4509 in an uncontested case to require petitioner to present evidence of fault after she has testified that the marriage has irreparably broken down".

We may now turn our attention to another provision of the Family Law Act which deals with the reconciliation and denial power. Section 4508 provides:

> (a) If from the evidence at the hearing and contained in the confidential questionnaire, the court finds that there are irreconcilable differences which have caused the irremediable breakdown of the marriage, it shall order the dissolution of the marriage, or a legal separation. If it appears there is a reasonable possibility of reconciliation, the court shall continue the proceedings for a period not to exceed 30 days. . . . At any time after termination of such 30-day period, either party may move for the dissolution of the marriage or legal separation, and the court may enter its judgment decreeing such dissolution or separation.

Two situations could be contemplated under the above section. In the first instance, if the court is satisfied upon evidence that there are irreconcilable differences which have caused the irremediable breakdown of the marriage, it is mandatory that the court grant the decree of dissolution. This is clear because in this clause the word "shall" is used. Under the second situation, if it appears to the court that there is a reasonable possibility of reconciliation, then the court is to continue the proceedings for a period not exceeding 30 days in an effort to bring about reconciliation. And, after the lapse of 30 days when either party asks for the decree, it is provided that the court "may" dissolve the marriage. In this clause the word "may" is used instead of the word "shall". This, it is submitted, may give rise to a cause for confusion. For, if under the first clause it is mandatory to pronounce a decree of divorce, it is all the more a reason that under the second clause when reconciliation was proved to be futile after the lapse of 30 days, the court must grant the decree. It is for this reason suggested that the word "may" in the second clause be dropped and the word "shall" substituted in its place.

Rheinstein[30] has strongly criticized the California statute because it fails to lay down any standard by which breakdown of marriage can be established. According to him the words "irreconcilable differences" and "irremediable breakdown" are vague and cryptic. In his view even when there is a serious marital discord the possibility of reconciliation is never completely exhausted, even though the probability may be extremely low. Therefore, he says that what the statute contemplate is a marriage breakdown with a low probability of being remedied.[31]

The impossibility of determining what constitutes irremediable breakdown of marriage, according to Rheinstein, has been overcome by the guidelines provided under English law, German and Scandinavian laws, such as adultery, separation for a certain period.[32] Citing well known instances of irreconcilable differences (differences in character, temperament, attitudes but not in height, health and sex characteristics) Rheinstein attacks the vagueness of the phrase with equal strength.[33] He enters thereafter into a semantic argument about the "grounds", "facts", "marital life in common" and "formal marriage bond". He fails to appreciate the rationality of "substantial reasons" for not continuing the marriage.[34]

The fact that some jurisdictions have specifically laid down the criteria and spelt out the situations in which marital breakdown could be presumed by the courts does not mean that the guidelines in the California statute are utterly devoid of content. The formulae of irreconcilable differences and irremediability of breakdown cannot be contoured with mathematical precision just as is true of the real life differences which have caused the breakdown. The phrases "irreconcilable differences" and "substantial reasons" have obviously been employed and are meant to suggest situations which are not frivolous or trivial. It has been so decided in the cases we have referred to above.[35] Irremediable breakdown seems to suggest in common language a breakdown beyond repair as opposed to a transient or momentary breakdown.

The analogies on the basis of which Rheinstein mounts his criticism of California law reflect a suspicion of wide judicial discretion. Irremediable breakdown, the learned writer says, is susceptible of a great variety of interpretations, especially when, as the statute says, the breakdown must be caused by irreconcilable differences.[36] There is an element of truth in what the writer says. But it may be asked : is it not true of all American divorce laws? There are many terms which are susceptible to different interpretations. For instance, we may take the case of "mental cruelty", fraud, or for that matter, incompatibility. None of these terms have been defined precisely in the statutes. Is it not a fact that both conservative as well as liberal judges have handled these statutes? Is it not also a fact that these terms have been construed differently by these judges? The point is that the law of divorce in American jurisprudence is based upon the premise that dissolution of marriage should take place under judicial autopsy. So long as this premise is accepted there is bound to be wide judicial discretion in favour of the court. In order to limit the discretion of the court and avoid diverse judicial interpretation a more objective criteria such as one year "living separate and apart" period may be provided to establish breakdown of the marriage. Or, if one wants to take divorce completely out of the court, divorce by registration seems to be the only alternative.

Rheinstein's arguments bring one straight into the eternal debate on the advisability of spelling out concrete situation in statutory provisions or adopting comprehensive "catch all" formulae which the judiciary can apply with discretion. The pros and cons of both the methods of legal craftmanship and judicial innovation have been demonstrated *ad nauseum* in the legal literature. The California drafter's preference for what Rheinstein considers vague and cryptic concepts is not different from the one chosen by the founding fathers of the American Constitution itself. Adopting laws which provide for judicial improvisation is a recognized technique to meet the needs of a fast moving technological society where concepts of conservatism and liberalism in community life (including matrimonial mores) are scarcely constant. The California statute refuses to put the court in a straight jacket but gives it a greater scope to handle complex marital problems. It represents a deliberate choice in favor of a comprehensive remedy to a complex marital situation in a dynamic social milieu in which it is supposed to operate. But Rheinstein chooses to view the vagueness designed "as a sop to the conservatives".[37]

THE UNIFORM MARRIAGE AND DIVORCE ACT, 1970

In 1970, the National Conference of Commissioners on Uniform State Laws in the United States promulgated an Act called the Uniform Marriage and Divorce Act, 1970.[38] This Act eliminates the notions of fault in divorce proceedings and substitutes "irretrievable breakdown" as the sole ground for divorce. The Family Law Section of the American Bar Association did not approve the Act as originally drafted by the Commissioners.[39] The Section's objections were not directed against the adoption of the non-fault divorce law nor aganist "irretrievable breakdown" as the exclusive ground for divorce. The Section opposition was mainly due to the fact that (a) breakdown was not defined, (b) that the Act did not prescribe meaningful guidelines to determine irretrievable breakdown,[40] (c) that the grant of decree of dissolution was mandatory as no discretion rested with the court to deny a decree and lastly, (d) that the Act did not provide for an effective conciliation and reconciliation procedure.[41]

In order to remedy the situation, the Family Law Section proposed an alternative draft which provided suitable guidelines to determine irretrievable breakdown and laid down an effective procedure for counseling and reconciliation. In 1971, a joint committee[42] selected by the Commissioners and the Family Law Section met to thrash out the issues and resolve their differences. As a result of successive meetings between these two bodies, the Act was amended, incorporating some of the suggestions of the Family Law Section relating to domicile, jurisdiction and reconciliation. The suggestions relating to other matters, namely, definition, guidelines, discretion of the court and reconciliation procedures were not included in the 1971 amendment. However, in 1973 the UMDA was further amended by providing guidelines to establish irretrievable breakdown.

To appreciate the objections raised by the Family Law Section against the UMDA as amended in 1971, and to understand the reasons behind those objections, it is necessary to juxtapose and compare the relevant provisions of the two versions of the divorce law. The 1971 amended version read:

Section 302.

(a) The court shall enter a decree of dissolution of marriage if:

(1) the court finds that one of the parties, at the time the action was commenced, was domiciled in this State, or was stationed in this State while a member of the armed services, and that the domicile or military presence has been maintained for 90 days next preceding the making of the findings;

(2) the court finds that the conciliation provisions of Section 305 either do not apply or have been met;

(3) the court finds that the marriage is irretrievably broken;

It may be noticed that the term "irretrievable breakdown," has not been defined. Also, no guidelines are provided to establish the breakdown of a marriage. To define "breakdown" with exactitude is an extremely difficult task. Every individual marriage differs from another in a variety of ways. So do the causes of breakdown. To encompass or anticipate every incident or eventuality in a married life and to delineate the contours of marital breakdown by a comprehensive definition is neither possible nor desirable. Confronted with the problem, it seems that the drafters of the UMDA thought it best to leave it to the courts to build up the concept of breakdown on a case by case study. True, the lack of definition or guidelines gives the court considerable leeway in judging the condition of marriage but it also opens the door for diverse judicial interpretation.

Under the above provisions the court is directed to enter a decree of dissolution if certain conditions are satisfied. If the parties state that there has been a breakdown of marriage and if other conditions relating to domicile and reconciliation are satisfied; the court is left with no discretion but to grant dissolution. In other words, the parties can dissolve the marriage at their own instance.

Let us look at the corresponding section of the proposed draft of the Family Law Section.[43] It provides, *inter alia*:

Section 302.

(a) The court shall enter a decree of dissolution of marriage if:

(2) the court finds that the marriage is irretrievably broken, which finding shall be established by proof (a) that the parties have lived separate and apart for a period of more than one year next preceding the commencement of this proceeding, or, (b) that such serious marital misconduct has occurred which has so adversely affected the physical or mental health of the petitioning party as to make it impossible for the parties to continue the marital relation, and that reconciliation is improbable; and

(3) the court finds that the conciliation provisions of Section 305 have been met and that past efforts at reconciliation have failed or that further attempts at reconciliation would be impracticable or not in the best interests of the family.

The difference between this section and section 302 of the UMDA is both apparent and significant. Section 302(a)(2) of the proposed draft provides for the dissolution of marriage if it is irretrievably broken. However, it provides certain specific guidelines to prove breakdown: living separate and apart for a period of more than one year or, serious marital misconduct which has so adversely affected the physical or mental health of the petitioning party as to make it impossible for the continuance of the marital relation. Under guideline (a) it is presumed that when parties have lived separate and apart for a considerable period it is a sufficient indication that the marriage is no longer viable. This guideline, according to the Family Law Section, gives some certainty and meaning to the term "irretrievably broken". The separation or waiting period enforced by law no doubt aids the court in arriving at the conclusion as to the fact of breakdown, but it must be said that the period can be manipulated by the parties who are desirous of obtaining divorce. In this way again, the marriage could be dissolved at the whim of the parties. The living apart requirement has been criticized on the ground that it might encourage migratory divorce.[44] A further point is that the fact that the parties have not lived separately and apart does not necessarily mean that the marriage is a "live" one. For, many couples due to economic reasons may choose to live together until they are forced to dissolve the marriage.[45]

However, enforced separation as proof of marriage breakdown has certain distinct advantages.[46] It affords an opportunity for the parties to resolve their differences and to try to start afresh their married life. They could seek counseling. If the parties have finally decided on a divorce the separation period provides an opportunity for them carefully to arrange their post-divorce "family" life.[47]

Guideline (2) comes to the aid of those people who do not want to wait before filing for divorce. The parties could plead that there has been serious marital misconduct which has so adversely affected their married life that it is no longer possible to continue it. The reference to "marital misconduct" in this guideline is unfortunate. There is no doubt that the courts will return to the old notions of "guilt" in order to be satisfied of the proof of breakdown. The Family Law Section seems to follow the pattern of the English Divorce Reform Act of 1969 in this respect.

Apart from giving content to the term "irretrievable breakdown" with these guidelines, the proposed draft provides that, before a marriage can be dissolved, the court must find that "the conciliation provisions of section 305 have been met and that past efforts at reconciliation have failed or that future attempts at reconciliation would be impracticable or not in the best interests of the family".

The UMDA as amended in 1971 provides:

Section 305.

(a) If both of the parties by petition or otherwise have stated under oath or affirmation that the marriage is irretrievably broken, or one of the parties has so stated and the other has not denied it, the court, after hearing, shall make a finding whether the marriage is irretrievably broken.

(b) If one of the parties has denied under oath or affirmation that the marriage is irretrievably broken, the court shall consider all relevant factors, including the circumstances that gave rise to filing the petition and the prospect of reconciliation, and shall:

(1) make a finding whether the marriage is irretrievably broken; or

(2) continue the matter for further hearing not fewer than 30 nor more than 60 days later, or as soon thereafter as the matter may be reached on the court's calendar, and may suggest to the parties that they seek counseling. The court, at the request of either party shall, or on its own motion may, order a conciliation conference. At the adjourned hearing the court shall make a finding whether the marriage is irretrievably broken.

(c) A finding of irretrievable breakdown is a determination that there is no reasonable prospect of the reconciliation.

Under section 305(a) the court must make a finding, after hearing, whether or not the marriage is broken irretrievably in two situations: when both the parties state that the marriage has broken irretrievably or if one of the parties has so stated and the other has not denied it. The only evidence that the court has in such a situation is the testimony of the parties as to the irretrievable breakdown. As no other evidence will normally be available to the court, it has to pronounce the decree dissolving the marriage. Hence the grant of a decree would be mandatory. The court has no discretion. This was one of the main objections of the Family Law Section which pointed out that in a provision formulated such as this, the grant of a decree would be automatic. It is submitted that when both the parties have under oath testified as to the existence of irrevocable breakdown and sincerely feel that their marriage should be dissolved, this by itself is a sufficient justification for the court to terminate the marriage.

Sub-section (b) deals with a situation where there is a dispute as to the fact of breakdown. The court, under these circumstances, is called upon to consider all factors relevant to marital breakdown including the petitioner's reasons for seeking a dissolution and the probability of reconciliation. Then, the court shall either find whether the marriage has irretrievably broken or order further hearing for not fewer than 30 nor more than 60 days. The court is authorized to suggest that the parties seek counseling. It may do so either at the request of the parties or on its own motion. It may be noticed, that the procedure provided under this section to order counseling or to adjourn the hearing is not available in cases falling under sub-section (a) of section 305. In other words, it is only when one of the parties has denied the fact of breakdown that efforts at reconciliation are made under this provision not when there is no dispute between the parties as to the existence of breakdown.

Let us now turn our attention toward the corresponding section of the proposed draft of the Family Law Section[48] and see how and in what manner this differs from the UMDA.

Section 305.

(a) No finding as to irretrievable breakdown of the marriage may be made under Section 302 of this Act until 3 months have elapsed after commencement of the proceedings and until the [Commissioner or court officer] has certified to the court that further efforts at reconciliation or conciliation are impracticable or not in the interest of the family. In order to determine such fact for certification the [Commissioner or court officer] may require the attendance of either or both parties at a conference or interview at which is explored the practicability or need for reconciliation or conciliation efforts.

(b) If the [Commissioner or court officer] find that the parties have lived separate and apart for one or more years, or is satisfied that past efforts at reconciliation were made but were unsuccessful, or that further effort would be impracticable or not in the interests of the family, he shall certify such fact to the court.

It may be noticed, that the above provisions contemplate an elaborate and effective procedure for the finding of the irretrievable breakdown. Section 305(a) requires as a condition precedent that no finding of breakdown is to be made until 3 months have elapsed after the commencement of the proceedings and until a Commissioner or a court officer has certified to the court that further reconciliation or conciliation are impracticable or not in the interests of the family. In order to determine whether further efforts at reconciliation are impracticable it is provided that the court officer may require the presence of the parties at the conference. This procedure is to be followed in all cases of dissolution, whereas under the UMDA, as we have mentioned above, the question of reconciliation will arise only when there is a denial of breakdown by one of the parties.

Section 305(b) deals with the situation where the parties have lived separate and apart for a period of one or more years. Here, the court officer has to certify that past efforts at reconciliation have proved futile and that future efforts would be impracticable. The provisions are formulated in such a way than an effective inquiry as to the condition of the marriage and the possibility of reconciliation is ensured. This feature, it must be said, is absent in the corresponding provisions of the UMDA. While both the proposed draft and the UMDA do provide for counseling, neither contemplate compulsory counseling. The proposed draft specifically states that a party who objects shall not be forced to submit to counseling.

The two versions of the law discussed above reflect different philosophies upon which divorce on the principle of breakdown should be granted. The difference in their respective approaches also marks the difference between the structuring of the reforms and the policies underlying them. The Family Law Section's draft attempts to eliminate differing judicial interpretation by providing suitable guidelines to breakdown. Under its scheme great care is taken before a marriage is pronounced "dead". The "cooling off" period prevents hasty actions by the parties. The court is not allowed to dissolve a marriage before the court officer has certified that past efforts at reconciliation have failed and that further efforts at reconciliation would be impracticable. In short, the Family Law Section's approach, it seems, is to make every endeavour to save the marriage so long as it is possible to do so. On the other hand, the Commissioners seem to rest the responsibility in the matter of divorce on the parties themselves. While the Family Law Section puts more faith in the reconciliation process, the Commissioners seem to rely upon sound judicial discretion. The Family Law Section is concerned more about the public interest involved in the dissolution of the marriage, while the Commissioners seem to give precedence to individual marriages over marriage as an institution. The Commissioner's approach may be regarded as individualistic and radical. It is because of these reasons that Foster remarks:[49]

> The amended Uniform Act caters to the private interest in divorce but downgrades the public concern as to marriage stability and the consequences of divorce.

However, the UMDA was subsequently amended in 1973. Most, if not all, of the suggestions made by the Family Law

Section have been incorporated by amending section 302. The law as it stands today provides:

Section 302.

(a) The court shall enter a decree of dissolution of marriage if:

(2) the court finds that the marriage is irretrievably broken, if the finding is supported by evidence that (i) the parties have lived separate and apart for a period of more than 180 days next preceding the commencement of the proceedings, or (ii) there is serious marital discord adversely affecting the attitude of one or both of the parties toward the marriage.

It may be noticed that the period of separation as proof of breakdown has been fixed as 180 days which is shorter than the period prescribed by the Family Law Section's proposed draft. Under guideline (ii) the words used in the current section 302 are "marital discord" and not "marital misconduct" as used in the proposed draft. With the amendment of this section the only substantial difference between the UMDA and that of the proposed draft is with regard to the counseling and reconciliation procedure.

Since the promulgation of the UMDA, several states have adopted the breakdown approach to marital dissolution. They have added irretrievable breakdown of marriage either as a sole ground or as an additional ground for divorce in their existing statutes. We shall deal with some of them below :[50]

Iowa

Iowa's non-fault divorce statute provides for the dissolution of the marriage if:

> ... there has been a breakdown of the marriage relationship to the extent that the legitimate objects of matrimony have been destroyed and there remains no reasonable likelihood that the marriage can be preserved.[51]

It is to be noted that the statute does not talk of irreconcilable differences and irremediable breakdown as does the California statute. It merely provides two broad guidelines : legitimate objects of matrimony have been destroyed and there remains no likelihood that the marriage can be preserved. Michigan too enacted similar provision as that of Iowa. These statutes do not refer or retain, as does the California statute, the evidence of misconduct to prove marriage breakdown. Therefore, the issues or the peculiar problems raised by the California law may not arise. Nonetheless what evidence or how much evidence of fault can be relied for establishing marriage breakdown will be an important question. Under the no-fault divorce statutes which do not refer or retain the evidence of fault it would be easier for the court to discard the fault evidence. For example in the *Williams* case[52] the respondent husband alleged that conduct of the spouses and particularly of the guilty spouse had not been removed as a criterion in determining the equitable disposition of property. The Supreme Court of Iowa held that the concept of "guilty party" had been eliminated by the new divorce law. It was also ruled that evidence of fault was not a factor in the determination of the parties' financial rights and obligation.[53]

Florida

The Florida divorce statute provides for the dissolution of the marriage if it has brokendow nirretrievably.[54] The statute does not define the term "irretrievable breakdown", nor does it provide any guidelines for establishing irretrievable breakdown. When the petition is based on the allegation that the marriage is irretrievably broken, the "court shall dispose of the petition for dissolution of marriage" in the following manner.[55]

When there are no minor children and when the respondent does not deny that the marriage is irretrievably broken, the court is authorized to dissolve the marriage but only on the finding that it has irretrievably broken.[56]

When there are minor children or when the respondent denies irretrievable breakdown, the court is directed either to order both the parties to seek counseling or continue the proceedings for a reasonable time not to exceed three months to enable the parties themselves to effect a reconciliation.[57] It is futher provided that if, at any time, the court finds that the marriage is irretrievably broken, it shall order dissolution.[58] If the finding is to the contrary, the court is empowered to deny the petition for dissolution.[59] Provisions are made in the statute to enable the court to take any action as may be in the best interest of the parties and the minor children.[60]

In *Ryan* v. *Ryan*[61], a case decided under the Florida statute, the word "irretrievably" was defined by the help of the Webster dictionary. Accordingly, it was held as "impossible to recoupe, repair or overcome". However, the court said that the fact of irretrievable breakdown of marriage was left to be determined by the Chancellor. It was observed:

> We do not view the matter of dissolution as being such a simple, unilateral matter of one mate simply saying "I want out".[62]

The new Act of Florida abolishes defenses of condonation, collusion and recrimination.[63] In the instant case the court had no difficulty in pronouncing that the defenses cannot be pleaded in an action for divorce under the new law. But, Roberts, J.,[64] seemed to have some trouble to agree to the majority view when he knew that an "unclean" spouse can under the new law force a divorce upon the innocent. His dissent is indicative of the judicial fury when he says:

> . . . the offending wife, after jumping from bed to bed with new found paramours, chronically drunk, and when at home nagging, brawling and quarreling, all against the wishes of a faithful husband who remains at home nuturing the children, is permitted to divorce her husband who does not desire a divorce, but rather, has one forced upon him, not because of anything he has done, but because the offending wife tells the trial court that her marriage is "irretrievably broken".[65]

Even when the statute explicitly mentioned the abolition of the defenses, he was able to say: "To hold otherwise would impute to the lawmakers a total lack of interest in the faithful spouse. . . ."[66]

Colorado[67] and Kentucky[68] have adopted a similar approach to the dissolution of marriage. Both of these statutes provide that irretrievable breakdown is a finding that there is no reasonable prospect of reconciliation: the only yard-stick for measuring whether there has been a breakdown of marriage. Finding of a breakdown is mandatory under both systems is undisputed. Where disputed a discretion is given to the court to grant 30-60 days continuance with the suggestion that the parties seek counseling. The Oregon statute[69] follows the California statute in providing irreconcilable differences which have caused the irremediable breakdown of the marriage. But, in Oregon irreconcilable differences have not been defined. Under its law the requirement of evidence of fault, when child custody is an issue or when the court finds such evidence necessary to prove irremediable breakdown, is retained as it is the case with California.

Oregon and New Hampshire

Oregon and New Hampshire do not follow the UMDA. Instead, they follow the California model by adopting "irreconcilable differences" as the proof of breakdown. In Oregon, irreconcilable differences causing irremediable breakdown of the marriage is a sole ground of dissolution[70], while in New Hampshire[71], irreconcilable differences between the parties causing irremediable breakdown of the marriage is an additional ground existing alongside the fault-based grounds.

The statutes of Oregon and New Hampshire do not define the terms "irreconcilable differences" or "irremediable breakdown". Lack of definition or the absence of any standards for determining the existence or irreconcilable differences leaves in the hands of the judges, an enormous discretion in the administration of divorce law. For this reason, the criticism heaped against the California law by Rheinstein referred to above,[72] applies with equal strength to the Oregon and New Hampshire statutes. Under these statutes, as is the case in California, evidence of specific acts of misconduct is admissible when the court finds that such evidence is necessary to prove irreconcilable differences. The problem created by retaining this provision, which runs counter to the breakdown principle, has been briefly touched upon while we dealt with the California law above. This problem is further discussed in detail in the section which follows hereafter.[73]

Missouri

In Missouri, irretrievable breakdown of marriage is the sole ground for dissolution.[74] The statute is modelled after the English Divorce Reform Act, 1969. Even the language used in some of the provisions is identical to that of the English divorce statute. Under the new law, a marriage is considered to have irretrievably broken if the court finds that "there remains no reasonable likelihood that the marriage can be preserved".[75] The court is called upon to find whether or not a marriage is irretrievably broken in two sets of circumstances, as is the case with most of the non-fault statutes, first, where both the parties have stated that the marriage is irretrievably broken, or one of the parties have so stated and the other has ot denied it;[76] and second, where one of the parties has denied the fact of breakdown. In the later case, the court has to consider all of the relevant factors including the circumstances which gave rise to the filing of the petition and the prospect of reconciliation.[77]

In order that the court may establish irretrievable breakdown, the petitioner, like his counterpart in English law, has to satisfy the court of one or more of the following facts:[78]

(a) That the respondent has committed adultery and the petitioner finds it intolerable to live with the respondent;

(b) That the respondent has behaved in such a way that the petitioner cannot reasonably be expected to live with the respondent;

(c) That the respondent has abandoned the petitioner for a continuous period of at least six months preceding the presentation of the petition ;

(d) That the parties to the marriage have lived separate and apart by mutual consent for a continuous period of twelve months;

(e) That the parties to the marriage have lived separate

and apart for a continuous period of at least twenty-four months.

It may be noticed that while the UMDA provides only two specific guidelines to support the evidence of breakdown, the Missouri statute furnish a long list of facts, some of which are the conventional grounds based on the concept of "fault". These facts, it may be noted, are to be regarded as criteria for establishing breakdown. They are not to be regarded as grounds upon which dissolution should be based.

Critical to the problem of introducing the breakdown principle into the divorce law is the question as to how to prove breakdown. Since "breakdown" reflects a condition or state of marriage, by what criteria should this condition be judged? In order to facilitate the proof of breakdown, the statute provides certain guidelines which would help the court in arriving at the conclusion as to the condition of the marriage. Such a technique has been adopted by the English Divorce Reform Act, 1969. We will discuss the English law in detail in the ensuing pages.[79] Since the Missouri non-fault divorce statute is identical to the English statute, a discussion of the former is avoided at this place.

Like most other non-fault statutes, the Missouri statute[80] makes provision for reconciliation when one party has filed for dissolution on the ground of irretrievable breakdown and the other has denied it. Under these circumstances the court is authorized to continue the hearing for not less than thirty days or for not more than six months and to suggest that the parties seek counseling. At the adjourned hearing, the court must determine whether or not there has been a breakdown of the marriage with the help of the guidelines provided under the statute.

Minnesota divorce statute[81] follows the same pattern as that of Missouri. The statute provides specific guidelines to establish irretrievable breakdown. The law provides that the finding of irretrievable breakdown has to be supported by evidence of the following:[82]

(1) A course of conduct detrimental to the marriage relationship of the party seeking dissolution;
(2) Sentence to imprisonment subsequent to marriage;
(3) Mental illness;
(4) Habitual alcoholism or chemical dependency for a period of one year;
(5) Continuous separation under an order of decree of separate maintenance for a period of one year;
(6) Serious marital discord adversely affecting the attitude of one or both the parties towards the marriage.

It may be mentioned in passing that the Divorce Act, 1968 of Canada supports its breakdown ground with specific guidelines. Under the Act[83] permanent breakdown of the marriage occurs by reason of one or more circumstances. These circumstances are: (a) imprisonment; (b) gross addiction to alcohol; (c) disappearance of the respondent; (d) non-consumption of the marriage and inability to consumate it; and (e) living separate and apart. But, unlike in Missouri or most of the non-fault statutes in the United States, breakdown of marriage is not the sole ground for divorce in the Canadian Act. The Divorce Act[84] provides two categories of grounds for divorce: fault and non-fault grounds.

Washington

Recently, Washington enacted the Marriage Dissolution Act, 1973,[85] which permits dissolution of the marriage on the sole ground of irretrievable breakdown. Under the new law when a petition for dissolution is filed alleging irretrievable breakdown, ninety days should have elapsed since the petition was filed and from the date when service of summons was made upon the respondent before the court can take action. The court is directed to proceed as follows:

Section 3.

(1) If the other party joins in the petition or does not deny that the marriage is irretrievably broken, the court shall enter a decree of dissolution.

It may be noticed that the grant of a decree of dissolution is mandatory if undisputed. There is no discretion given to the court, as the provision explicitly provides that "the court shall enter a decree of dissolution". The court does not, as is the case under the UMDA, make a finding "after hearing"[86] whether or not the marriage has irretrievably broken. In fact under the above provision the court is not required to decide anything with respect to irretrievable breakdown.[87] The result is that where there is a mutual allegation of breakdown by the parties, dissolution is automatic, granted merely for the asking. In none of the statutes that we have referred to above would such a situation arise. For, under those statutes, despite the fact of mutual allegation, the court has to determine, based upon evidence and after a hearing, whether or not the marriage has irretrievably broken. In other words, the law under these statutes contemplate that the determination of breakdown has to be a judicial determination,[88] whereas, under the Washington Dissolution Act, such a notion is not retained. The Washington Act, it is clear, rests the responsibility entirely upon the parties in the matter of divorce. It is only when there is a dispute as to the fact of breakdown that the court's judgment is called for. Accordingly, the law provides:

Section 3.

(3) If the other party denies that the marriage is irretrievably broken the court shall consider all relevant factors, including the circumstances that gave rise to the filing of the petition and the prospects of reconciliation and shall:

(a) Make a finding that the marriage is irretrievably broken and enter a decree of dissolution of the marriage; or

(b) At the request of either party or on its own motion, transfer the cause to the family court, refer them to another counseling service of their choice, and request a report back from the counseling service within sixty days, or continue the matter for not more than sixty days for hearing. If the cause is returned from the family court or at the adjourned hearing, the court shall:

(i) Find that the parties have agreed to reconciliation and dismiss the petition; or

(ii) Find that the parties have not been reconciled, and that either party continues to allege that the marriage is irretrievably broken. When such facts are found, the court shall enter a decree of dissolution of the marriage.

The court under the above provisions has to perform different role in different circumstances when there is a dispute by one of the parties as to the existence of breakdown. First, it has to consider all relevant factors including the circumstances which gave rise to filing the petition and the prospects for reconciliation. Based upon this evidence, the court is authorized to dissolve the marriage if the finding is that the marriage has irretrievably broken. Secondly, the court may either transfer the cause to the family court or direct the parties to seek counseling, requesting that the parties submit the report of the counseling service within sixty days. If the parties are not referred to the family court or to counseling services, the court may continue the matter for hearing for not more than sixty days. If the cause is returned from the family court or at the adjourned hearing, again the court has two options. If it finds that the parties have agreed to reconciliation, it can dismiss the petition. If the parties have not been reconciled then the court can dissolve the marriage.

In these respects the law under the Washington statute is the same as that laid down under the UMDA or, for that matter, under most of the non-fault divorce statutes.

Section 3(2) of the Dissolution Act embodies a principle of public policy. It simply states that if the respondent alleges that the petitioner was induced to file the petition by fraud, or collusion, the court shall dismiss the petition. The necessity to incorporate this principle of public policy explicitly into the statute is due, it appears, to the fact that it has sometimes been argued that under the breakdown principle there should be no objection to the obtaining of a divorce by fraud or collusion.

Such a question did arise in California in *In Re Marriage of McKim*[89] and in Florida in the case of *Ryan* v. *Ryan*.[90] In both the cases the courts relying on policy maintained that collusion or fraud between the parties would disentitle them from obtaining dissolution.

It should be mentioned that none of the states which have adopted the breakdown standard of marital dissolution follow the UMDA in its exact form. Some statutes do not provide any specific guidelines to irretrievable breakdown.[91] Some provide specific guidelines to irretrievable breakdown.[92] The guidelines are a long list of facts to be alleged and proved before breakdown can be established. Most statutes make provision for counseling and reconciliation services.[93] In a majority of cases counseling is either voluntary or may be ordered by the court. In Iowa, counseling is mandatory.[94]

JUDICIAL INTERPRETATION OF BREAKDOWN OF MARRIAGE

We have examined above the various no-fault statutes and their different approaches to marital breakdown. It is now proposed to deal with the cases that have arisen under these statutes which will give us an insight into the judical interpretation of the concept of breakdown. The inquiry will thus relate to : What constitutes "marriage breakdown".[95] In other words, when and under what circumstances have the court found that the marriage has, in fact, ended.

In Iowa, couples can dissolve their marriage if the legitimate objects of matrimony are destroyed and there is no reasonable likelihood of reconciliation.[96]

In *In Re Marriage of Morgan*,[97] the wife's petition for separate maintenance was granted and the husband's counter claim for dissolution was denied. The husband appealed. He testified that he no longer loved his wife. He was living with another woman and avoided his wife and the family. The fact that the husband was openly living with another woman and completely disregarded his responsibility as father with a view to "get away" from his wife was considered sufficient to establish that the objects of matrimony have been defeated. Since there was no reasonable likelihood that the marriage could be preserved, it was dissolved.

In *In Re Marriage of Boyd*[98], the husband sought a divorce decree on the ground of breakdown of marriage. The parties were married in 1950 and separated in 1970. There was continuous conflict in the home since 1961. When the husband instituted proceedings for divorce the court had ordered conciliation. The conciliators concluded that there was no such possibility. The court was of the opinion that there had been a breakdown of marriage and hence a decree dissolving the marriage was pronounced.

In *In Re Marriage of Tucker*[99], the petitioning husband stated that the love in his household had been a "dying thing". He hated to go home from work. The marriage had lasted for almost 24 years during which time the husband had made every effort to save the marriage but failed. He strongly felt that the marriage deteriorated beyond repair. His daughter, a witness for petitioner, was asked by the court whether the marriage could be saved. The witness replied "No, your Honour, I don't see any hope".[100] The testimony of the husband together with the testimony of the daughter was sufficient to sustain the decree dissolving the marriage.

In *In Re Marriage of Collins*,[101] the wife petitioned for divorce pleading breakdown of marriage. The parties were married in the year 1958, had several children. The suit was instituted in 1970. It was alleged that the parties could not agree to family economics. There was testimony of physical abuse of children. The petitioner testified that she had been beaten and slapped. Further, it was also found that there were philosophical differences over religion. The husband had insisted that his wife and the childern follow his religious inclinations. The court had ordered conciliation between the parties which proved futile. The marriage was dissolved. The court said :

> We conclude the record was replete with evidence from which the court could find the marriage relationship of the parties had broken down beyond hope of reconciliation.[102]

Whenever one of the parties to a marriage seeks dissolution alleging breakdown the other party who wants to continue the relationship invariably denies that the marriage has broken down beyond salvage. In fact, that is the only valid ground of defense that can be pleaded under the no-fault divorce law.[103] Under the Florida statute[104] as mentioned earlier, if the respondent denies that the marriage is irretrievably broken, the court can either continue the proceedings for a certain period not exceeding three months or order conciliation. If the court finds that the marriage is irretrievably broken, the court "shall enter a judgment of dissolution of the marriage". Otherwise, the court is entitled to deny the petition for divorce. In *Nooe* v. *Nooe*[105], the wife contested the petition failed against her for dissolution by her husband on the ground that the marriage had not irretrievably broken. The parties were married in 1961. They had encountered marital difficulties for a considerable period. The husband had been living separate and apart from the wife since [1968. He had taken up residence in a motel for about three years when the petition for dissolution was filed. The wife was asked by the court whether in light of the facts she was satisfied that the marriage was broken. She categorically denied that the marriage had reached its terminal stage and expressed a hope that her husband might still come back. The court, however, held that the marriage was irretrievably broken, that there was no hope of reconciliation and that it was in the best interests of the parties, and particularly the teenage children, that the marriage relationship be terminated. The court took support from the decision in *Riley v. Riley* where it was stated :

> If refusal of dissolution would amount to a legal perpetuation of a relationship which has ceased to exist in fact, the petition should be granted.[106]

In Oregon,[107] dissolution of marriage could be ordered "when irreconcilable differences between the parties have caused the irremediable breakdown of the marriage". In the case of *Dunn*,[108] the wife petitioned for divorce alleging irreconcilable differences which had resulted in an irremediable breakdown. The lower court granted the decree. The husband appealed the decision. He contended that there was no sufficient evidence to support the court's finding of irreconcilable differences. It was further contested that such differences were irremediable. The Oregon statute,[109] unlike the California statute does not define "irreconcilable differences". The California statute defines irreconcilable differences as "grounds which are determined by the court to be substantial reasons for not continuing the marriage and which make it appear that the marriage should be dissolved". The court relied on this definition and ruled that once the existence of a difference or differences claimed by the petitioner have been established it was for the court to investigate whether or not such differences were apparently irreconcilable. If the court was satisfied of the irreconcilability of the differences, it could conclude that there was an irremediable breakdown of marriage. In *Dunn's* case the court found the evidence sufficient to support the finding that irreconcilable differences did exist in the mind of the wife and that such differences had caused irremediable breakdown so as to warrant a decree of dissolution.

In the no-fault divorce laws when one of the parties desires a divorce on the ground of breakdown and the other does not deny or contest, the task of the court is easier. But considerable difficulty arises, as we have seen, when the petition is contested for insufficiency of evidence to support a finding of breakdown. In such a case the court can order conciliation and if efforts toward reconciliation have failed, it is again not difficult for the court to presume that marriage, in fact, has been terminated. But what happens if both the parties to a divorce proceeding agree that there has been a breakdown of marriage, but one of them who wants a divorce refuses marriage counseling and had no desire to continue the marital relationship, while the other is willing to have marriage counseling ? Should the court grant a decree of dissolution under these circumstances ? In *Kretzschmar* v. *Kretzschmar*,[110] the court was faced with such a situation. The plaintiff husband testified that marital arguments and conflicts continued for several years. The defendant allegedly called him mentally incompetent and described him as a drug addict and an abortionist. The plaintiff was living separate and apart for about two years when the action for divorce was brought. The wife contended that the marriage could still be saved and she was willing to try reconciliation. But the husband refused to have mediation and conciliatory services. He maintained that he had no desire for reconciliation. It is interesting to note that both the parties testified that the marriage had broken.

The trial court denied relief to the plaintiff. The court was of the opinion that even though there had been a breakdown of marriage, since the wife testified that the marriage could be saved and was willing to undergo reconciliation, there was a "reasonable likelihood" that the marriage could be saved. Hence the relief of divorce was denied to the plaintiff. On appeal the question again hinged upon the possibility of reconciliation and the likelihood of saving the marriage. The appellate court concluded that in addition to the testimony of the parties to the effect that the marriage had broken, evidence was overwhelming that there was no reasonable likelihood that the marriage could be preserved. Thus, while reversing the judgment of the trial court, the appellate court stated :[111]

> The trial court, instead of applying the proper statutory criterion of "reasonable likelihood", erroneously utilized as a standard the possibility that this marriage could be preserved.

A similar problem arose in the Iowa Supreme Court in the *Penney* case.[112] The Iowa Dissolution of Marriage Act[113] requires the court to order conciliation for a certain period. Under the Act conciliation procedure is mandatory. However, conciliation may be waived by the court upon a showing of good cause provided that it shall not be waived if either party objects.[114] In the instant case, the trial court granted a divorce to the plaintiff husband after his application to waive conciliation was approved. The respondent wife was willing to undergo reconciliation and objected to the waiver of conciliation by the court. The court was of the opinion that since the parties had counseling services earlier to the filing of the divorce petition and since they have lived separate and apart for a considerable period, it served no useful purpose to order further conciliation. On appeal, the Supreme Court agreed with the conclusions arrived at by the trial court but interpreting the mandatory conciliation provisions stated that a party's right to conciliation is absolute. A waiver of conciliation is prohibited if either party objects.[115] Since no conciliation was ordered by the trial court, its decision was reversed.

Both in the *Kretzschmar* case and in the *Penney* case the petitioners refused counseling. In the former, a divorce was pronounced; in the latter, dissolution was denied. The difference is due to the fact that the *Penney* case is governed by a statute where conciliation is mandatory whereas *Kretzschmar* was decided under a statute[116] which does not envisage mandatory court counseling.

Commenting upon the decision of the Iowa Supreme Court in the *Penney* case relating to the waiver of conciliation, Stephen L. Sass[117] advocates the drawing of a distinction between the rights of the petitioner and those of the respondent. In his view, since it is usually the petitioner who requests a waiver and the respondent who objects, dissolution should be denied to the petitioner as he has failed to cooperate with the court. If it is the respondent who refuses to cooperate in a conciliation, his or her refusal amounts to a waiver of the right to conciliation and, as such, should not have any consequences upon the dissolution proceedings. It is submitted that if we accept the contention of the learned writer then, it would amount to denying the petitioner a right to obtain divorce simply because he requests a waiver of conciliation and refused to cooperate with the court. The interpretation given by the Supreme Court to the effect that the right of the party to conciliation is absolute and that a waiver of conciliation cannot be allowed if either party objects seems to be a good solution to the problem.

Under the Family Code of Texas, one of the non-fault grounds of divorce is insupportability. The code provides:[118]

Section 3.01.

> On the petition of either party to a marriage, a divorce may be decreed without regard to fault if the marriage has become insupportable because of discord or conflict of personalities that destroys the legitimate ends of the marriage

relationship and prevents any reasonable expectation of reconciliation.

In *Bakken* v. *Bakken,*[119] the wife obtained a decree of divorce on the ground that her marriage had become insupportable and that there was no reasonable expectation of reconciliation. The wife testified in support of her allegations that there was incompatibility. She contended that her husband did not support her and the children, the husband's employment was irregular and that he had taken to excessive drinking. There were also marital problems for a number of years. The court found justification based on the evidence to decree divorce. The court stated:

> It is not necessary for one seeking a divorce to testify specifically that "the marriage has become insupportable because of discord or conflict of personalities. . ." Neither is it necessary for any witness to testify specifically that there is no reasonable expectation of reconciliation. These are factual conclusions which the court may properly reach after hearing all the evidence.[120]

An examination of the case law thus reveals that all sorts of matrimonial wrangles ranging from separation to incompatibility, irreconcilable differences to family disagreement on matters of economic and religion and from cruelty to infatuation for another woman have been pleaded. And, in every case, it was found upon evidence that there had been a breakdown of marriage. As a matter of fact there was hardly any case where breakdown was pleaded that a decree of dissolution was denied.[121] Where it was denied in a few cases such as *McKim* and *Penny,* it was due to non-compliance of the procedural formalities and not on merits. A husband may leave the matrimonial home, start living with another woman, refuse marriage counseling and yet force a divorce upon the wife who nevertheless wants to continue the marital relationship. It is the facility and the ease with which dissolution is obtained under the no-fault system that caused Foster to suggest putting "brakes on breakdown".[122]

In the interpretation and application of the new statutes the question regarding the extent of corroborative evidence required to prove breakdown has arisen. The Supreme Court of Iowa in the *Collins* case[123] had to construe the provision under the new law which requires corroboration of the petitioner's testimony before granting dissolution.[124] Under the prior law also divorce could not be granted without corroborating evidence of the plaintiff's testimony. The question was whether the requirement of corroboration in a no-fault divorce law was necessary and essential. It was held in the instant case that the requirement of corroborative evidence was repugnant to the concept of no-fault divorce. It was further held that corroboration required for divorce may be furnished by direct or circumstantial evidence or by the testimony of the other spouse, or by his or her failure to deny the evidence presented by the petitioner.[125] However, the Supreme Court ruled that corroboration was required mainly to prevent collusion between the parties. This is the position in Iowa where there is an express provision respecting the petitioner's testimony. In most of the statutes, no such provision exists in this regard.[126] However, where corroboration was necessary to support the testimony of the petitioner and in cases where it was available the courts seemed to have included such evidence.[127] Otherwise, generally speaking, courts are unanimous in their stand that under the no-fault divorce law corroboration is not required.

The question as to whether the defense of collusion has been eliminated under the no-fault divorce also came up for determination. For example, in *In Re Marriage of McKim*,[128] the wife contended, *inter alia*, that the Family Law Act and the defense of collusion were mutually exclusive. It was alleged that any agreement by the spouses that their marriage would be dissolved established irreconcilable differences and the breakdown of their marriage. Therefore, it was argued that under the new enactment collusion was not a defense for the denial of the decree of dissolution. But the Supreme Court rejected the wife's contention and ruled that obtaining of a decree of dissolution by such an agreement would be a fraud on the court. Similarly, it was stated in *R*ı*an* v. *Ryan*,[129] that the courts would not knowingly become a party to contrivance or fraud.

While determining the fact of breakdown, the courts have

to a large extent depended upon the subjective state of mind of the parties.[130] Such dependence is necessary as the irreconcilable differences standard is necessarily subjective.[131] The Legislature in California has also described "irreconcilable differences" as "descriptive of the frame of mind of the spouses in a marriage which is no longer viable".[132] It was held in *Walton*[133] and in *McKim*[134] that in view of the legislative mandate the existence of irreconcilable differences must be pleaded generally and without reliance on specific acts of misconduct. In fact the evidence of acts of misconduct has been made admissible only in two cases, namely, where the issue is one related to child custody or where it is determined by the court to be necessary to establish irreconcilable differences. It is obvious, therefore, to the extent the court is restrained from admitting the evidence of fault, it has to necessarily depend upon the subjective state of mind of the parties in order to establish irreconcilable differences between them.

The Attorney's Guide to Family Law Act Practice[135] also recommends the type of questions that should be asked to establish irreconcilable differences :

Q. 1. You have stated that there are irreconcilable differences between you and your spouse. Is it your belief that your marriage has completely broken down ?

Q. 2. Do you believe that conciliation, the assistance of this court, or a waiting period can restore the marriage ?

The judges of the Los Angeles County Superior Court have granted dissolution if the answer to question No. 1 was "Yes" and to question No. 2 "No". If the party has answered "No" to question 1 and "Yes" to question 2, the court has directed the parties to conciliation court in order to determine whether the prescribed period for counseling could save the marriage.[136]

It must be pointed out that the subjective standard was not all that the courts have considered sufficient to establish the irreconcilable differences which resulted in an irretrievable breakdown. The court had to make an independent determination of the viability of the marriage. For example, in *Walton*[137], it was held that the determination of the existence of irreconcilable differences causing the irremediable breakdown of marriage was a judicial determination and not a ministerial function. Also, the Supreme Court of New Hampshire in *Woodruff* v. *Woodruff*[138] stated that although the state of mind of the parties is considered, it was not for them to decide if the breakdown was irremediable.

As respects the question whether one party only or both should view the differences to be irreconcilable, it was held in *In Re Dunn*[139] that it was not necessary that both should view the differences to be irreconcilable. It might under certain circumstances be unilaterally so viewed. Such an approach by the judiciary is in tune with the legislative policy as evidenced by the Report of the 1969 Divorce Reform Legislation of California which states that an absolute refusal on the part of one spouse to live with the other, despite a conciliatory attitude and effort on the part of the latter, is sufficient reason for dissolution.[140]

The most significant aspect of divorce reforms has been the anxiety to eliminate the notion of "fault" or "matrimonial guilt" from the dissolution proceedings and to substitute "marital breakdown" as the basis for granting divorce. It is for the same reason that the new statutes specifically prohibit the introduction of misconduct for the purpose of proving marriage-breakdown. The California[141], Oregon[142] and the New Hampshire[143] statutes do adhere to this principle. But, while they do so, they also allow evidence of specific acts of misconduct "at the hearing where it is determined by the court to be necessary to establish the existence of irreconcilable differences".

The incorporation of such a provision, it is to be noted, is peculiar to the statutes which allow dissolution based upon irreconcilable differences causing irremediable breakdown. It is interesting to note how and under what circumstances this provision was finally retained under the California enactment. The Family Law Act was based on the recommendation of the Governor's Commission on the Family.[144] Under its scheme it was envisaged that the court would dissolve the marriage after the parties have taken certain procedural steps and that a certain period of time had passed. It was thought by the Asssembly Judiciary Committee that under such a scheme the parties and not the court would be entitled to dissolve the marriage. Further under such a scheme, the court would be performing a ministerial function rather than judicially determine the fact of breakdown. Therefore, the Assembly Committee rejected the proposals of the Governor's Commission.[145] One of the objectives of the new legislation was to eliminate the evils of adversary procedure and reduce acrimony and hostility between the parties. When the ground of irreconcilable differences was adopted as the basis for dissolution, it was feared that the court might apply the test perfunctorily. It must have been for the same reason that the Legislature might have engrafted this exception by way of abundant caution.

The provisions in the Oregon and New Hampshire statutes which are modelled on the California Act and which introduce the fault evidence necessary to establish the existence of irreconcilable differences might have been enacted for similar reasons. Whatever reasons might have prevailed upon the reformers, the fact remains that such evidence is extraneous to the no-fault divorce considerations and could be regarded as inconsistent with the main objective of the no-fault divorce legislation.

The admissibility of the evidence of misconduct under these statutes may cause confusion and difficulty in their judicial construction. For example, Judge Martin F. Loughlin of Manchester has recently forwarded to the State Supreme Court of New Hampshire his finding of the facts in a divorce case and asked for a ruling on whether he was authorized to grant divorce under the New Hampshire no-fault divorce statute.[146] The law enacted in New Hampshire in 1971 provides:[146(a)]

Section 458 : 7-a

> A divorce from the bonds of matrimony shall be decreed, irrespective of the fault of either party, on the ground of irreconcilable differences which have caused the irremediable breakdown of the marriage. In any pleading or hearing of a libel for divorce under this section, *allegation or evidence of specific acts of misconduct shall be improper and inadmissible*, except where child custody is in issue . . . *or at a hearing where it determined by the court to be necessary to establish the existence of irreconcilable differences.* If upon hearing of an action for divorce under this section,

> both parties are found to have committed act or acts which justify a finding of irreconcilable differences, a divorce shall be decreed and the acts of one party shall not negate the acts of the other, nor bar a divorce decree.

The wife[147] filed for divorce under this statute claiming irreconcilable differences. She testified that her husband did not work regularly. At the time of the wife's pregnancy, he had suggested to put the child for adoption if it were not a boy. Subsequently, a daughter was born and the father became very much attached to her. He was visiting her regularly and complying with the support order imposed upon him at the time of separation decree. The wife claimed that she no longer loved her husband, but admitted that her husband was an industrious worker. The husband testified that he loved his wife and that he did not want a divorce. The contradictions in the statements made by the wife and the husband, the inconsistency with regard to the admissibility of evidence of acts of misconduct, coupled with some ambiguity in the language of the statute, seem to have troubled the judge who preferred to refer the case to the Supreme Court.

No case had come up squarely before the courts which called for the judicial construction of these provisions which, while prohibiting fault evidence for the determination of the fact of the "marriage breakdown" in the same breath gives a discretion to the court to introduce such evidence to prove the existence of irreconcilable differences. However, we have some solutions and suggestions coming from some judges and a few writers. MacFadan,[148] Presiding Judge of the Los Angeles County Domestic Relations Department, is reported to have said that his court would construe section 4509 of the California Family Law Act, 1970 "as if the above-portioned phrase were not contained therein". Marvin A. Freeman,[149] another judge from California, suggests that the court "may bifurcate the trial and hear evidence on the granting of the divorce, the awarding of support, and the issue of alimony before allowing the custody matter to be heard". In that way "fault" would only come into the custody determination, not into the question of divorce.

Commenting upon this aspect of the question, one writer

states that as a general rule fault evidence would be unnecessary to establish the existence of irreconcilable differences and the exception contained in section 4509 of the California Act should be confined to circumstances where objective evidence of fault could persuade the judge to disregard his initial inclination to refer the parties to conciliation court.[150] In his view "any broader interpretation could nullify the purpose of the new law by giving the trial courts uncontrolled discretion to revive the evils of the fault based system, including bitterness, perjured testimony, and disrespect for the courts". According to Stephen Sass,[151] in exceptional cases an irretrievable breakdown of the marital relationship might have no other significant symptoms but the acts of marital wrong. Only in such cases should marital misconduct be proved. According to Roger J. Leo[152], admission of evidence of misconduct is most appropriate in the case of the "hold out" spouse, when dissolution may be warranted in fact but one party continues to oppose dissolution out of spite or in hope of a more favorable post-dissolution settlement. Perhaps the best way to justify the inclusion of the fault evidence in a non-fault divorce statute is to regard the proof of misconduct as a factor demonstrative of marital breakdown rather than to treat the misconduct itself as the basis upon which dissolution has occurred. Such is the approach adopted under the English Divorce Reform Act, 1969. But under the statute, this is the only way of proving breakdown.

From the survey of the cases it appears that the no-fault divorce statutes have not created any significant problems in their application. One might have expected that the exception which allows admissibility of misconduct to prove the fact of breakdown would have led more attorneys to try introduce such evidence in order to conclusively establish breakdown. Surprisingly enough, this does not seem to have happened. The courts too have not been tempted to invoke their discretionary power by introducing the fault-related evidence into the proceedings. In fact, they have neatly avoided this question. The judges of the Los Angeles County Superior Court, Family Law Department,[153] have maintained that where one spouse affirms the existence of irreconcilable differences while the other denies, marriage has obviously broken. By this way the necessity of including "evidence of specific acts of misconduct" has been avoided.

The notion that it is not for the parties but for the court to dissolve the marriage or that the determination of the fact of breakdown is a judicial function has been preserved. However, such a notion appears to exist only in theory; in actual practice unilateral divorce has become a reality. In an undefended case marriage breakdown is presumed because of the lack of interest of the other spouse to continue the marital relationship. In contested cases, denial of the spouse as to the existence of irreconcilable differences or as to the fact of breakdown was considered by the courts as a sufficient reason to conclude that the marriage is no more viable.

Although courts have not abdicated that power either to grant or refuse a decree of dissolution, they seem to be convinced of the fact that no useful purpose would be served by forcing upon married persons a tie which no longer endures. An idea is gaining currency that:

> It takes two people in a marriage to say "I do". If one party says "I don't", then there is no marriage performed. This applies to dissolutions, in that if one says "I don't" (i.e., I don't want to stay married), then there is no marriage either.[154]

Is this an appropriate attitude to be adopted by a court of law? Is it a sound policy to be laid down by the legislature? The courts, as seen above, however, have demonstrated some concern for restoration of marital relations. They have advised the parties to seek counseling and on the basis of the evidence that there were no possibilities for reconciliation they have dissolved the marriage. But constituted as they are it is probably idle to expect a healing touch from the judicial hand. The counseling services, too, cannot perform the function of the psychiatrist. Nevertheless, it is wholly legitimate to expect of the judiciary that the standard of irreconcilable differences is not construed frivolously nor applied perfunctorily.

While it is true that marriages cannot be imposed on unwilling parties nor prolonged when one of them wants to quit, a good deal of friction that arises normally out of constant company can be magnified by a party into "irreconcilable differences", especially when the party has different designs. The function of the court lies in drawing that line perceptibly, and try to save those marriages that fall within the right side of the line. This, it is submitted, seems to be the legislative policy underlying reforms. On the one hand the policy is to remove adversary procedure and eliminate fault notions from divorce proceedings, recognizing the fact that an absolute refusal of one of the parties to live with the other is a sufficient justification for the court to pronounce a marriage as dead. On the other hand, the policy also dictates that dissolution should not be granted lightly. This is the legislative dilemma which confronts the courts in the administration of no-fault divorce law.

The no-fault divorce law has been in operation only for a short period. Accordingly, no considerable data is available with respect to its empirical efforts. However, some information is available on the effects of the new law in jurisdictions of California[155] and Iowa.[156] In California, in 1969 the number of petitions for divorce decreased from the normal rate and in 1970, after the Family Law Act came into operation, the number rose again.[157] This, we are told, is due to the reason that many couples may have postponed filing the petitions for divorce in 1969 in anticipation of the Act which makes divorce less difficult and without having to prove any specific matrimonial wrong on the part of the respondent. The Family Law Act[158] of California requires that in all cases where conciliation is involved, the parties must file a confidential conciliation questionnaire. This procedure, it appears, has had a good effect on the parties who are desirous of availing themselves of the conciliation services. In 1970 the conciliation filing in Los Angeles county increased by 12½ per cent over 1969.[159] It appears that the trial of contested matters under the Act has been more pleasant for the parties, counsel and the court since the fault considerations have been eliminated. Of course, in cases involving custody of children bitterness seems to have continued as it is only natural to expect.

The Iowa no-fault dissolution statute has not increased petitions.[160] It seems that the respondents are aware of the fact that under the new law the parties no longer have to be concerned about the consequence of fault upon issues of support and property divisions.[161] If they have contested, it was only to have the issues tried in the court. The average duration of hearing on the merits of a case in uncontested proceedings was five to thirty minutes.[162] This can be explained by the fact that the courts could presume breakdown of the marriage without probing deep into the evidence in those cases.

It appears that judges still continue to consider fault evidence in the administration of the no-fault divorce law. Of the twenty judges who were asked to answer whether they admit fault evidence in an effort to determine the marital breakdown, sixteen indicated that they had introduced fault considerations to be convinced of irremediable breakdown.[163] One attorney is reported to have queried: "How else can you show a breakdown?"[164] The reliance by the judges upon "fault" may have been due to the statutory exception which allows the court to admit evidence disclosing that there has been an irretrievable breakdown.[165] Further, since evidence of misconduct helps the judge to arrive at a decision on breakdown with less difficulty, the tendency must have been to introduce such evidence.

SEPARATION, INCOMPATIBILITY AND IRRETRIEVABLE BREAKDOWN AS NON-FAULT GROUNDS : A REAPPRAISAL

Separate and living apart of the parties to a marriage for a specified period without any intention to ever come together as a cause for divorce has distinct advantages. First, it reflects the attitude of the parties to terminate the marital tie. Secondly, it avoids the painful process of adversary procedure in which the parties have to establish misconduct in order to obtain a divorce. But this non-fault separation ground, as we have seen, was qualified by an adjective "voluntary" in some of the jurisdictions. The additional requirement of voluntariness greatly reduced the utility of this ground as courts took a stance that unless the parties had mutually and voluntarily separated no decree of divorce could be granted.

In jurisdictions where separation was not qualified, still the courts tended to look into the conduct of the plaintiff before he or she could be awarded a decree of divorce. Under these circumstances the great force and rationality of separation as a ground for divorce was lost. Another drawback to the separation statutes lies in the fact that it discourages attempts at reconciliation. We have pointed out while dealing with separation ground that where one of the parties had made honest efforts at reconciliation, it was held that such efforts negatived the intention to separate voluntarily. Further, the problem whether attempts were made in good faith or not also cropped up. The principal problem of intention when breakdown occurred for the purpose of counting the continuity of the prescribed period remains to be combated by the courts.[166] Whatever may be the shortcomings and pitfalls visiting the separation ground, its adoption in the framework of fault-based divorce law is definitely an advantage and improvement in the present system. Separation as one of the indications of "irretrievable breakdown" of marriage is always an asset. The English law provides living apart for a specified period as an evidence of irretrievable breakdown.[167] The Uniform Marriage and Divorce Act as recently amended incorporates living separate and apart of the parties as evidence pointing towards the irretrievable breakdown.

Incompatibility as a non-fault alternative to the present divorce law is a further improvement towards reforms. But this apparently simple remedy ran into difficulties when put into actual practice.[168] We saw that the concept of mutual incompatibility was introduced by judicial legislation. Another problem attendant upon the incompatibility ground was one related to the defense of recrimination. The problem is solved in some jurisdictions having incompatibility as a ground by abolishing this defense. In other jurisdictions the court took a bold posture and declared that recrimination could not be pleaded as a defense to a divorce action. But in New Mexico, the problem remains in a somewhat attenuated form. Reliance by the courts in introducing fault considerations in incompatibility cases caused Wadlington to remark :

> Regardless of legislative intent, many courts simply cannot conceive of eliminating fault from consideration without an unequivocal legislative mandate to that effect, and perhaps not even then. But the main difficulty is the impossibility of introducing incompatibility into the existing fault-oriented

> framework of divorce law, since to a large extent they cannot stand together.[169]

But, in fairness to the judiciary, it must be pointed out that before the time when Wadlington commented as well as todate, courts have consistently discarded fault considerations in cases arising on incompatibility.

Recognition of incompatibility as a ground for divorce can facilitate a fair settlement in cases which would not be covered by the rule of mutual consent. Suppose that a marriage has utterly broken down, but one of the parties is unwilling to acknowledge the fact, or perhaps holding out for an unreasonable financial settlement. If incompatibility is a ground, a court can override the wishes of the stubborn party. Thus, even if divorce by mutual consent were recognized, it would be advisable to include incompatibility also; still more should incompatibility be recognized in American law, which does not allow divorce by mutual consent.

The question that confronts us is: should we have non-fault grounds alongside with the fault grounds in a divorce statute ? It is submitted that when one wants to get rid of the evils of adversary system and bring divorce law more in conformity with the needs and realities of human need, it is better to start off with a clean slate. When the non-fault grounds of separation or incompatibility exist alongside with the conventional grounds there is a danger that the judiciary, in the absence of a clear mandate, might tend to be obsessed by fault-notions and deny a decree of divorce when it is most needed in the interest of the parties themselves. As Rutman points out:

> . . . where a non-fault ground of divorce exists side by side with fault grounds, and it is in such a situation that the courts, particularly if their predisposition lies along traditional lines, will tend to approach what are different problems with the same instruments and similar preconceptions.[170]

Further, in those jurisdictions which have incompatibility alongside with the fault grounds, the former has been a favorite remedy. For instance, when incompatibility was added to the books in Delaware, the fault grounds were seldom used.[171] Sometimes a husband might prefer to sue on fault ground in an effort to escape the alimony award that might be allowed if he was to sue on incompatibility or on separation ground. This ingenious technique by the cunning husbands was done away by the Supreme Court where it was held that a separation caused by the misconduct of one spouse cannot be regarded as voluntary.[172]

Neither separation nor incompatibility as an alternative to the present divorce system, particularly when these grounds were encircled within the clouds of "fault" could satisfy the urge of the reformers to find a solution to the complex marital problems. A step forward was taken by modernizing further the divorce law.

Irretrievable breakdown of marriage became the basis for divorce. In order to encompass complex marital situations indicative of breakdown, irreconcilable differences between the spouses came in handy. Some statutes define "breakdown" in terms of irreconcilable differences, others provide that breakdown of marriage will ensue when legitimate objects of matrimony have been destroyed and there remains no likelihood that the marriage can be preserved.

The progress made by reforming the divorce law in tune with the social philosophy and mores of the American society is laudable. The new law has taken away many of the scathing arrows that the bow of fault contains. It has given to the society in which it has to function a clean and more honest workable solution to marital discontentment. Other significant aspects of reform are : first, the provisions which direct the parties to wait for a specified period before the termination of the marriage bond; secondly, the provisions which are meant to encourage reconciliation. A caveat must be entered here. The success of reforms depends upon many factors : establishment of Family Courts, effective conciliation process, protection of the children and the weaker party. Since under the new law a guilty party can force a divorce upon the faithful and the innocent it is of utmost importance that the law protect the faithful, honest but unfortunate spouse. Considerable progress has been made in this direction in jurisdictions which have adopted community property concept.[173]

NOTES AND REFERENCES

1. See generally Clark, Jr., *Divorce Policy and Divorce Reform*, 42 Colo.L.Rev. 403 (1971); McCurdy, *Divorce: A Suggested Approach with Particular Reference to Dissolution for Living Separate and Apart*, 9 Vand. L.Rev. 685 (1956); Bodenheimer, *Reflections on the Future Grounds for Divorce*, 8 J.Fam.L. 179 (1968); Wadlington, *Divorce without Fault without Perjury*, 52 Va.L.Rev. 32 (1966); Bradway, *The Myth of the Innocent Spouse*, II Tulane.L.Rev. 377 (1937); see by the same author *Family Dissolution—Limits of the Present Litigious Method in Selected Essays on Family Law*, 881 (Association of American Law School, Brooklyn, The Foundation Press, Inc. 1950); Lichtenberger, *Divorce Legislation*. Ibid. at 862. For further articles on the subject see:
   Schoenlaub, *No-Fault Divorce : A Practical Approach to the Problem of Marital Failure*, 27 Mo. B.J. 579(1971); Honigman, *What No-Fault Means to Divorce Law*, 51 Mich. S.B.J. 16 (1972); Note, *No-Fault Divorce: A Time for Change* ? 7 Suffolk U.L.Rev. 86 (1972).
2. See Goldstein and Gitter, *On Abolition of Grounds For Divorce: A Model Statute* and *Commentary*, 3 Fam.L.Q. 75 (1969); Freeman, *The Search For A Rational Divorce Law*, 24 Cur.L.Prob. 178 (1971); Couch, *Toward a More Realistic Divorce Law*, 43 Tul.L.Rev. 243, 254 (1969,; See further Morris Ploscowe, *A Mordern Divorce and Judicial Separation Act for New York*, 30 Alabany L.Rev. 1 (1966).
3. Traynor, *Law and Social Change in a Democratic Society*, U.Ill.L.F. 230 at 236 (1956).
4. Alexander, *Family Life Conference Suggests New Judicial Procedures and Attitudes Toward Marriage and Divorce*, 32 J.Am.Jud. Society, 38 at 40 (1948). See further by the same author, *Let's Get Embattled Spouses out of the Trenches*, 18 Law & Contem. Prob. 98 (1953).
5. Sayre, *Divorce for the Unworthy: Specific Grounds for Divorce*, 18 Law & Contem. Prob. 26 at 28 (1953).
6. Rheinstein, *Trends in Marriage and Divorce Law of Western Countries*, 18 Law & Contem. Prob. 3 at 19 (1953).
7. Squire, *The Shift from Adversary to Administrative Divorce*, 33 Boston U.L.Rev. 141 at 143 (1953).
8. See Ch. III, Section C at 88. The divorce law based on the concept of breakdown in England is dealt with in Ch. IV at 120. With regard to other countries such as Germany, Poland and Switzerland see generally Rheinstein, *Marriage Stability, Divorce and the Law* 345 (1972); See also Rheinstein, *Divorce Around the World in Divorce and After* 143 (Bohannan ed. 1971).
9. This has been discussed and commented upon in Ch. III Section B at 63.
10. Ibid. See Ch. III pp. 51-88.
11. *Jay* v. *Jay*, 67 Misc. 2d 371 at 372, 323 N.Y.S. 2d 387 at 388 (1971).

12. *Berlin* v. *Berlin*, 64 Misc. 2d 352, 314 N.Y.S. 2d 911 (Sup. Ct. 1970).
12a. See Ch. II at pp. 42-44.
13. For an evaluation, comments and criticism on the new divorce law see Hogoboom, *The California Family Law Act of 1970; 18 months Experience*, 27 Mo.B.J. 584 (1971); Krom, *California's Divorce Law Reform: A Historical Analysis*, 1 Pac.L.J, 156 (1970); Walker, *Disarming the Litigious Man: A Glance at Fault and California's New Divorce Legislation*, 1 Pac.L.J. 182 (1970); Goddard, *A Report on California's New Divorce Law: Progress and Problems*, 6 Fam.L.Q. 405 (1972); Note, *Untying the Knot: The Course and Patterns of Divorce Reform*, 57 Cornell L.Rev. 649, 658 (1972); Brody, *California's Divorce Reform: Its Sociological Implications*, 1 Pac.L.J. 223 (1970). See Cal. Civ. Code, Sec. 4506 to 4509 (West-Supp. 1975).
14. See Max Rheinstein, *Marriage Stability, Divorce and the Law*, 368-73 (1972).
15. See Hogoboom, supra note 13, at 584-585.
16. Ibid.
17. *In Re Marriage of Walton*, 28 Cal. App. 3d 108, 104 Cal. Reptr. 472.
18. Rheinstein, supra note 14 at 370.
19. *In Re Marriage of Walton*, 28 Cal.App. 3d 108 at 116, 104 Cal. Reptr. 472 at 481.
20. For a thorough discussion of this aspect of the question see Comment, *The End of Innocence: Elimination of Fault in California Divorce Law*, 17 U.C.L.A.L.Rev. 1305 (1970).
21. *McKim* v. *McKim*, 6 Cal. 3d 673, 100 Cal.Reptr. 140 (1970).
22. Ibid. 6 Cal. 3d 673 at 680, 100 Cal. Reptr. 140 at 145.
23. Ibid. 6 Cal. 3d 673 at 679, 100 Cal. Reptr. 140 at 143.
24. Ibid. 6 Cal. 3d 673 at 683, 100 Cal. Reptr. 140 at 146.
25. Ibid.
26. Ibid. 6 Cal. 3d 673 at 685, 100 Cal. Reptr. 140 at 148.
27. See Comment, supra note 20 at 1326-27.
28. Ibid. at 1327.
29. Ibid.
30. Rheinstein, supra note 14 at 368-73.
31. Rheinstein says, "... what is meant in the statute is obviously a marriage breakdown with a low probability of being remedied. But how low must the probability be: 20 per cent, or 1, or 49 ?" Ibid, at 368.
32. Ibid. at 369.
33. Ibid.
34. Ibid. at 370.
35. *McKim* and *Walton*, supra nn. 17 and 21.
36. Rheinstein, supra note 14 at 373.
37. Ibid. at 373.
38. See for the critical examination of the breakdown theory and the recommendations made for its adoption into the Divorce Reform Act, 1970, Levy, *Uniform Marriage ana Divorce Legislation : A Preliminary*

Analysis 88 (1968); For the legislative history of the Act, see Foster, *Divorce Reform and the Uniform Act*, 18 S.D.L.Rev. 572 at 577 (1973); Frederick P. O'Connell, *Marriage, Divorce and the Uniform Marriage and Divorce Act*, 17 N.Y.L.F. 983, at 1014 (1971); Commissioner's Prefactory Note, *Uniform Marriage and Divorce Act*, 9 ULA 455 (Master ed. 1973). The Uniform Marriage and Divorce Act will hereinafter be referred to as UMDA.

39. For the objections raised by the Family Law Section of the ABA against the UMDA, their comments and recommendations see, *1971 Midyear Report and Recommendation of the Family Law Section to the ABA House of Delegates on the Uniform Marriage and Divorce Act*, 5 Fam.L.Q. 133 (1971).

40. As no guidelines were provided to the irretrievable breakdown in the Act of 1970, its provisions were the subject of criticism by many writers. For example, Rheinstein says:

    "No guidance is given for the determination of this vague term. Irretrievable breakdown of marriage means whatever a court chooses it to mean. So it may mean one thing in a liberal court and another in a conservative."

    See Rheinstein, *Marriage Stability, Divorce and the Law* 385 (1972); For similar reasons Bodenheimer says :

    "The indefiniteness of the breakdown standard opens anew the whole gamut of divergent and conflicting views on divorce. . . ." See Bodenheimer, *Reflections on the Future of Grounds for Divorce*, 8 J.Fam.L. 179 at 202 (1968); She says further: "But we cannot count on many Solomans, nor could we administer a case-by-case system of justice for the more than one-half million divorce cases filed in this country every year". Id. at 203-206.

41. See H. Merill, Section 305 : *Genesis and Effect*, 18 S.D.L.Rev. 538 (1973); Ralph J. Podell, *The case for the Revision of Uniform Marriage and Divorce Act*, 18 S.D.L.Rev. 601 (1973); Monrad G. Paulsen and Walter Wadlington, *Statutory Materials on Family Law*, 13-18 (Second ed. 1974); King, *Marriage, Divorce and Custody Reform in South Dakota*, 18 S.D.L.Rev. 654 (1973); See further Zuckman and Fox, *Ferment in Divorce Legislation*, 12 J.Fam.L. 515, 559-64 (1973); Foster, supra note 38, at 583-85. Staff, *Reconciliation and the Uniform Marriage and Divorce Act*, 18 S.D.L.Rev. 611 (1973).

42. See the Report on Uniform Marriage and Divorce Act of the Joint Meeting between the Representative of the Section of Family Law and the National Conference of Commissioners on Uniform State Laws held in New Orleans on April 3 and 4, 1971, in 5 Fam.L.Q. 125 (1971).

43. ABA-Family Law Section, *Proposed Revised Uniform Marriage and Divorce Act* (Apopted by the Family Law Section Council Nov. 9, 1972), reprinted at Symposium—*The Uniform Marriage and Divorce Act*, 18 S.D.L.Rev. 693 at 697 (1973).

44. See *Zuckman and Fox*, supra note 41, at 596-97.

45. See Merill, supra note 41, at 545.
46. See Foote, Levy and Sander, *Cases and Materials on Family Law*, 134 (Suppl. 1971).
47. Ibid. at 134.
48. Section 305 of the Proposed Revised Draft, supra note 43, at 698-99.
49. Foster, supra note 38, at 592.
50. At the time of this writing as many as twenty states have adopted the breakdown approach to marriage dissolution. Breakdown of marriage is the sole ground for dissolution in the following states : Arizona, Colorado, Delaware, Iowa, Kentucky, Michigan, Minnesota, Missouri, Nebraska, Oregon, Washington, Virgin Islands. Insanity is a separate ground in addition to breakdown in California and in Florida. In Hawaii breakdown of marriage and living separate and apart for a specified period of time are the two non-fault grounds for divorce. In the following states, breakdown of marriage is added to the existing fault grounds : Alabama, Connecticut, Georgia, New Hampshire and Texas.
51. Iowa Code ANN. Sec. 598.17 (Supp. 1973).
52. *In Re Marriage of Williams*, 199 N.W. 2d 339 (Iowa 1972).
53. Ibid. at 345.
54. Fla. STAT. ANN. Sec. 61.052 (1)(a) (West Supp. 1975).
55. Ibid. Sec. 61.052 (2).
56. Ibid. Sec. 61.052 (2)(a).
57. Ibid. Sec. 61.052 (2)(b) 1 & 2.
58. Ibid. Sec. 61.052 (2)(b) 3.
59. Ibid.
60. Ibid.
61. *Ryan* v. *Ryan*, 277 So. 2d 266 at 270 (Fla. 1972).
62. Ibid. at 271.
63. Fla. STAT. ANN. Sec. 61.044 (West Supp. 1975).
64. See supra note 61 at 276.
65. Ibid. at 278.
66. Ibid. at 277.
67. Ch. 130, Sec. 46-1-10 (1971) Colo. Sess. Laws 523.
68. Ky. Rev. STAT. ANN. Sec. 403. 170 (Supp. 1974).
69. Ore. Rev. STAT. Sec. 107.025 (1971). For a discussion on the new law see Comment, *Oregon's No-Fault Marriage Dissolution Act*, 51 Ore. L. Rev. 715 (1972).
70. Ore. Rev. STAT. Sec. 107.025 (1971).
71. N.H. Rev. STAT. ANN. Sec. 458:7 and 458:7-a (Supp. 1973).
72. See Rheinstein, supra note 14 and the accompanying text.
73. See Ch. III Section C. Judicial Interpretation of Breakdown of Marriage ?
74. Mo. STAT. ANN. Sec. 452.305 (Vernon Supp. 1975).
75. Ibid. Sec. 452.305 (2).
76. Sec. 452.320.1.
77. Sec. 452.320.2.

78. Sec. 452 320.2 (1).
79. See Ch. IV on Divorce Reforms in England at 116.
80. Sec. 452.320.2 (2).
81. Minn. STAT. ANN. Sec. 518.06 (Supp. 1975).
82. Ibid. Sec. 518.06, Subd. 2.
83. Sec. 4 of the Divorce Act, 1968. See R.W. Reville, *The Divorce Act, Annotated* (1973). For a detailed account of the divorce law in Canada see Costa, Derek Mendes da, *Divorce in Canada* (1972). (Unpublished S.J.D. thesis available in the Harvard Law School Library). For comments on the Divorce Act, 1968, see Bodenheimer, *The New Canadian Divorce Law*, 2 Fam. L.Q. 213, 220 (1968).
84. Sec. 3 of the Divorce Act, 1968 provides the following grounds : (a) Adultery, (b) Sodomy, bestiality, rape, or a homosexual act; (c) going through a form of Marriage with other person; and (d) physical or mental cruelty.
85. R.C.W.A. Ch. 157, Sec. 3 (Supp. 1973).
86. See UMDA, Sec. 302. To prescribe that a decision be made "after hearing" is to prescribe that it be made "upon evidence". See Merill, *Section 305: Genesis And Effect*, 18. S.D.L. Rev. 538 at 562 (1973). See also Commissioner's *Note on the Uniform Marriage and Divorce Act*, *9 ULA*, 485 (Master ed. 1973).
87. Rieke, *The Dissolution Act of 1973: From Status to Contract*, 49 Wash. L. Rev. 375, 385 (1974).
88. *In Re Marriage of McKim*, 6 Cal. 3d 673, 100 Cal. Reptr. 140 (1972).
89. Ibid.
90. *Ryan* v. *Ryan*, 277 So. 2d 266 (Fla. 1972).
91. E.g., Kentucky, Colorado and Michigan.
92. E.g., Missouri and Minnesota.
93. In California, counties having Conciliation Court, the petitioner is required to file a questionnaire approved by the Judicial Council. A copy of the questionnaire shall be served upon the respondent. The respondent is required to complete and file the questionnaire with his responsive pleading. See Cal. Civ. Code Sec. 4505 (West Supp. 1975). See also Cal. Civ. Pro. Code Sec. 1720 et seq. Under the UMDA the Court either at the request of the parties or on its own motion may order conciliation conference: See Sec. 305(b) 2 of the UMDA (Revised version 1971).
94. Iowa, Code ANN. 598.16 (Supp. 1974).
95. As to what constitutes "marriage breakdown" it was observed:

    We have found no more graphic definition than that of Senator Leonard in the debate on the bill when he said, "This law goes back to the real cause for divorce—they just absolutely cannot get along". See *Rodrique* v. *Rodrique*, 300 A. 2d 312 at 314 (N.H. 1973).
96. Iowa Code ANN. Sec. 598.17 (Supp. 1973).
97. *In Re Marriage of Morgan*, 218 N.W. 2d 552 (Iowa 1974).
98. *In Re Marriage of Boyd*, 200 N.W. 2d 845 (Iowa 1972).
99. *In Re Marriage of Tucker*, 213 N.W. 2d 498 (Iowa 1973).

100. Ibid. at 500.
101. *In Re Marriage of Collins*, 200 N.W. 2d 886 (Iowa 1972).
102. Ibid. at 890.
103. Traditional defenses such as recrimination and condonation have been abolished under the new divorce statutes. See for example, Fla. STAT. ANN. Sec. 61.004 (Supp. 1973). Iowa Code ANN. Sec. 598.18 (Supp. 1973).
104. Fla. STAT. Sec. 61.052 (a) (West Supp. 1975).
105. *Nooe* v. *Nooe*, 277 So. 2d 835 (Fla. App. 1973).
106. *Riley* v. *Riley*, 271 So. 2d 181 at 183 (Fla. 1972).
107. Ore. Rev. STAT. Sec. 107.025 (1971).
108. *In Re Dunn*, 511 P. 2d 427 (Ore. App. 1973).
109. Supra note 107.
110. *Kretzschmar* v. *Kretzschmar*, 48 Mich. App. 279, 210 N.W. 2d 352 (1973).
111. Ibid. 48 Mich. App. 279 at 286, 210 N.W. 2d 352 at 353.
112. *In Re Marriage of Penny*, 203 N. W. 2d 380 (Iowa 1973).
113. Iowa Code ANN. Sec. 598.16 (Supp. 1973).
114. Ibid.
115. Supra note 112, 203 N. W. 2d 380 at 382.
116. See Fla. STAT. 61.052 (2) (b) (1973).
117. Sass, *The Iowa No-Fault Dissolution of Marriage Law in Action*, 18 South Dakota L. Rev. 629 at 641-42 (1973).
118. Tex. Code ANN. Sec. 3.01 (Vernon 1975).
119. *Bakkan* v. *Bakkan* 502 S. W. 2d 315 (Tax. 1973).
120. Ibid. at 316.
121. Based upon personal interviews with California practitioners and a review of the literature Foster says that there was no case in which petition was denied because of failure to prove irremediable breakdown. See Foster and Freed, *Divorce Reform*: *Brakes on Breakdown*, 13 Jl. of Fam. L. 443 at 449 (f. n. 30) (1974).
122. According to Foster, there should be some objective proof of marriage breakdown particularly when there are children of the marriage. In his view the best proof of breakdown is separation due to marital difficulties. He advocates strongly that court should provide conciliation and counseling services. Other proposals include appointment of a professional staff in the divorce court, appointment of a court officer to protect the welfare of children and to have independent counsel for the child in contested cases. See supra note 121 above at 491.
123. *Collins* v. *Collins*, 200 N. W. 886 (Iowa 1972).
124. Iowa Code ANN. Sec. 598.10 (Supp. 1973). This section is a re-enactment of section 598.7 of the earlier Code of 1966.
125. Supra note 123 at 890.
126. It may be pointed out that under Florida statute the evidence at the hearing need not be corroborated except for the purpose of proving residence requirement. See Fla. STAT. ANN. 61.052 (2) (West Supp. 1975).

127. See for example, *Nooe* v. *Nooe*, 277 So. 2d 835 (Fal. App. 1973).
128. *In Re Marriage of McKim*. 6 Cal. App. 3d 673, 100 Cal. Reptr. 140 (1972). The retention of the defense of collusion in this case has been deplored by Baron. He says "When divorce is viewed as involving two transactions, that of release from the present situation and the desire to create a new domestic life, the collusion rule, especially in light of the new Act, seems ill-conceived and artificial". See Note, *In Re Marriage of McKim—Playacting and the New Family Law Act*, 4 Sw. U. L. Rev. 325 at 329 (1972).
129. *Ryan* v. *Ryan*, 277 So. 2d 266 (Fla. 1973).
130. See *In Re Marriage of Morgan*, 218 N. W. 2d 552 at 560 (Iowa 1974); *Woodruff* v. *Woodruff*, 320 A. 2d 661 at 663 (N. H. 1974).
131. One writer points out that the necessity of a subjective standard in the context of a no-fault system becomes apparent when one considers the alternative to a determination based on state of mind. If irreconcilable differences is not an individual respresentation that one partner has assessed his marital situation and had decided that the marriage cannot continue, then the trial court must make an independent determination of the viability of the marriage. Since no standard for the exercise of the trial court's discretion was provided by the legislature, the writer says that a *prima facie* case for dissolution would be satisfied by the declaration of petitioner that he or she sincerely believes that marriage has irreparably broken down. See Comment, *The End of Innocence: Elimination of Fault in California Divorce Law*, 17 U. C. L. A.L. Rev. 1306 (1970).
132. See California Assembly Committee on Judiciary, Report of 1969 Divorce Reform Legislation, 4 Cal. Assem. J. 8054 at 8057 (Aug. 8, 1969) in Comment, supra note 131 above at 1319.
133. *In Re Marriage of Walton*, 28 Cal. App. 3d 108, 104 Cal. Reptr. 472 (1972).
134. See *McKim* supra note 128.
135. Attorney's Guide To Family Law Act Practice, pp. 129-30 Sec. 2.26 (C. Brosnahan & Isadore-Rosenblat 1970).
136. See Note, *Irreconcilable Differences: California Court Respond to No-Fault Dissolutions*, 7 Loyola of Los Angeles L. Rev. 453 at 464-65 (1974).
137. *In Re Marriage of Walton*, 28 Cal. App. 108 at 117, 104 Cal. Reptr. 472 at 480.
138. *Woodruff* v. *Woodruff*, 320 A. 2d 661 (N. H. 1974).
139. *In Re Dunn*, supra note 108.
140. See the Report of the 1969 Divorce Reform Legislation of the Assembly Committee in Judiciary, 4 Assm. J. 8054, 8058 (1969) in Note, supra note 128, at 327-28.
141. Cal. Civ. Code Sec. 4509 (West 1970).
142. Ore. Rev. STAT. ANN 107.036 (Supp. 1971).
143. N. H. Rev. STAT. ANN. 458:7-a (Supp. 1973).
144. For a short discussion, see Walton supra note 133, 28 Cal. App. 3d 108 at 117-118, 104 Cal. Reptr. 472 at 480.

145. Ibid.
146. See Boston Sunday Globe, Aug. 4, 1974 at 72, Col. 1 to 4.
146A. N.H. Rev. STAT. ANN. See, 458 : 7-a (Supp. 1973) Emphasis added).
147. See Boston Sunday Globe. supra note 146.
148. See the remarks of Mac Faden, J., in Saul, *Proof of a No-Fault Divorce Case*, Los Angeles B. Bull. 99 at 127 (1970).
149. Ibid. at 127.
150. See Comment supra note 131, at 1328.
151. Sass, supra note 117, at 646.
152. Leo, *Oregon's No-Fault Marriage Dissolution Act*, 51 Ore. L. Rev. 715 at 721 (1972).
153. See supra 136, at 466.
154. Interview with Commissioner Reese in Note, supra note 136 at 466.
155. See Hogoboom and Goddard, supra note 13.
156. See Sass, supra note 117. See also Peters, *Iowa Reform of Marriage Termination*, 20 Drake. L. Rev. 211 (1971).
157. See Goddard, supra note 13, at 409-410.
158. Col. Civ. Code. Sec. 4505 (West 1970).
159. See Hogoboom, supra note 13, at 588.
160. See Sass supra note 117, at 639.
161. Ibid. at 639.
162. Ibid.
163. Ibid. at 643.
164. Remarks of an anonymous attorney in Sass, supra note 117, at 644.
165. For a discussion on this aspect of the question see Ch. III, Sec. A at 58-59.

D. A. Reappraisal

166. See Wadlington, *Divorce without Fault without Perjury*, 52 Va. L. Rev. 32 at 68-70 (1966).
167. The Divorce Reform Act, 1969, Sec. 2(1)(d) and (e).
168. See Rutman, *Departure from Fault*, 1 J. Fam. L. 181 at 183-90 (1961).
169. See Wadlington, supra note 166, at 52.
170. Rutman, supra note 168 at 187.
171. Gallagher, *No-Fault Divorce in Delaware*, A.B. A. J. 873 (1973).
172. *Wife V. v. Husband V*, 291 A. 2d 277 (Del. 1972).
173. Arizona, California, Idaho, Louisiana, Nevada, New Mexico, Texas and Washington have the system of community property. See Foote, Levy and Sander 317-323 (1966). *Cases and Materials on Family Law*. See also H. Clark, *Law of Domestic Relations*, pp. 219-229, Sec. 7.1 to 7.2 (1968).

Divorce Law Reform in England* 4

BACKGROUND TO THE DIVORCE REFORM ACT, 1969

THE Anglo-Saxon law before the Norman conquest allowed divorce by mutual consent or on the ground of the wife's infidelity and recognized a right to remarry.[1] The ecclesiastical courts during the reign of Queen Elizabeth[2] have granted a divorce *a vinculo mattrimonii* (divorce absolute) as distinguished from divorce *a mensa et thoro* (separation from bed and board) on the ground of adultery and permitted the parties to marry again.[3] As early as the tenth century the law of marriage and divorce was cast in a rigid mould because of the complete dominance of the church over matrimonial matters.[4] The ecclesiastical courts could pronounce a marriage void *ab initio*, but they had no power to pronounce a divorce *a vinculo* if there had been a valid marriage.[5]

Under the canon law, from the Council of Trent to the Reformation, the marriage tie was universally regarded as indissoluble, and *separatio tori* was the only remedy given for adultery in the courts of Church.[6] The Canonical theory of indissolubility of marriage did not allow divorce, instead, it allowed only divorce *a mensa et thoro* on the ground of adultery which was considered as a serious breach of marriage vow.[7] In the days of Victoria, divorce was regarded by those in exalted position as a low place, from which those who descended to it, even as petitioners emerged with soiled fingers.[8]

The procedure to obtain divorce during the seventh century till 1857 was like this. The husband seeking divorce on the ground of his wife's adultery was first to obtain a decree

*This section has appeared under the title, "A Look at the Divorce Law Reform in England". See *Kurukshetra Law Journal*, Vol. 2 p. 80 (1976).

of divorce *a mensa et thoro* from the ecclesiastical court and then petition the parliament for divorce *a vinculo*.[9] But, before he could obtain the decree from the ecclesiastical court, he had to file a suit against the adulterer in an action for criminal conversion and after having proved the charge against his wife and the co-respondent, he could obtain the decree from the church's court. The procedural formalities, the time that was involved and the expenses that had to be incurred in order to obtain a divorce decree fell into disrepute. Divorce became the luxury of the rich people.[10] The demand for cheaper and simpler form of divorce started during the years following Waterloo.[11] The stage was set and the decks cleared for further relaxation in the grounds of divorce.

The Matrimonial Causes Act, 1857 was the first inroad made in the ecclesiastical divorce law. A Royal Commission was appointed in 1850 to look into the question of reforms in the matrimonial law. The commission recommended cruelty and desertion in addition to adultery as grounds upon which divorce could be granted. The Act was passed in the teeth of opposition. For instance, when the bill was introduced, Gladstone, a powerful antagonist to liberal divorce observed :

> It is opposed, to the law of church, to the law of nature, and to the law of God.[12]

Even Lord Cranworth who recommended the passage of the bill had his own reservations. He struck a note of caution and expressed fear by stating :

> I think recognition of the sanctity of marriage underlines the essentials of our quality as a people. No measure could be more injurious or more calculated to interfere with the social welfare of the country than one which tended to shake the solidarity of marriage and the strength of the marriage tie.[13]

Be that as it may, the Act took away the jurisdiction of the ecclesiastical courts over matrimonial matters and gave powers to the secular courts to dissolve the marriage. The Act, for the first time, provided divorce by judicial process. Divorce *a mensa et thoro* was substituted by a decree of judicial separation on the same grounds on which divorce could have been obtained. In short, in the words of Dicey[14] "The Divorce Act of 1857 was a triumph of individualistic liberalism and of common justice. It did away the inequity of law which theoretically permitted divorce, but in reality conceded to the rich a right denied to the poor". It may be mentioned here that before the Matrimonial Causes Act, 1857 was passed a husband could obtain divorce on the ground of adultery *simpliciter* whereas a wife had to prove adultery coupled with incest, bigamy, cruelty or alternatively, rape or an unnatural offence.[15] The Act of 1857 retained this distinction until 1923 when another Matrimonial Causes Act of that year put the husband and the wife on an equal footing.[16]

A.P. Herbert's Matrimonial Causes Act of 1937 further extended the grounds for divorce. Under the Act,[17] divorce or judicial separation could be obtained for cruelty, or desertion without cause for three years, or incurable insanity. It is of significance to note that divorce on the ground of insanity was not based upon the theory of matrimonial guilt. It was of the essence of the English law of divorce that the petitioner had to prove some matrimonial offence committed by the respondent before he could be granted a divorce. But, divorce on the ground of insanity can in no way be regarded as a ground based upon the principle of matrimonial guilt.

From that time onwards various Royal Commissions were appointed to enquire into the law of matrimonial causes. By a touch here and a twist there, the law was altered and consolidated in the Matrimonial Causes Act, 1950. The law was further amended, repealed and finally consolidated in the Matrimonial Causes Act of 1965.[18] Although, the basic structure of the law of divorce remained unchanged, that is divorce shall be granted solely upon the ground of one spouse's fault.

The enormous social changes following the world wars had already caused a great upheaval into the very fabric of social unit—the family. Added to it, the industrial era completely polluted the social and cultural climate. Values changed, ideas got transformed, the relative roles of men and women in a progressive society attained different postures.[19] The age old doctrine that divorce should be available only to the "innocent" and not to the "guilty" spouse was challenged. The very foundation of the recognition of the conventional grounds as the basis for divorce was shaken. After all, the laws of marriage and divorce were not written by the finger of God on tables of stone, but they were made and altered again and again by men, for their own convenience, moved by separate and changing prejudices, in the clash of conflicting views and warring creeds, and under the stress of expediency.[20]

THE DIVORCE REFORM ACT, 1969

The grounds for divorce, as we have seen were, before the passing of the Divorce Reform Act of 1969, based on the concept of fault. This concept owes its origin to the ecclesiastical conception of marriage. In order to dissolve a marriage, law must find some justification and that justification was sought in the "innocence" or the "guilt" of the spouses. While divorce was made available and the grounds slowly and surely expanded, it also became necessary to restrict the grant of decrees to such petitioners who did not come to the court with "clean hands". Thus many of the bars such as condonation, connivance and collusion were really the ingenious expedients employed by the ecclesiastical law to retain the marriage tie on one hand and to discourage or check the proclivity of the spouses seeking divorce on the other. These discretionary bars were retained in the statutory law from its inception till the Divorce Reform Act of 1969 came to be passed.

The law of divorce based solely on "fault-notion" was found to be unsatisfactory. It was realised that many of the causes on which the parties pull apart were not necessarily the guilty conduct of the one or the other spouse. The causes could be emotional or psychological which had resulted in the breakdown of marriage. In order to find out an alternative to the present divorce law, a group was appointed by the Archbishop of Canterbury in January 1964 and the report of the group was published in July 1966.[21] While trying to find out a new basis for divorce which was the task of the group, it was observed :[22]

Unsatisfactory as the law based on the matrimonial offence

has proved in practice to be, it has yet to be shown that the substitution of some other basis would improve the situation. It is after all conceivable that the only alternative to the frying-pan might turn out to be the fire—in which case it would be safer to stick to the frying-pan.

The group stuck to the frying-pan, as it was safer in their own estimation and recommended that breakdown of marriage should be the sole ground for divorce as it was by far the better alternative. Therefore, under the scheme of putting asunder Canterbury-style, the existing grounds of divorce were to be abolished and breakdown substituted in their place. Furthermore, the proposal envisaged breakdown with inquest, that is to say, that the court was to assume an inquisitorial role in order to justify itself that the breakdown of marriage was irretrievable.

Meanwhile, the Law Commission was also seized of the matter relating to matrimonial causes with a view to reforming the law by codification. The Commission too gave its report : "Reform of Grounds of Divorce: Field of choice" in November 1966. Endorsing the views of the Archbishop's group that the law based on the concept of fault was unsatisfactory, the Law Commission observed :[23]

> It does not achieve the maximum possible fairness to all concerned, for a spouse may be branded as guilty in law though not the more blameworthy in fact. The insistence on guilt and innocence tends to embitter relationships, with particularly damaging results to the children, rather than to promote future harmony. Its principles are widely regarded as hypocritical.

However, the proposal of the group that divorce should be based upon "breakdown with inquest" was rejected by the Commission as it would involve enormous expenditure and was procedurally impracticable. The Commission, after examining the law on the subject, concluded that a good divorce law should be able to achieve two objectives:[24]

(i) To buttress, rather than to undermine, the stability of marriage; and

(ii) When, regrettably, a marriage has irretrievably broken down, to enable the empty shell to be destroyed with the maximum fairness, and the minimum bitterness, distress and humiliation.

Eventually, the Commission accepted the proposal that irretrievable breakdown of marriage should form the basis for divorce.

The Divorce Reform Act received the Royal assent in October 1969 and came into effect on January 1, 1971. As recommended by both the Archbishop's Group and the Law Commission, the Act has adopted the breakdown approach to marital dissolution. But, in its present form it neither follows the scheme of "breakdown with inquest" envisaged by the Archbishop's Group nor the Law Commission's proposal of "breakdown without inquest". The Act follows a different procedure for establishing the irretrievable breakdown. Under the Act, certain facts have to be proved in order to raise a presumption of irretrievable breakdown. Some of the facts resemble the grounds for divorce under the prior law. In fact, the scheme adopted under the Act represents a compromise between the "matrimonial wrong" principle and the breakdown theory.[25] It may be pointed out that the Archbishop's Group has stated that apart from making an inquiry into the history of the marriage, its condition or the causes for its failure, other factors such as the matrimonial offences, could also be considered as providing evidence of irretrievable breakdown.[26] Since the procedure of "breakdown with inquest" was abandoned as being impracticable, the Act provided an alternative technique contemplated by the Archbishop's Group for establishing breakdown. Accordingly, the prior matrimonial offences were incorporated under the Act as guidelines to facilitate the proof of irretrievable breakdown of the marriage.

The Act abolishes the conventional grounds of divorce based on matrimonial guilt. Section 1 of the Act provides that the sole ground on which a petition for divorce may be presented to the court by either party to a marriage shall be that the marriage has broken down irretrievably. However, section 2 lays down that the court shall not hold the marriage to have broken down irretrievably unless the petitioner satisfies the court of one or more of the five facts. Some of these facts resemble the former grounds for divorce. But, since irretrievable breakdown has been made the sole ground for divorce, they should not be regarded as grounds. Instead, they should be treated as "guidelines" which will assist the court to determine whether or not there has been a breakdown of the marriage.[27]

The guidelines to irretrievable breakdown

Under the Divorce Reform Act, 1969, the petitioner has to prove one or more of the following facts :

Guideline 1. Sec. 2(1)(a) "that the respondent has committed adultery and the petitioner finds it intolerable to live with the respondent".

Much controversy has centered round the interpretation of this guideline. We have a conflict of judicial decisions as well as a difference of opinion among writers and commentators. The fact to be proved under this head is that the respondent has committed adultery *and* the petitioner finds it intolerable to live with the respondent. There are, therefore, two matters which must be established before the fact could be proved: (1) the respondent's adultery and (2) petitioner's intolerability to live with the respondent. The question that arises is as to whether there is any link or some connection between adultery and intolerability or whether the two factors are independent of each other. In other words, should the petitioner merely prove adultery and say that he found the life intolerable due to other reasons than adultery of the respondent or is it necessary for him to prove adultery and establish that it was by reason of the adultery that his living with the respondent had become intolerable. In *Goodrich* v. *Goodrich*,[28] it was held that the phrase "has committed adultery" and the phrase "and the petitioner finds it intolerable to live with the respondent" were independent of each other. The facts of the case briefly stated were as follows:

The husband filed a petition for divorce on the ground of his wife's adultery and alleged that he found it intolerable to live with her. The wife contended, as she was entitled to under section 2(3) of the Divorce Reform Act, 1969[29] (hereinafter referred to for short as the Act) that the husband had condoned the adultery and that his contention was inconsistent with the fact that he had offered her reconciliation. The court on evidence found that the husband had made offer of reconciliation and that the wife had spurned the offer. The court granted a decree *nisi* for divorce notwithstanding the fact that the husband found living with his wife intolerable for a reason other than adultery. On the other hand the Family Division of the High Court in *Roper* v. *Roper*[30] came to a contrary conclusion interpreting the same guideline. The *Goodrich* case was referred and Faulks, J., said that the two facts that have to be proved are : [31]

> (1) the respondent has committed adultery, and (2) the petitioner finds it intolerable to live with the respondent : . . . She may find it intolerable to live with him because he blows his nose more often than she likes. There is no necessary nexus between the committing of the adultery and the finding that it is intolerable to live with the respondent . . . I think common-sense tells you that where the finding that has got to be made is that the respondent has committed adultery, and the petitioner finds it intolerable to live with the respondent, it means, "*and in consequence* of the adultery the petitioner finds it intolerable to live with the respondent".

Text writers such as Rayden[32], Tolstoy[33], Bromley[34] and Passingham[35] subscribe to the view taken in the *Goodrich* case. But some writers have taken a contrary view. Barton[36] has advocated that there must be some connection between adultery and intolerability. Rosenbaum[37] states that to construe guideline (a) such that there need to be no casual link between adultery and intolerability seems, *prima facie*, to betray the intention of the drafter of the Divorce Reform Act.

The difference of opinion has arisen, it would seem, due to the word "and" used in this guideline. Gramatically speaking "and" is a disjunctive word and the guideline read as it is, would mean that there need be no link between adultery and intolerability. To borrow the words of Lord Denning in the context of statutory interpretation "strawberries *and* cream" means "strawberries *and* cream" not "strawberries *with* cream".[38]

Now let us take a look into the Parliamentary debates and find out whether they throw any light on the matter. Some of the Law Lords, for instance, Viscount Dilhorne[39] pointed out that the guideline as drafted would be susceptible to a wider interpretation in the sense that the petitioner could find it intolerable to live with the respondent for reasons wholly unconnected with adultery. It was therefore proposed to amend the guideline to read "The respondent has committed adultery and by reason of that adultery the petitioner finds it intolerable to live with the respondent. But Lord Reid emphatically objected to the proposal. He said:[40]

> In a common case, there has been bickering in the family for a long time. The wife finds it very near to being the last straw. Then the husband rather blatantly commits adultery with some one. She says, "This is the last straw. It is not so much the adultery I object to; but the whole thing added together". If this amendment were passed, you would not be allowed to say that. You would have to concentrate on the adultery and nothing else. I do not believe that this is what, in most cases. wives in that position would feel. . . A wife would say: "I cannot say that I find the adultery by itself intolerable but I find the whole situation intolerable".

A majority in the House of Lords agreed with Lord Reid and thus the move to amend the guideline was voted down. The Parliamentary debates no doubt support the decision in *Goodrich* case, but it must be pointed out that the implications of this decision and the views expressed by many who support it may have far reaching effects. This has been neatly explained by David Morris by a picturesque illustration. The writer can do no more than to quote from his work :[41]

> Suppose, as has happened in these enlightened days, husband and wife go to a wife-swapping party. At the end of convivial evening the husband goes off to bed with Mrs. X

> knowing that his wife is going to bed with Mr. X. Next morning husband and wife meet on amicable terms and recount to each other the pleasures and amusements of the preceding night. All is happy between them. Suppose, however, that during the next two months the husband begins to regret the whole incident because he finds that his wife is repeatedly comparing his sexual performance unfavourably with that of Mr. X. What could be more intolerable than that ?

That in the above situation the husband could be granted a decree of divorce under the Act nobody can dispute. But if such a case were to come up for decision under the prior law, clearly the husband's conduct would have amounted to connivance and a decree refused. One really wonders why all this confusion could not be removed. One way to deal with it is to amend the guideline in such a way as to make it clear that the petitioner should establish that it was by reason of the adultery of the respondent that he found his life intolerable. The other way is perhaps to simply retain the guideline as a fact of adultery to be proved whereupon the court could regard that the marriage has broken down. And, perhaps the best way is to simply remove this guideline from the statute. But adultery which is regarded as an offense *par excellence* and which seems to be so dear to the English reformers that any suggestion to drop the guideline from the Act may not be appealing.

Guideline 2. Sec. 2(1)(b), "that the respondent has behaved in such a way that the petitioner cannot reasonably be expected to live with the respondent".

This guideline covers a large range of acts which may include most of the matrimonial offenses such as cruelty, conduct which could be regarded as "grave and weighty", constructive desertion and unnatural offenses. In interpreting this guideline the courts will necessarily draw inspiration from the principles and precedents hitherto followed in adjudicating matrimonial reliefs. The concept of "legal cruelty" or what amounts to constructive desertion or what causes could be grave and weighty have all been defined and developed. The courts will have little difficulty in the application of the law to the facts of each case before they could find whether the marriage has really broken down. Unlike in the first guideline, here the test is objective. It is for the court to determine whether the petitioner can reasonably be expected to live with the respondent in a given set of circumstances. Each case naturally will have to be decided on the facts and merits and judicial discretion is given a free play under this guideline. However, in cases of cruelty it will not be necessary to establish the principle or rather standard laid down in *Russell* v. *Russell*.[42] For under the new Act there is a shift from the concept of "fault" to that of "breakdown". That the test is not the same under the old law and under the Act has been rightly driven home by Justice Ormrod in *Pheasant* v. *Pheasant*.[43] It was observed :

> . . . [T]he test to be applied. . . is closely similar to, but not necessarily identical with, that which was formerly used in relation to constructive desertion. . . . It would be consistent with the new legislation if this problem were now to be approached more from the point of breach of obligation than in terms of the now out-moded idea of the matrimonial offence.[44]

The above observations were made in relation to constructive desertion and what is true of a case of constructive desertion is equally true in respect of other matrimonial misconduct.

Guideline 3. Sec. 2(1)(c) "that the respondent has deserted the petitioner for a continuous period of at least two years immediately preceding the presentation of the petition".

Under this guideline, desertion will be limited to cases of actual desertion.[45] Cases of constructive desertion, i.e., where the respondent's conduct had forced the petitioner to withdraw from cohabitation can be proved and covered under guideline (b). For, it will not be necessary for the petitioner to wait until the separation has lasted for the full statutory period of desertion. Under the earlier law the period of desertion was three years which has now been reduced to two years. However, under the Act, while considering whether the period of desertion is continuous no account is to be taken of any period not exceeding six months or any two or more periods not exceeding six months in all during which the parties resumed living with each other, but no period during which the parties lived with each other shall count as part of the period of desertion or of the period for which the parties lived apart, as the case may be.[46]

Guideline 4. Sec. 2(1)(d) "that the parties to the marriage have lived apart for a continuous period of at least two years immediately preceding the presentation of the petition and the respondent consents to a decree being granted".

It is under this guideline as well as in guideline (e) that the real progress in divorce law is seen. Living apart without any matrimonial misconduct for a period of two years provided the respondent consents to a decree being granted is regarded as a breakdown upon which a court is authorized to grant a decree of divorce. Separation statutes in varying forms have appeared in American jurisprudence since about the middle of the nineteenth century. We have also examined some of the common problems connected with separation statutes, namely, what constitutes separation, when can it be said to be voluntary separation and what is the effect of fault on the part of the spouse seeking divorce in a proceeding. The basis for the recognition of "living apart" as an index of marital breakdown is also accepted under this guideline. The important question under this guideline is, whether simply "living apart" for a period of two years is enough to ground a petition for divorce if the respondent consents to a decree being granted or something more is required. In other words should the parties who have lived apart for the prescribed period have "lived apart" with the intention to sever the marital relationship ?

In *Santos* v. *Santos*[47] the court was of the view that the phrase "living apart" did not mean physical separation. It said, that in addition to establishing the fact of separation, the petitioner had to prove that he "had ceased to recognize the marriage as subsisting and intended never to return". This decision is likely to be followed should cases on the point arise in future. It may be pointed out in the context that under the law of desertion, intention to desert is one of the essential element. When intention to bring cohabitation permanently to an end for a prescribed statutory period was established, then the petitioner was entitled to a decree of judicial separation or divorce. The English judges were well aware of this principle and it came in handy to the judge who was called upon to construe this guideline. It is not at all surprising. But, it could be argued whether this interpretation will not go against the concept of "breakdown" which has been accepted as a sole ground for divorce. The court in the instant case was conscious of the absurdities that would result if "living apart" was to be construed as mere physical separation. It is quite understandable. It is no doubt true that some injustice or absurdity is involved in such an interpretation. But the fundamental question in the context is how far is the court justified in refusing the decree when both the parties out of their free will and choice decide to get rid of each other. Unfortunately, neither the Law Commission nor the Archbishop's group has dealt with this aspect of the question in detail. The decision in *Santos* case deserves merit only on one count. That is, under the scheme of the Act reconciliation has been given a prominent position. The preamble says "An Act. . . to facilitate reconciliation in matrimonial causes". Therefore, we can accept the interpretation given in *Santos* case as encouraging reconciliation. Yet, as MacKenna advocates "the fact that the two parties to a contract or to any relation wish to be released from it *is a reason,* though not necessarily a conclusive one, for giving the relief, but *never a good reason for withholding it.*[48]

Further difficulty in bringing in the element of intention under this guideline is at what point of time could one say that the necessary intention "never to return" was entertained in the mind of the petitioner. The principal problem, as stated by Wadlington,[49] becomes one of proof of time when the breakdown occurred. It may be pointed out here that the Full Court of New South Wales in *Macrae* v. *Macrae*[50] held that breakdown occurred from the date the parties lived apart and not from the date when the intention never to live again was formed. According to Freeman,[51] since the Act is concerned with the state of marriage at the petition and not at the date, of parting a decree can be pronounced if the two facts under the guideline are proved, namely, living apart for two years and the consent of the respondent.

Guideline 5. Sec. 2(1)(e) "That the parties to the marriage have lived apart for a continuous period of at least five years immediately preceding the presentation of the petitition".

This guideline too has been the subject of much controversy as it would enable a guilty spouse to force a divorce against the wishes of an innocent party. For centuries the hallmark of English law of divorce had been that no one should be allowed to take advantage of his own wrong. But according to the noble Lord who introduced the Bill which has now become the law, the principle that a man would not get the benefit of his own wrong was "really senseless".

To many who detest this guideline because it hits the innocent party with a sharper edge, it must be told that the fact that a lady found herself divorced after waiting for 5 long years for her husband who was discharged from the hospital or from jail, must be viewed not as a punishment to the faithful lady but as one of those frolics in which fate often delights.

The great merit of the guideline in the estimation of the Law Commission[52] lies in the fact that it enables many stable illicit unions to legalize their relation and also confers a status of legitimacy to their children who have been born outside lawful wedlock. But the fact remains, as the law now stands, that a man who is weary of his wife can simply go, stay happily with his mistress, beget children and divorce his wife after five years. This is perhaps the prize that the reformistic legislation had to pay.

Bars and defences

No petition for divorce can be presented until three years have elapsed after the solemnization of the marriage.[53] Since the Divorce Reform Act has incorporated the principle of irretrievable breakdown as a sole ground for divorce, the conventional bars of condonation, connivance and collusion have been abolished.[54] Conduct of the parties will be relevant only for consideration of questions of financial provision, property and the interest of the children.[55] The real defences are those provided in section 2(1) and section 2(3) of the Act. Section 2(1) provides that the court shall not hold the marriage to have broken down irretrievably unless the petitioner satisfied the court of one or more facts specified in sub-sections (a) to (e). Section 2(3) provides that the court shall grant a decree *nisi* "if satisfied on the evidence of any such fact as is mentioned in sub-section (1) of this section: then, unless it is satisfied on all the evidence that the marriage has not broken down irretrievably, it shall ... grant a decree *nisi* of divorce."

The defences which a respondent can plead are provided in sections 4 and 6 of the Act.[56] It is laid down in these sections that the respondent could oppose that the grant of the decree, where the petitioner alleged the facts mentioned in (d) and (e) (i.e., that parties have lived apart for a period of at least two years and the respondent has consented for divorce; that the parties have lived apart for a period of at least five years) would involve grave financial or other hardships. The financial hardships are those which relate to the loss of pension rights or other property matters. But such hardships must be "grave".[57]

As respects, what would be the other hardships, we have a recent case, *Banik* v. *Banik*,[58] involving an Indian (Hindu) couple. The husband filed a petition for divorce on the ground that he and his wife had "lived apart" for a period of five years and upwards. The lower court granted the decree *nisi* of divorce. The wife appealed. She opposed both on the ground that the grant of the decree would not only result in financial hardships but other hardships too. The other hardships which she alleged were that a divorced woman in the Hindu society was regarded as an outcast and carried a stigma. She could not marry according to the customs and traditions of her caste and community. The court readily accepted her contention and set aside the decree *nisi* granted by the lower court.

It should not be imagined that the Divorce Reform Act has made divorce easy. There are, as we have seen, ample safeguards provided in the Act itself. The cases mentioned above are pointers in this direction. Furthermore, the courts will not pronounce a decree as a matter of course even if there has been a breakdown of marriage. The case of *Richards* v. *Richards*[59] illustrates this point. The wife filed a petition for divorce on the ground that her husband had behaved in such a way as to make her life intolerable [i.e., under section 2(1)(b)]. She alleged that the husband had become mentally ill, suffered from moodiness, taciturnity and insomnia. He had also slapped her on one occasion. All this was proved by evidence. Dismissing the petition the court said that the wife had, in all circumstances, failed to establish that the husband behaved in such a way that she could not reasonably be expected to live with him.

All told, the Divorce Reform Act is certainly a step forward towards reforming the divorce law. It has abolished the concept of "fault" and substituted it with "irretrievable breakdown". But the ghost of "guilt" walks into other provisions relating to financial matters, property and custody of children as the conduct of the parties is a relevant consideration in such proceedings. The way, says Frank Bates,[60] in which these sections have been drafted is unlikely to encourage the judiciary to abandon the matrimonial offense. This is particularly true in respect of guidelines (a), (b) and (c), though as we have stated earlier that they exist not as grounds but as facts to be proved as evidence of marriage breakdown. Section (1) of the Act boldly declares that after the commencement of the Act the sole ground on which a petition for divorce may be presented shall be that the marriage has broken down irretrievably. This might gladden the heart of a liberal but soon he comes to dismay when his eyes are cast upon the first three paragraphs of section 2(1). It is perhaps due to this reason that Bromley[61] remarked that the Act "represents an unhappy compromise between the matrimonial offence theory and the irretrievable breakdown theory which is unlikely to commend itself to the supporters of either".

One of the objectives of the Law Commission which recommended the adoption of breakdown concept as the basis for divorce was "to take the heat out of the matrimonial proceeding," To what extent this objective would be achieved is doubtful particularly when proceedings are initiated under the first three guidelines.[62] So far as the custody of the child is concerned hostilities would continue. But, to be fair, "fault" will become less and less relevant as many a couple would prefer to get rid of each other by mutual consent after having lived apart for two years or five years as the case may be. By this process the Act prevents slinging of mud against each other and saves the spouses from public scandal. Many dead marriages could be given a decent burial with less embarrassment and bitterness.

Writing on marriage and divorce in 1936, Lord Merrivale concluded with the following observation :

> When judgment comes to be given upon serious proposals for the amendment of the law of marriage, let us make sure that any change to be made shall be beyond question a beneficial change. Our English people have experience enough, and sense enough, to determine the matter. Past generations have supplied us with knowledge, the facts of everyday life supply the problems which that knowledge guided by honest minds, must solve. Let us bear in mind that marriage is an outstanding means of profit, and that divorce is its enemy. So may we be guided in the right way.[63]

To what extent the solemn aspiration of Lord Merrivale has been translated into reality is an open question. It may be that with the ever-accumulating "sense" and "experience" the English people have taken steps in what they perceive to be the right direction. It may be pointed out that the reforms that touch the very basic fibre of social life cannot be responsibly and realistically appreciated in a brief span of their operation. Yet while commenting upon these reforms one cannot escape the task of presenting their evaluation in analytical and comparative terms. Accordingly, an attempt is made in the following chapter to present such an evaluation in comparison with the divorce reforms in the United States.

NOTES AND REFERENCES

1. See 2 W. Holdsworth, *A History of English Law* 90 (4th ed. 1936); F. Pollock and F. Maitland, *The History of English Law* 393 (2nd ed. 1959); S.B. Kitchin, *A History of Divorce* 171 (1912). J.F. Worsley Boden, *Mischief of the Marriage Law* 217 (1932).
2. See the First Report of the Royal Commission, *The Law of Divorce* (1853) (Minutes of evidence given by Stephen Lushington before the Committee of House of Lord, pp. 35-47. See also the evidence given by J. Stoddard at 53).
3. See O.R. McGregor, *Divorce in England* 1-34 (1957); J. Jackson, *The Formation and Annulment of Marriage* 8, 31 *et seq.* (2nd ed. 1969).
4. See 1 Wordsworth, *A History of English Law* 621-623 (Seventh ed. Rev. 1956).
5. Ibid. at 623.
6. See A. Wood Renton and G. Phillimore, *The Comparative Law of Marriage and Divorce* 857 (1910).
7. The ecclesiastical courts, however, claimed the power to dissolve the marriage on the ground of the wife's adultery in the case of Marquis of Northampton in 1542. He had to obtain recognition of his marriage by an Act of Parliament which declared divorce pronounced by the church court as valid. Subsequently, in 1602 in Fuliambe's case that Act was repealed overriding that the decree granted by the ecclesiastical court in Northampton's case did not dissolve the marriage. See *Rye* v. *Fuliambe*, 3 Salk. 138; Moore's Report 683; 72 E.R. 838 (K.B. 1907).
8. Alfred Fellows, *The Case Against the English Divorce Law* 76 (1932).
9. See Devid Morris, *The End of Marriage* 16 (1971).
10. The cost involved to get a divorce in those days was anything between 100 pounds to 5,000 pounds. See C. Gasquoine Hartley, *Divorce* (*Today and Tomorrow*) 6 (1957); McGregor, supra note 3 at 17. Don. Flood, *The Dissolution of Marriage* 75 (1962).
11. See R.H. Graveson, *The Background of the Century in A Century of Family Law* 6 (1957).
12. As quoted by Lord Merrivale at his *Marriage and Divorce* 37 (1936).
13. Ibid. at pp. 37-38.
14. Dicey, *Law and Public Opinion in England during the Nineteenth Century* 347 (2nd ed. 1920).
15. Matrimonial Causes Act, 1857, Sec. 27.
16. Matrimonial Causes Act, 1923, Sec. 1.
17. Matrimonial Causes Act, 1937, Secs. 2 and 3.

18. Matrimonial Causes Act 1965, Sec. 1.
19. For a lively account of the various factors which affected the law of divorce, see Rheinstein, *Marriage Stability, Divorce and the Law*, pp. 317-321 (1972).
20. Hartley, supra note 10, at pp. 10-11.
21. Putting as under : *A Divorce Law for Contemporary Society*. The Report of a Group appointed by the Archbishop of Canterbury in January 1964 (S.P.C.K. 1966).
22. Ibid. para 46 at 33.
23. The Law Commission, *Reform of the Grounds of Divorce : The Field of Choice*. Cmnd. 3123, para 28 at 16 (1966).
24. Ibid. para 15 at 10.
25. Letter from Anderson to the Sunday Time in B.H. Lee, *Divorce Law Reform in England* 104 (1974).
26. See putting as under supra note 21, para 28 at pp. 18-19.
27. See Passingham, *The Divorce Reform Act 1969*, para 6 at 4 (1970).
28. *Goodrich* v. *Goodrich*, [1971] 2 All E.R. 1340; [1971] 1 W.L.R. 1142.
29. Divorce Reform Act, 1969 provides :

    Sec. 2(3) If the court is satisfied on the evidence of any such fact as is mentioned in sub-section (1) of this section, then, unless it is satisfied on all evidence that the marriage has not broken down irretrievably, it shall. . . grant a decree nisi of divorce.

    The Divorce Reform Act 1969 has been repealed by the Matrimonial Causes Act, 1973. However, the law as embodied under the Divorce Reform Act, 1969 has been retained under the new enactment. Citations herein will be to the Divorce Reform Act, 1969.
30. *Roper* v. *Roper*, [1972] 3 All E.R. 668; [1972] 1 W.L.R. 1314.
31. Ibid. [1972] 3 All E.R. 668 at 670; [1972] 1 W.L.R. 1314 at 1317 (Emphasis as added in the report).
32. Reyden on Divorce, 205 (eleventh ed. 1972).
33. Tolstoy on Divorce, 54, Sec. 4-06 (seventh ed. 1971).
34. Bromley, *Family Law* 209 (fourth ed. 1971).
35. See Passingham supra note 27, para 8 at 17.
36. Barton, *Questions on the Divorce Reform Act, 1969*, 86 L.Q.R. 348 (1970).
37. Rosenbaum, *Divorce Reform in England : The Decline of the Matrimonial Offense*, 12 J. Fam.L. 365 at 370 (1972-73). See further Freeman, *Adultery and Intolerability*, 35 M.L.R. 100 (1972).
38. Per Lord Denning as quoted in Rosenbaum, Ibid. at 371.
39. See 303 Parl.Deb.H.L (5th Ser.) 1222 (1968-69).
40. Ibid. at 1238.
41. David Morris, *The End of Marriage* 86-87 (1971).
42. *Russell* v. *Russell*, [1895] p. 315; [1897] A.C. 395.
43. *Pheasant* v. *Pheasant*, [1972] 1 All E.R. 587; [1972] 2 W.L.R. 353.
44. Ibid. [1972] All E.R. 587 at 591; [1972] 2 W.L.R. 353 at 357.
45. See Passingham supra note 27, para 37 at 16.

46. The Divorce Reform Act, 1969, Sec. 3 (5).
47. *Santos* v. *Santos*, [1972] 2 All E.R. 246; [1972] 2 W.L.R. 899. (C A).
48. MacKenna, *Divorce by Consent and Divorce for Breakdown of Marriage*, 30 M.L.R. 121 at 122 (1967) (Emphasis added).
49. Wadlington, *Divorce without Fault without Perjury*, 52 V.A.L.Rev. 32, 70 (1966). The author made the point while commenting upon separation statutes as ground for divorce in American jurisprudence.
50. *Macrae* v. *Macrae*, 9 F.L.R. 441 (New South Wales 1967).
51. Freeman, *The Search for a Rational Divorce Law*, 24 C.L.P. 178 at 196 (1971).
52. See the Law Commission Report, supra note 23, para 33 to 36 at pp. 18-19. See also Bromley, supra note 34, at 213.
53. Section 2(3) of the Divorce Reform Act, 1969 read with section 5(5) of the Matrimonial Causes Act, 1965.
54. See Sec. 9(2) and Schedule 2 of the Divorce Reform Act, 1969.
55. The Divorce Reform Act, 1969, Secs. 4 & 6.
56. For a discussion on the subject see Ch. V at 144.
57. This aspect of the question is dealt with in Ch. V at 144.
58. *Banik* v. *Banik*, [1973] 3 All E.R. 45; [1973] 1 W.L.R. 860.
59. *Richards* v. *Richards*, [1972] 3 All E.R. 695: [1972] 1 W.L.R. 1073.
60. Bates, *Divorce Reform in England*, 3 Tasmania U.L. Rev. 343 (1970).
61. See Bromley, supra note 34 at 213.
62. In the opinion of Brown, the Act is a success in that it has achieved to remove the heat from the divorce proceedings. See Brown, *The Act of 1969—The First Year*, 122 New.L.Jl. 528 at 529 (1972). According to Levin if separation becomes a favorite ground then the element of fault would decline. See Levin, *The Divorce Reform Act, 1969*, 33 M.L R. 632 at 648 (1970).
63. See Merrivale, supra note 12, at 71.

An Analysis of the Divorce Reforms in the United States and England 5

THE basic premise upon which the marital breakdown concept is founded under both the American and English legal systems, to borrow the words of the Law Commission (England) is "To buttress, rather than to undermine, the stability of marriage, and when, regrettably, a marriage has irretrievably broken down, to enable the empty legal shell to be destroyed with maximum fairness, and the minimum bitterness, distress and humiliation".[1] The objectives to be achieved under both systems have been:

- (i) the substitution of the concept of breakdown of marriage as the sole ground of divorce in place of conventional causes;
- (ii) to minimize the evils of an adversary procedure; and
- (iii) to bury without much fuss a defunct marriage and to save as far as possible a marriage having a flicker of life.

It is interesting to note that while the premise upon which the breakdown is founded and the objectives to be achieved are the same, the approach to breakdown concept has been on different lines. While under the English law "breakdown" is a finding of a long list of facts[2] to be alleged and proved in order to dissolve a marriage, under the American legislation irretrievable breakdown is a finding of that fact supported by only two or three guidelines, namely, separation, serious discord and non-reconciliation.[3]

The difference in the respective apporaches may have been due to various reasons. For instance, it may have been due to moral, social, religious or philosophical reasons. Another reason which can account for the difference in the approach from the historical standpoint may perhaps be due to the fact that matrimonial law was entrenched in the ecclesiastical setting in England. It must have been extremely difficult for the reformers to steer the divorce law from the ecclesiastical influence by throwing overboard the whole basis of "matrimonial guilt" concept at one stroke. No doubt the Divorce Reform Act, 1969[4], boldly declares that sole ground for dissolution shall be "irretrievable breakdown" of marriage, but enacts the former fault grounds as facts to be proved before breakdown could be presumed.

There are, if we examine closely the development of divorce law in England, two stages. First, the transfer of matrimonial matters from the ecclesiastical courts to secular courts (i.e., from the church to the state) and secondly, a shift from the matrimonial misconduct to marital failure. It is perhaps due to these historical antecedents and the influence of common law that a more violent break from the past is not witnessed in the English divorce law. Instead, the Divorce Reform Act, 1969 is a compromise between the claims of Christianity on the sanctity of marriage on one hand and the interest of society and the individual parties on the other.

Looking at the American divorce law we know that the corresponding first stage seen in England is absent. In the United States, canon law has never been adopted and the ecclesiastical court system never recognised.[5] Many jurisdictions in the United States had e rlier the use of non-fault ground such as the living separate and aprat ground. As pointed out by Levy,[6] in America both the assertion of civil jurisdiction and the utilization of canonical principles for separation as grounds for absolute divorce came much earlier than in England. Further, the reformers in the United States must have been greatly influenced by the various reports given by the Law Commission of England recommending reform in divorce law from time to time. Therefore, there was no need for the reformers to take a rather hesitant step toward radical reforms. The divorce law could take just one step forward toward reforms and could completely discard the fault-based grounds.

By retaining fault related grounds as guidelines for proving breakdown, the Divorce Reform Act, 1969 may not succeed in removing completely the hostilities and acrimony from the divorce proceedings. To this extent it has failed to achieve one of the objectives of reform, namely, "to take the heat out of the matrimonial proceeding". On the other hand, the Uniform Marriage and Divorce Act and the no-fault divorce statutes in the United States do not incorporate the fault-related guidelines and thus eliminate completely the possibility of introducing into the divorce proceedings hostility and acrimony. We have noticed[7] the difficulty and the confusion that has arisen in the English courts in the interpretation of the phrase "adultery and intolerability" under guideline (a) of the Divorce Reform Act, 1969. The fate of the English spouses hung on the interpretation of the disjunctive word "and" provided in that guideline. The very basis of matrimonial relief—breakdown—rested on the technicalities and the niceties of judicial interpretation. The courts were swayed by the cannons of interpretation rather than face the main issue, namely, whether in a given case, marriage has irretrievably broken down. The Uniform Marriage and Divorce Act does not suffer from such technicalities. By providing less complicated guidelines to determine the fact of breakdown, the Act gives ample opportunity to the court to make to a rational judgment about the viability of the marriage relationship. Under guideline (b) of the English statute[8] it is for the petitioner to prove that the respondent has behaved in such a way that the petitoner cannot reasonably be expected to live with the respondent; whereas under the American statute a serious marital discord can affect one or both the parties.[9] Therefore, any party can go to a court and allege that the serious marital discord has affected him or her irrespective of the attitude of the other party toward the marriage.

Living apart under both the systems has been made a criterion for a finding of the breakdown. But there are some fundamental differences, leaving aside the difference in the period of time, that these statutes prescribe. Under the English law two different separation periods are provided. One provision provides for a two-year or longer separation period and the other for a period of five years or longer. Under the former it is necessary that the respondent consents to divorce; under the latter no such condition is imposed. The effect of such a scheme is that in cases where the parties have lived separate and apart for two years or more and the respondent does not consent to divorce there is a safety valve. That is, the petitioner will have to wait for another three years before he can obtain a divorce irrespective of the wishes of the other party. The American statute provides for a single separation period.

Each marital situation under the English statute has to be tailored to suit the characteristic guidelines provided by it. This reminds one of the pigeon-hole theory which was applied in England for determining tortuous liability. The necessity to prove the facts, to fit the legal formulae greatly diminishes the value of reforms based on the doctrine of breakdown. On the other hand, the progress made by the Uniform Marriage and Divorce Act when compared with its counterpart is commendable.

It is significant that a "hardship clause" adopted in the English divorce law is conspicuously absent in the Uniform Marriage and Divorce Act, 1970. Nor does this exception find a place in any of the no-fault divorce statutes in the United States. In the context of divorce law reform based solely upon the breakdown concept, it is important to know the purpose, the advantage or desirability or otherwise of having such a "hardship clause". An examination of this aspect of the question is particularly relevant in view of the fact that divorce, as we have noticed earlier, under the no-fault system in the United States, has become unilateral or automatic.

The relevant provisions adopting the "hardship clause" under the Divorce Reform Act, 1969, are :

Section 4. Decree to be refused in certain circumstances.

(1) The respondent to a petition for divorce in which the petitioner alleges any such fact as is mentioned in paragraph (e) of section 2(1) of this Act may oppose the grant of a decree *nisi* on the ground that dissolution of the marriage will result in grave financial or other hardship to him and that it would in all the circumstances be wrong to dissolve the marriage.

(2) Where the grant of a decree *nisi* is opposed by virtue of this section, then,

(a) if the court is satisfied that the only fact mentioned in the said section 2(1) on which the petitioner is entitled to rely in support of his petition is that mentioned in the said paragraph (e), and

(b) if apart from this section it would grant a decree *nisi*,

the court shall consider all the circumstances, including the conduct of the parties to the marriage and the interests of those parties and of any children or other persons concerned, and if the court is of opinion that the dissolution of the marriage will result in grave financial or other hardship to the respondent and that it would in all the circumstances be wrong to dissolve the marriage it shall dismiss the petition.

(3) For the purposes of this section hardship shall include the loss of the chance of acquiring any benefit which the respondent might acquire if the marriage were not dissolved.

These provisions, it is evident, seek to protect the respondent, in a divorce suit by allowing him or her to oppose the grant of a decree of dissolution on the ground that it would result in a grave financial and other hardship. The English courts have had to deal with a number of petitions in which the respondents invariably the wives, have sought to invoke the provisions contending that the grant of a decree of dissolution would not only result in a grave financial hardship but that it would in all circumstances be wrong to dissolve the marriage.

The usual type of financial hardship likely to be suffered by the respondent wife is her widow's pension. What amounts to "grave financial hardship" is a question of fact and each case has to be decided according to its merits. In considering whether in a given set of circumstances the hardships alleged are grave, the court has to take into account various factors such as age, capacity to earn, chances of remarriage, conduct of the parties and the interest of the childern. Courts have adopted a subjective view of such hardship.[10] For example, in *Dorrell* v. *Dorrell*[11] the grant of a divorce decree would have resulted in a loss of a widow's pension to the wife of only two pounds a week. Sir George Baker P. observed:

> When a woman is living on £6 or £8 a week, £2 a week is a third or a quarter of her income. It is as important to her as 100,000 may be to a millionaire. . . . I think the loss of this pension of £2 a week, small though it is, would be a grave financial hardship to the wife.[12]

The wife in this case was in her fifties and there was a great possibility of her surviving the petitioner to qualify for the widow's pension. The fact that she was receiving a small amount by way of social security was of no consequence in arriving at the conclusion as to the "grave financial hardship". On the other hand, in *Mathias* v. *Mathias*[13] the wife opposed the grant of a decree on the ground that dissolution of the marriage would result in grave financial hardship to her. She relied mainly upon the loss of her army and widow's pension which she might be entitled to, should she survive the petitioner as his widow. By a court order the husband was paying the wife a maintenance of £ 11.50 a week for her and the child. The wife was young, about 32 years. It was held that the loss to the wife of her army and state widow's pension "bearing in mind that she was a young wife who could take a part-time job, was not such a loss as would constitute 'grave financial hardship' to her within the meaning of section 4(1) of the Divorce Reform Act, 1969". The husband in this case had deserted the wife for many years and was intending to marry another woman. Under these circumstances, the court considered public interest and broad policy of the law which required to put an end to the "empty tie" and concluded that it would not be wrong to dissolve the marriage.

In *Julian* v. *Julian*,[14] the parties were aged 61 and 58 years respectively. The husband left the matrimonial home in 1965 and petitioned for divorce on the ground that he had lived separately and apart from his wife for more than five years. The wife opposed the petition on the ground that she would suffer grave financial hardship as she would lose a right to a police widow's pension of £790 per annum. She was receiving £65 per month from her husband. She was in poor health and unable to work. The husband was willing to purchase an annuity of £ 215 with his capital assets in the event of dissolution of the marriage. As there was a substantial difference between the amount of pension which the wife would receive if she survived the petitioner and the amount of annuity, the court was of the opinion that under those circumstances it would amount to grave financial hardship to the wife. On the other hand, in *Parker* v. *Parker*[15] on similar facts, the court granted the decree of divorce to the husband. The husband in this case was able to compensate the possible loss to his wife of her widow's pension by purchasing a deferred annuity and a policy providing specified sum on maturity. The court was also satisfied that the husband's obligation to pay the annual premium could be secured, if necessary, by a mortgage on his house.

There are two things that have to be established to the satisfaction of the court before the respondent could successfully oppose the grant of the divorce under section 4 of the Divorce Reform Act, 1969. First, that dissolution will result in a grave financial and other hardship and secondly, that it would in all circumstances be wrong to dissolve the marriage.[16] Therefore, even if the respondent suffers such hardship, yet unless the court is satisfied that it would be wrong to dissolve the marriage, it would grant dissolution. For example, in *Brickell* v. *Brickell*[17] the husband petitioned for divorce on the ground of living separate and apart for five years. The wife opposed the grant of decree *nisi* on the ground that she would suffer a loss of widow's pension in the amount of some £200. The court admitted that such a loss to the wife would be a grave financial hardship but concluded that it would *not be wrong to dissolve the marriage*. The decision in the instant case turned on another important aspect of the question. According to section 4(2)(b) of the Divorce Reform Act, 1969, conduct of the parties to a marriage is made a relevant consideration in deciding whether or not it would be wrong to dissolve the marriage. The question that arose was whether "conduct" used in the Act was to be understood in the sense of the old matrimonial offense. Davies, LJ.,[18] held that "conduct" was not confined to conduct in the sense of the old matrimonial offenses, but must clearly include it. The learned judge said that if very gross conduct were shown, or if misconduct were shown, then it was one of the matters to which the court must have regard in deciding whether or not it was wrong to dissolve the marriage.[19] The wife in this case used to visit the nursing home run by her husband in association with a woman who was a matron. The wife spied on the husband. She caused great annoyance to the husband and the patients as a result of which the business of the nursing home was closed down. In the opinion of the court the wife's conduct was disgraceful. Under these circumstances, the petitioning husband was granted a divorce despite the fact that the grant of a decree would result in "grave financial hardship to the wife".

It may be pointed out that in an earlier decision of *Dorrell* v. *Dorrell*,[20] Sir George Baker P. interpreted the words "conduct of the parties" not in the sense of the old matrimonial offence. According to the learned judge "having regard to this Act as a whole, conduct cannot mean conduct in the sense of the old matrimonial offence; because if it does, then it would be impossible to carry out one express purpose of the Act, namely, divorce after living apart continuously for five years". Davies, LJ., rejected this interpretation in *Brickell* v. *Brickell* (a decision of the Court of Appeal) overruling *Dorrell* v. *Dorrell*.

The grave financial or other hardship must stem from the grant of the decree of dissolution. If the hardships suffered by the respondent are the result of a prior separation then the court will not deny divorce to the petitioner. The case of *Talbot* v. *Talbot*[21] is in point. The parties were married in 1957. A child was born in 1965. In the same year the husband left the matrimonial home. The wife, in an undefended suit, obtained a decree of judicial separation in 1966 on the ground of her husband's adultery. She was granted £590 per annum as maintenance for herself and £130 per annum for the child. The wife also received £600 as her share from the sale of the matrimonial home. The husband had taken up a job in Italy. He was living with another woman. He petitioned for divorce in 1970 under the Divorce Reform Act, 1969 on the ground of five years separation. The wife opposed the petition alleging financial hardship. On the question whether the wife would suffer grave financial hardship if the marriage were to be dissolved, Dunn, J., said :[22]

> Grave financial hardship meant exactly what the words said and had to be considered subjectively in relation to the particular marriage and the circumstances in which the parties lived while it subsisted. Section 4(1) of the Divorce Reform Act provided that the hardship should be the result of the dissolution of the marriage. *Such hardship as the wife had already suffered was the result of the breakdown of the marriage and she would suffer no further hardship from its dissolution.*

The fact that the "hardship clause" has not become an impediment to the progress made by divorce law reform in England does not necessarily justify its adoption into the no-fault divorce system in the United States or, for that matter, in any future law reforms. For, dissolution of marriage necessarily involves some hardship (economic or other). In every case where the wife is confronted by a divorce petition on the ground of five years separation, she may be tempted to seek protection afforded by this clause. This might encourage unnecessary litigation. Further, a vengeful wife may use this exception as a prop to keep the husband in a matrimonial limbo. The subjective standard of "financial hardship" may give rise to diverse judicial interpretation and certain value judgment may unconsciously creep into the law. The interpretation of the phrase "conduct of the parties" would revive the old concept of "matrimonial guilt". All these unhappy developments can be avoided if the "hardship clause" is not adopted in any future divorce legislation.

We may recall that both the Archbishop group and the Law Commission of England, while suggesting divorce reforms were highly earnest to safeguard and protect the interest of the weaker party. They were conscious of the fact that in a system of law which forces a divorce upon the unwilling party, particularly the "innocent wife" it was absolutely imperative to protect the economic interest of such party. Thus, the rationale for adopting the "hardship clause" was mainly to put the disadvantaged party on an equal economic footing. If the law could achieve this objective by providing an appropriate remedy and safeguard the "economic future" of the parties concerned, including the interest of the children of divorced marriages then adoption of such a clause in the scheme of "breakdo wn' would seem to be redundant. As rightly pointed out by Giesen[23], in the context of divorce law reform in Germany, we cannot dispense with a financial hardship clause unless it is rendered useless by reforming the laws related to the consequences of divorce.

We have before us two pieces of legislation adopting different approaches to marital breakdown. Under the Divorce Reform Act, 1969 the principle of breakdown is introduced by means of a long list of facts including separation as guidelines for proving breakdown. The Uniform Marriage and Divorce Act, 1970 incorporates a fixed period of separation and a general rule as to the proof of breakdown. Both the approaches have certain advantages and disadvantages. For example, if a statute provides specific guidelines they would aid the court in the determination of irretrievable breakdown. The court would feel more secure while handling the ground of breakdown. But it is also possible that if the standard set by a specific guideline is not met, even though there has been in fact an irretrievable breakdown of the marriage, a decree of dissolution might be refused. The case of *Richard* v. *Rechard*[24] decided under the English statute illustrates this point. There, as we have noticed earlier, the petitioning wife did prove by sufficient evidence that the marriage had irretrievably broken down. The court admitted that the marriage had broken down irretrievably, yet was not satisfied of the fact mentioned in section 2(1)(b) of the Divorce Reform Act, 1969, namely, that the respondent has behaved in such a way that the petitioner cannot reasonably be expected to live with the respondent. Therefore, the petition for dissolution was dismissed. Should a case with similar facts arise under the American law where breakdown isdefined by a general rule : serious marital discord adversely affecting the attitude of one or both of the parties toward the marriage, a decree of dissolution would be granted.

A survey of the case law under both the jurisdictions reveal that a good deal of discretion has been used by the English courts in the administration of divorce. This is particularly true in the cases that have arisen under the hardship clause referred to above. Where the marriage had lasted for a longer period and the parties were comparatively older, a decree of divorce was refused. But, where the marriage had lasted for a shorter period, the wives relatively young, had the capacity to earn and the chances for remarriage were present, the courts had granted dissolution despite the financial hardship clause.

In order to obviate the shortcomings under both the approaches, namely, supporting irretrievable breakdown with specific guidelines or adopting a general rule for establishing breakdown it is sometimes suggested that the better alternative to these approaches would be to introduce the breakdown principle by means of a single separation period which can be the sole ground for divorce. Some writers such as Goldstein[25] and Bodenheimer seem to subscribe to this approach. Bodenheimer says :[26]

> If all the old brush is cleared away and a fresh start is made, the "breakdown" ground in the form of "living separate and apart" as the only ground for divorce would seem to hold the greatest promise for a better divorce law for the future.

In her view the separation ground could replace all other grounds if the "idea that divorce shall be available only if marriage relationship has irretrievably broken down would be declared to be the guiding principle". She suggests a procedure which, in sum and substance, allows unilateral and bilateral divorce after a certain period of separation. Under the scheme the parties will be able to obtain divorce after the court has made them become aware of the seriousness of the consequences of divorce and after it has directed the parties to avail of the counseling opportunity. The procedure envisaged by Bodenheimer comes very close to obtaining divorce by registration with waiting period.

Rheinstein limits the concept of breakdown to separation and abandonment. He says :[27]

> We are concerned with marriage breakdown as a mass phenomenon and the problem of how, if at all its incidence might be reduced. It is for this compelling reason of statistical observability that we shall limit ourselves to inquiry concerning marriage breakdown in the sense of physical cessation of the spouses' life in common, i.e., of abandonment and separation.

Abel[28] does not agree with the conceptual formulation of breakdown as contemplated by Rheinstein. He says geographic separation is not a necessary condition for divorce. He points out that many disaffected couples live together until they are divorced; many remain separated without going in for divorce due to economic or other reasons such as want of accommodations.[29] Both the views put forward by these writers merit consideration. While under Rheinstien's conceptual formulation, the vagueness and uncertainty is eliminated, under Abel's formulation the breakdown concept is given a latitude and flexibility which covers all those cases of marital breakdown which may not be the result of separation and abandonment.

It is an acknowledged fact that the best approach to divorce is through the acceptance of the breakdown principle. The concept of breakdown has so much appeal and charm that it has spread like an epidemic in that western world[30] and it continues to extend in the United States. Both England and the United States have travelled a hazardous path starting with the "matrimonial guilt" to "matrimonial breakdown". But still, under both these jurisdictions the State retains control of the dissolution of the marriage. Even in a case of matrimonial breakdown, the court is the final arbiter.[31] Will there be a further breakthrough in divorce law ? Will the State concede its right in favor of the parties themselves to terminate the marriage when it has broken down ? At least some of the trends that we witness today in the United States are pointers in this direction.

We know that there is a shift in the State's conception of marriage : from marriage as an institution to marriage as a private contract. In 1971, there was an attempt in the state of Maryland to bring into existence a three year renewable "contract marriages".[32] The idea that the rights and obligations of parties could be determined on the basis of a formal legal contract entered into by them before marriage is in vogue. The State's serious interference into the privacy of the married persons in inveighed.[33] Considering the thrust of reforms, the judicial liberalism, the mood and the social mores in this country, it would not be rash to speculate that divorce by registration, after a certain period of delay, will become an accepted norm.[34]

NOTES AND REFERENCES

1. See the Law Commission Report, *Reform of the Grounds of Divorce : Field of Choice*, Cmnd. 3123, para 15 at 10 (1966).
2. See Sec. 2(1) of the Divorce Reform Act, 1969.
3. The Uniform Marriage and Divorce Act, Secs. 302 and 305 (1973 version).
4. The Divorce Reform Act, 1969, Sec. 1. This Act has been repealed by the Matrimonial Causes Act, 1973 which consolidates the law relating to divorce, nullity and other matrimonial suits. However, the law as embodied in the Divorce Reform Act, 1969 is retained under the new enactment. Citations herein will be to the Divorce Reform Act, 1969.
5. See. Ch. 1, Section A at 7.
6. See R. Levy, *Uniform Marriage and Divorce Legislation : A Preliminary Analysis* 43 (1968).
7. See the discussion in Ch. VI at 124 to 130.
8. The Divorce Reform Act, 1969, Sec. 2(1)(b).
9. The Uniform Marriage and Divorce Act, Sec. 302(2).
10. Manchester, *Divorce and Grave Financial or Other Hardship*, 118 Sol. J. 193 (1974).
11. *Dorrel* v. *Dorrel*, [1972] 1 W.L.R. 1087 at 1093.
12. Ibid. at 1093.
13. *Mathias* v. *Mathias*, [1972] 3 All E.R. 1; [1972] 3 W.L.R. 201.
14. *Julian* v. *Julian*, 116 Sol. J. 763 (1972).
15. *Parker* v. *Parker*, [1972] 1 All E.R. 410; [1972] 2 W.L.R. 21.
16. *Mathias* v. *Mathias*, [1972] 3 All E.R. 1 at 4; [1972] 3 W.L.R. 201 at 205.
17. *Brickell* v. *Brickell*, [1973] 3 W.L.R. 602 (C.A.).
18. Ibid. at 606.
19. Ibid.
20. *Dorrell* v. *Dorrell*, supra note 11, at 1092.
21. *Talbot* v. *Talbot*, 115 Sol. J. 870 (197.).
22. Ibid. at 870 (Emphasis added).
23. Giesen, *Divorce Reform in Germany*, 7 Fam. L.Q. 351 at 368 (1973).

24. *Richards* v. *Richards*, [1972] 3 All E.R. 695; [1972] 1 W.L.R. 1073.
25. See Goldstein and Gitter, *On Abolition of Grounds for Divorce : A Model Statute & Commentary*, 3 Fam. L.Q. 75, 89 (1969).
26. Bodenheimer, *Reflections on the Future Grounds for Divorce*, 8 J. Fam. L. 179 at 211-12 (1968).
27. Rheinstein, *Marriage Stability, Divorce and the Law* 263 (1972).
28. See Abel, *Book Review*, 26 Stanf. L. Rev. 175 at 197 (1973).
29. Abel (citing Fiefer, Justice in Moscow, 154, 1964) says that because of the housing shortage in Russia divorced couples are often unable to find accommodation and continue to live together sometimes for several years. He also points out (citing *Berman* v. *Berman*, 101, N.Y.S. 2d 206) that a decree of legal separation was refused on the ground of intolerable cruelty when couple was still living together for want of a separate apartment. Ibid. at 197 (f.n. 93).
30. See generally Rheinstein, supra note 27. See further Jan Gorecki, *Divorce in Poland* (1970). Geisen, supra note 23. Rheinstein, *Divorce Around the World, in Divorce and after* 140 (Bohannan ed. 1971).
31. But see Ch. 111 Section C at pp. 107-108.
32. See note, *Untying the Knot : The Course and Patterns of Divorce Reform*, 57 Cornell L. Rev. 649 at 662 (1972). See also note, *The No-Fault Concept : Is this the Final Stage in the Evolution of Divorce ?* 47 Notre Dame Lawyer, 959, 970 (1972).
33. For example, Dona J. Zenor says :

    > Although theoretically the breakdown standard underscores the uniqueness of each marital relationship, there is a danger that its implication may entail serious state intrusion into the privacy of the marriage.

    Ibid. note, Untying the Knot at 659-60. It is interesting to note that recently the Divorce Reform Task Force of the Council on Family Relations has strongly urged for the removal of divorce from the courts. See 1 F.L.R. 2026 (Nov. 1974).
34. For a detailed proposal as to how and in what manner registration divorce should be allowed into divorce law see Goldstein and Gitter, supra note 25, at 89-93. Cantor says "Divorce should be made a right to be granted automatically after a fixed period of time by a court, upon the filing of a notice of intention to procure a divorce by a person who wishes to obtain one. No explanation for why the divorce is desired should be required by this notice". See Cantor, *The Right of Divorce*, Atlantic Monthly, November 1966, 67 at 68.

Divorce Laws and Reforms in India 6

GENERAL

DURING the colonial rule in India the British judges who were called upon to apply an alien law in an alien country, were fully alive to the fact that inhabitants of the country believed their law to be of divine origin. They were mindful that the relations between law and religion had taken different course in the west, tending to a separation of these subjects. They realized, however, that such separation could not be applied in the Indian context.

The British rulers having known the enormous influence of religion upon Indians left the religious laws of both Hindus and Muslims untouched, while gradually replacing other branches of law, e.g., law of crimes, evidence and contracts, by modern laws of western origin.[1] On the contrary, Warren Hasting's plan of 1772[2] expressly stated that both the Muslims and Hindus of India would be governed by their respective personal laws. This was a policy which the British rulers learned from the Moghal Emperors.

The Hindu and the Muslim laws became almost static particularly in matters relating to family during the British period. However, in Hindu law as well as in Muslim law certain enactments affecting the law of marriage and divorce were passed. For instance, as early as in 1846, the Hindu Widows' Remarriage Act[3] was passed which declared that all marriages contracted by the widows were valid. Prior to this enactment, according to traditional Hindu law, a widow was not allowed to marry at all. If she did, the marriage was treated as invalid. Under Muslim law, the wife could not dissolve the marriage if her husband was cruel, impotent or had deserted her. Again, during the British regime the Muslim Dissolution of Marriages Act, 1939[4] was passed which gave rights to the Muslim women to dissolve the marriage on those grounds. Apart from these and a few other legislative enactments which affected the personal laws of Hindus and Muslims no significant change in the law of divorce was made. It was only after India became independent that the Hindu law of marriage and divorce was drastically modified.[5] Muslim law remains as it was at the time when the British left. Nonetheless, some efforts are being made to change the traditional Islamic law as applied to the Muslims in India.[6]

THE HINDU LAW OF DIVORCE

Position before the passing of the Hindu Marriage Act, 1955

According to traditional Hindu law divorce was not known. This was due to the fact that marriage among Hindus is regarded as an indissoluble tie. Although divorce was not allowed by the general Hindu law, it was recognized in certain castes of the Hindu community based upon custom.[7] Before the passing of the Hindu Marriage Act, 1955 many states such as Madras[8], Bombay[9] and Saurastra[10] had their own state laws which allowed divorce on certain grounds. In all other states divorce was denied to the Hindus.

The need for reforms in the Hindu law of marriage and divorce was felt even during the British regime.[11] The reforms hesitantly initiated in some states of India did not satisfy the whole Hindu community. There was a clamoring on the part of the enlightened and progressive Hindu women that the law of marriage and divorce were too stringent and caused considerable hardship in the family life. This strengthened the hands of the reformers who were always so concerned with removing the inequality between the sexes.

In 1941 a committee under the chairmanship of Sir B.N. Rau was formed to submit a report on the feasibility of codifying Hindu law.[12] The report of the committee was accompanied by a draft report which dealt, *inter alia*, with marriage and divorce. The Hindu code was referred to a select committee and after various changes and suitable amendments a part of the Hindu code was adopted by the Parliament. The first Act passed by the Parliament was the Hindu Marriage Act, 1955, followed by other Acts relating to minority, succession and adoption.

Divorce under the Hindu Marriage Act, 1955

The Hindu Marriage Act, 1955 is a piece of central legislation and thus applies to all Hindus uniformly. The various grounds on which a husband or the wife can obtain divorce are provided in section 13 of the Act. They are: living in adultery[13], conversion[14] to another religion, insanity[15], incurable leprosy[16], venereal disease[17], renunciation[18], disappearance[19], failure to resume cohabitation for a period of two years after the passing of the decree of judicial separation[20] and failure to comply with the decree of restitution of conjugal rights.[21] Thus, in a way, the grounds of divorce parallel with those of the American law. In addition to these grounds a wife has been given a right to obtain divorce on some special grounds such as rape, sodomy and bestiality. Since polygamy was valid before the Act was passed, any of the previously married wives can obtain divorce under the Act, if she proves that her husband had married her before the Act and that any of the other wives of the husband was alive at the time she files a petition for divorce.[22]

Cruelty and desertion were not made grounds for divorce earlier. In this respect, the Hindu law of divorce differed from that of American law. Cruelty and desertion were made grounds for judicial separation.[23] Nevertheless, after the passing of the decree of judicial separation on these grounds and if there has not been reconciliation for a period of two years or more then either party can file a petition for divorce.[24]

Adultery

Adultery is a wrong against marriage and every legal system recognizes adultery as a ground for divorce. But adultery in the context of matrimonial law is different from the adultery as a criminal offense. Under section 497 of the Indian Penal Code,[25] a person is guilty of adultery when he has sexual intercourse with another who is and whom he knows or has reason to believe to be the wife of another person. Thus under the penal law only a man can commit the offense of adultery and not a woman. But under the matrimonial law either spouse can be guilty of adultery if he or she has sexual intercourse with a third person whether married or unmarried.

According to section 13(1)(i) of the Hindu Marriage Act, adultery *simpliciter* was not a ground for divorce. The section provided that either party could present a petition for divorce on the ground that the other party "is living in adultery". The words "living in adultery" are significant. It would mean that the respondent must be at the time of presentation of the petition be "living in adultery". A single act of sexual intercourse by a spouse outside the lawful wedlock was not a sufficient ground for the grant of the decree, but was a valid ground for judicial separation.[26] The Bombay High Court in *Rajani* v. *Prabhakar*[27] has held that the words "living in adultery" means a continuous course of adulterous conduct. In this case the wife had committed adultery some time in the past. There was no evidence of such a conduct thereafter for a few years. Even at the time when the husband filed a petition it could not be proved that she had persisted in such a conduct. Under these circumstances the court denied the decree of divorce to the husband. The law has since been amended. Now voluntary sexual intercourse with any person other than his or her spouse is a ground for divorce.

Since adultery is considered a very grave matrimonial offense in India, a very high degree of standard of proof is required.[28] The courts have insisted that the offense of adultery should be proved beyond reasonable doubt. Thus, the Supreme Court rejected the proof as insufficient to establish adultery of the wife where there was an evidence merely of love letters written by one of her near relatives.[29] The fact that the *panchayat* of the community condemned the wife's conduct is not a ground for the judge to base his finding that adultery had been committed.[30] The standard of proof as required under English law need not necessarily be the same in the Indian context. This has been pointed out in *Subbarama* v. *Saraswathi*.[31] The court ruled that the English decisions provide a very useful guide for basic principles but they must not be extended any further as moral, social and cultural outlook of the Hindus is markedly different from the English.

Even if adultery of the respondent is proved, the court has to see before granting the decree that the petitioner has not condoned the offense or that he has not connived at or has been accessory to the commission of the offense. Section 23 of the Hindu Marriage Act provides that in any proceedings under the Act, if the court is satisfied that the ground for granting relief exists, then it shall be the duty of the court to see whether the petitioner is not in any way taking advantage of his/her own wrong or disability for the purpose of the relief.[32]

Cruelty[33]

The law relating to cruelty has been developed in India on the lines on which it was developed under the English law, or, for that matter, under the American law. The legal standard of cruelty laid down in *Russell* v. *Russell*[34] has been statutorily embodied under the Hindu Marriage Act.[35] The standard of cruelty according to Hindu law was different than what it is today. Changes in the concept of cruelty are also found in the modern Hindu society. In *Kamala* v. *Amar*,[36] it was held that the concept of cruelty had undergone changes due to changes in social customs and standard of behaviour. Again, in *Shyamsunder* v. *Shantamani*,[37] it was held that the concept of cruelty is fast changing and the courts have to take cognizance of the changes that are witnessed with regard to the attitudes of Hindus toward marriage. In short, under the Hindu Marriage Act, apart from physical cruelty, false allegation of unchastity, constant nagging, threat of violence or a reasonable apprehension of bodily or mental harm have been held to amount to cruelty.[38] Intention to injure was held to be an irrelevant factor to a charge of cruelty.[39] Insanity has been held by the Supreme Court as not a valid defense to a charge of matrimonial cruelty. In *Bhagwat* v. *Bhagwat*,[40] the husband was suffering from insanity during which period he beat his wife on diverse occasions. The wife filed a suit for judicial separation on the ground of cruelty. She alleged that there was a reasonable apprehension in her mind that the husband might relapse at any time into mental aberration. The husband invoked the M'Naghten rules as defense relying on the English cases. But the Bombay High Court followed *Williams* v. *Williams*[41] and ruled that the object of the court was to protect the victim from the respondent. It was held that M'Naghten rules could not be invoked by way of defense to a charge of cruelty.

Desertion[42]

The elements of desertion are the same as enunciated by the English principles and precedents. The decisions of the English courts have a great persuasive value in India particularly in the law of desertion as this remedy as also other remedies have been borrowed from the English law. The constituent elements of desertion as laid down in Halsburry's laws[43] have been approved and followed in *Bipinchander* v. *Prabhavati*[44] by the Supreme Court. Also, the concept of constructive desertion embodied in English law have been followed in Indian matrimonial law. In *Leela* v. *Manohar*,[45] it was held that the question of desertion cannot be decided by merely inquiring as to which party left the matrimonial home first. The test as to the conduct which drives the other spouse away is the same as that found in English law, namely, the causes must be grave and weighty. In *Narayan Prasad* v. *Prabhadevi*,[46] the husband petitioned for judicial separation on the ground of desertion. He alleged that the wife quarrelled and disobeyed his mother and made his life unhappy. The court, following the dictum of Lord Porter in *Lang* v. *Lang*,[47] held that such idiosyncrasies are part of the lottery in which every spouse engages on marrying, and taking the other partner of the marriage for "better or worse".

Apart from the above conventional grounds which are similar to the grounds in American law, we have certain other grounds under the Hindu Marriage Act which are peculiar to Hindu society. According to the Act, either party can petition for divorce on the ground that the other party has renounced the world by entering a religious order.[48] Renunciation according to Hindu law operates as a "civil death" effecting a complete severence from this mortal world. So, the Hindu Marriage Act recognizes the right of a party who has not renounced the world to obtain divorce from the one who is supposed to have been "civilly died". Also, under section 13(1)(ii) of the Act, either party can sue for divorce on the ground that the respondent has ceased to be a Hindu by conversion to another religion. It is significant that the right to obtain divorce is given only to the party who remains a Hindu. The convert himself cannot sue and obtain divorce.

Divorce according to custom[49]

According to the Hindu religious scriptures custom is regarded as transcendent law. Time-honored institutions, the usages and the practices which have been followed by the people for generations have been a fruitful source of Hindu law. In fact the whole superstructure of the Anglo-Hindu jurisprudence has been erected on the edifice of a valid custom. During the British period of administration of justice custom which was not opposed to public policy or considered immoral or which did not run counter to the spirit of Hindu law was upheld in the courts. The Privy Council declared that "clear proof of usage will outweigh the written text of law".[50]

Although not allowed by the general Hindu law, divorce was permitted if supported by valid custom. In an earlier Madras decision the court observed that there was nothing immoral in a custom which sanctioned divorce by mutual consent.[51] Before the passing of the Hindu Marriage Act, many states such as Madras, Bombay and Saurastra had enacted laws permitting divorce on certain grounds. Those custom-based forms of divorce were preserved under section 29(2) of the Hindu Marriage Act.[52]

The usual and more prevalent customary practices of obtaining divorce may be mentioned. They are : (a) by mutual consent; (b) by deed of divorce called *char-chitti*; (c) by the intervention of *panchayat* (caste tribunals); and (d) by simply abandoning the wife or by unilateral act.

The custom of obtaining divorce by mutual consent is prevalent among the inferior castes in Bombay, Madras, Mysore and Kerala. In Madhya Pradesh also it has been held that divorce by mutual consent is a valid custom among the *Patwas* of that state. Perhaps, ths more popular form by which divorce is effected is by the intervention of the *panchayat*. But it must be proved according to custom that the *panchayat* had the authority to dissolve the marriage. When once this fact is proved then the courts will not interfere with the jurisdiction of the *panchayat*. This is illustrated by *Pemanbai* v. *Channoolal.*[53] In this case the *panchayat* had dissolved the marriage based on the mutual consent of the parties. Thereafter, the wife filed a suit for a declaration that the marriage still subsisted on the plea that when she gave the consent for dissolution she was only 14 years of age. The court rejected her contention and held that divorce had taken place under the authority of *panchayat* and that she had sufficient understanding at the time when she gave her consent.

Divorce by execution of the deed is also prevalent among the lower castes in south India. It is also prevalent in the *Jat* community belonging to Punjab. Recently the Supreme Court in *Gurjit Singh* v. *Mst. Angrez Kaur,*[54] has held valid a deed executed by the husband divorcing his wife. The Allahabad High Court in *Madho Prasad* v. *Shakuntala*[55] has held that there is a valid custom in the community known as *Barai Chaurasiya* where divorce can be obtained by agreement popularly called *Chhuttam Chhutta.*

According to the custom prevailing in Manipur, it has been held that a husband can dissolve the marriage without any reason or at his pleasure. This kind of customary divorce is called *Khaniba.* Sometime, the husband abandons his wife and does not take care to provide her maintenance. He does not even bother if his wife is living with some one else. In such a case it was presumed by the court that the husband had repudiated his wife. According to the custom prevalent among *Rajput Gujratis* in *Khandesh,* marriage is dissolved if the husband abandons or deserts his wife. The custom which permits dissolution of marriage on payment of money to the wife has been held as invalid.[56] Also, a custom which allows the wife to marry another husband during the subsistence of a valid marriage with her first husband, is invalid. The Bombay High Court has rejected a custom which allows a woman to divorce her husband without any reason. It has been held that a divorce obtained by the permission of the caste assembly, without the consent of the husband, is invalid. Customary divorce practices have been duly accepted by the courts among the *Vellans* of *Palanis* and the *Marvars*, the *Kallans*, the *Pallans*, the *Malalis* of North Arcot, the *Rhat Rajas*, barbers and other lower caste Hindus.[57]

The courts have exercised a good deal of judicial scrutiny and discretion in upholding or rejecting such customary divorce practices. In so doing they have applied strict test for the validity of such custom. When the existence of a custom sanctioning divorce in a particular form was not proved or where the custom could be regarded as immoral or against public policy, the courts had declared such custom as invalid.

Where dissolution of marriage takes place according to custom, the parties can remarry immediately. But not where divorce is obtained under the Hindu Marriage Act alleging specific grounds. The parties have to wait after obtaining the decree of divorce for at least one year.

Retention of customary forms of divorce under the Hindu Marriage Act is advantageous particularly to those castes and communities whose customs permits of such divorce. They are speedy and cheap. It also saves time and the money involved in the litigation. However, it must be said that this practice is hard on women than men, as it seems that it is men who have divorced their wives against their wishes. The reason is not far to seek. A vast majority of Indian women are totally dependent economically or otherwise upon their husbands.

Divorce in Islamic Law

Talaq,[58] an arbitrary measure in the hands of a jealous husband in Islamic law, was treated as the most potent weapon to disrupt the unity of marriage. It was a constant threat to the wife which could, at any time, throw her into a state of social insecurity. This absolute and unlimited power of a Muslim husband to dissolve the marriage by resorting to the magical three word formula hangs like a Damocles' sword over the head of a wife. In early Arabia, the Arabs use to pronounce *Talaq* and revoke it.[59] They often took recourse to resorting to this unbridled power of pronouncing and revoking in order to satisfy their sadistic pleasure by teasing and preventing women from marrying others. Wives did not know when they were free nor whether they were tied to the matrimonial bond.

In order to put an end to the barbarous practice of the

pagan Arabs Prophet Mohammad declared that "of all the permitted things the most detestable is divorce in the eyes of God".[60] He effected many reforms in the institution of *Talaq*. In the words of Ameer Ali :

> The reforms of Mohammad marked a new departure in the history of Eastern legislation. He restrained the power of divorce possessed by the husbands; he gave to the women the right of obtaining a separation on reasonable grounds; and towards the end of his life he went so far as practically to forbid its exercise by the men without the intervention of arbiters or a judge.[61]

The reforms made by the Prophet of Islam and the law as expounded and interpreted by the jurists of renowned authority have been followed by Muslims in India both during the colonial rule and thereafter. The Shariat Act of 1937[62] declares, *inter alia*, that in all questions regarding marriage and dissolution of marriage, "the rule of decision in cases where the parties are Muslim shall be the Muslim Personal Law (*Shariat*)".

Forms of Talaq[63]

The pronouncement of *talaq* may be revocable or irrevocable. The revocable forms of *talaq* are considered as the "approved" ones. Prophet Mohammad is said to have favored this mode over the irrevocable forms. A revocable pronouncement of divorce gives a *locus poenitentiae* to the husband and an irrevocable pronouncement entails serious consequences. Under the latter, divorce becomes effective from the moment the pronouncement is made.

The forms of *talaq* are classified as follows :

1. *Talaqus-Sunna* (i.e., in conformity with the dictates of the prophet)
   (i) *Ahsan* (the most approved).
   (ii) *Hasan* (approved).
2. *Talaqu-l-Bida* (not approved)
   (i) Three declarations (the triple divorce) at one time.
   (ii) One irrevocable declaration (generally in writing).

Ahsan : This form consists of a single pronouncement made during a period of *tuhr* (i.e., when the woman is free from her menstrual course) followed by abstinence from sexual intercourse for a period of three months. *Talaq* pronounced in the *Ahsan* form is revocable during this three months period. It may be revoked either by express words or by conduct. After the lapse of three months divorce becomes effective if revocation has not followed after the pronouncement.
Hasan : This is also an approved form though less approved than the first, *Ahsan*. It consists of three successive pronouncements during three consecutive periods of purity (i.e., *Tuhr*). Each of these pronouncements should have been made at a time when no intercourse has taken place during that particular period of purity. It can be explained by an illustration :[64]

> The husband H pronounces *talaq* on his wife W for the first time during the period when W is free from her menstrual courses. The husband and wife had not come together during this period of purity. This is the first *talaq*. H resumes cohabitation or revokes this first *talaq* in this period of purity. Thereafter, in the following period of purity, at a time when no intercourse has taken place, H pronounces the second *talaq*. This *talaq* is again revoked by express words or by conduct, and the third period of purity is entered into. In this period, no intercourse having taken place, H for the third time pronounces the formula of divorce. This third pronouncement operates in law as a final irrevocable dissolution of the marital tie.

Talaqu-l-Bida (Disapproved form): When three pronouncements are made in a single *tuhr* either in one sentence, e.g., 'I divorce thee triply or thrice" or in three sentences, "I divorce thee, I divorce thee, I divorce thee", it operates as a single irrevocable divorce from the moment it is pronounced. This form although disapproved and considered as sinful is nevertheless valid.

The legal consequences respecting reconciliation and remarriage between the parties are different depending upon the form in which *talaq* is pronounced. In the *Ahsan* form of divorce reconciliation is possible before the expiry of three months. The waiting period which is incumbent upon a wife in order to contract a valid marriage after she has been divorced is called *Idda,* which is three months. Therefore, in the *Ahsan* form of divorce when *talaq* becomes effective after three months, a regular marriage is necessary should the parties prefer to marry again. In the *Hasan* form the *talaq* becomes effective after the third pronouncement. Here too the parties can marry again by a formal form of marriage.

If the *talaq* is in an unapproved form then the consequences are serious. The wife, after she has been divorced, has to wait for a period of three months, she has to be lawfully married to a second husband, this second husband must divorce her, she must wait for a period of three months and after that period she can remarry her first husband. This procedure suggested by Prophet Muhammad was to make the Arabs realize the seriousness of the consequences if *talaq* is pronounced in an unapproved form. This procedure was intended to check the proclivity of the husband to pronounce *talaq* in that undesirable form.

Talaq-i-Tawfeez

While the husband under Islamic law had an absolute power to divorce his wife, a corresponding right was not given to women. They could dissolve their marriage only in a limited way. That is, either when the husband has delegated his right of pronouncement of *talaq* to a third party or to the wife herself or by mutual consent. When the husband has delegated the right of *talaq* to the wife on the happening of certain specified conditions it is called *talaq-i-tawfeez* (delegated divorce). The right of the wife under a delegated divorce to free herself has been held to be valid provided the option is not absolute and unconditional. Further, it must be reasonable and not opposed to public policy. Thus, an agreement by which the husband authorizes the wife to divorce herself in the event of his marrying subsequently has been held to be valid and enforceable by the courts. Women desirous of freeing themselves when their husbands choose to marry a second wife may take advantage of this provision.

Khul is a form of divorce by mutual consent. If it is at the instance of the wife, it is called *Khul*; if both husband and wife agree to dissolve the marriage it is called *Mubarh*. In case of *Khul* the wife has to pay some compensation to the husband in order to get a release from him. Usually she forfeits her claim to dower. There is a difference of opinion among the Muslim jurists as to whether in case of a *Khul* the wife has necessarily to part with some consideration. Some hold that she has to forfeit the dower. Others are of the opinion that she need not.

The dissolution of muslim marriages Act, 1939

According to Hanafi law as applied to Muslims in India, inability of the husband to maintain the wife did not give her the right to dissolve the marriage. Following the traditional law, the courts in India had denied the wife the right to obtain divorce in cases where the husband has failed to provide her maintenance or has deserted her. On the other hand the *Maliki* law (another school of Islamic law) allowed the wife to dissolve the marriage when the husband had neglected her or had failed to provide maintenance.

Taking advantage of the law as enunciated by the *Malikis* and *Shafii*, the Dissolution of Muslim Marriages Act, 1939 was passed. This Act recognized the right of the wife to dissolve the marriage on various grounds such as cruelty, desertion, impotence, imprisonment. The Act also gives a remedy to a wife to dissolve the marriage if she had been given in marriage by the father or other guardian before she had attained the age of fifteen years. This right which is known as *Khyar-al-bulugh* (option of puberty) was recognized by the traditional law. Countless Muslim women have availed of the remedies provided by the Act. By far the most frequently used are the provisions relating to option of puberty and the provision relating to failure to provide maintenance. Let us take a look at these provisions.

Option of puberty : According to traditional Muslim law if a minor wife had heen given in marriage by the father or the father's father, the marriage was binding and valid. The wife had no right to repudiate the marriage on attaining puberty unless it could be shown that the father or the father's father had acted negligently and fraudulently. But if the minor was given in marriage by any other guardian she had the right to void the marriage on attaining puberty. The Act had modified the law in this regard. Under the Act, a minor wife, whether she has been given in marriage by her father or any other guardian, she has a right to repudiate on attaining puberty and before she had attained the age of 18 years. It is provided that the marriage should not have been consummated.

Courts have interpreted this provison in favor of females by invoking rules of equity and justice. They have interpreted the law liberally. This attitude is reflected in the following cases.

A married Muslim woman can seek dissolution of her marriage on the ground :[65]

> that she, having been given in marriage by her father or other guardian before she attained the age of fifteen years, repudiated the marriage before attaining the age of eighteen years : provided that the marriage has not been consummated.

In *Gulam Sakina* v. *Falak Sher Allah Bakhsh*,[66] a minor girl was married to the defendant. The marriage was consummated before the girl had attained the age of fifteen years; but before she attained the age of eighteen years she filed a suit for divorce under the Act. The defendant contended that she had lost the right to exercise the option of puberty as the marriage was consummated. The court proceeded on the basis of the presumption that a girl attained puberty at the age of fifteen years. Accordingly, it was held that consummation of marriage before she had attained puberty was no consummation and hence she did not lose the right of option to repudiate the marriage.

It has also been held[67] that mere consummation of the marriage is not sufficient; it must have been with the consent of the wife. Therefore, when there was consummation against the will of the wife or when consummation took place by force, it was held that it was not a valid consummation so as to take away the right of the wife to dissolve the marriage. Again, the courts[68] have recognized as valid the exercise of option of puberty even in a suit filed by the husband for restitution of conjugal rights; though some courts[69] have insisted upon the filing of a separate suit for dissolution by the wife in such a proceeding by the husband.

Failure to provide maintenance: The Dissolution of Muslim Marriages Act, 1939 provides that a woman married under Muslim law is entitled to obtain a decree of divorce on the ground:[70]

> that the husband has neglected or failed to provide her maintenance for a period of two years

This provision has given rise to conflicting judicial decisions.

The words "has neglected" and "failed to provide maintenance" have been interpreted by the courts in varying ways. This was due to the fact that under Islamic law a wife was entitled to maintenance even if she refused to live with the husband for a just cause. For example, a wife who refuses cohabitation on the ground that her prompt dower has not been paid is entitled to be maintained.[71] But if the wife does not obey reasonable instructions of her husband, she is not entitled to maintenance.[72]

There is a cleavage of juristic opinion as to whether a wife has a right to dissolve her marriage on the ground of the husband's neglect or failure to provide maintenance even if she has no right to maintenance under the principles of Islamic law. In *Badrunnisa* v. *Mohd. Yusuf*,[73] the Allahbad High Court held that the word "neglect" implies "wilful failure" and the words "has failed to provide" imply "an omission of duty"; therefore, where the wife's conduct was such as to absolve the husband from his duty to provide maintenance, the wife would have no right to seek a divorce on that ground. The Nagpur[74], Calcutta[75] and Bombay[76] High Courts have taken the same view. It was held by these courts that unless there was a duty on the part of the husband to maintain the wife, it could not be alleged that the husband had failed to provide maintenance. On this reasoning these courts took the view that a wife has no right to ask for a divorce when she has refused to stay with the husband without reasonable cause. The Sind High Court[77] had first taken a similar view, but in a later decision[78] it held that the wife would be entitled to dissolution of the marriage in spite of the fact that on account of her conduct in refusing to live with the husband she would have been entitled to enforce her claim to maintenance.

The question whether a wife who has wrongfully left the matrimonial home has the right to seek dissolution of the marriage merely on the failure of the husband to maintain her for two years came up recently before the Kerala High Court in *A. Yousuf* v. *Sowramma.*[79] Holding that it was a "popular fallacy" that Muslim husbands had unbridled authority in the matter of divorce and recognizing the right of a Muslim wife to seek dissolution on the ground of the husband's failure to provide maintenance for two years, Krishna Iyer, J. observed :[80]

> . . . [T]he Islamic law's serious realism on divorce, when regarded as the correct perspective, excludes blameworthy conduct as a factor and reads the failure to provide maintenance for two years as an index of irreconcilable breach, so that the mere fact of non-maintenance for the statutory period entitles the wife to sue for dissolution.

The dissolution of Muslim Marriages Act, 1939 is undoubtedly an important landmark in the Anglo-Mohammadan jurisprudence, but its scope is limited to the right of a Muslim wife to obtain dissolution of her marriage in a court of law. The Act does not in any way restrict the arbitrary power of a Muslim husband to pronounce *talaq*.

NOTES AND REFERENCES

1. See generally W.H. Morley, *Administration of Justice in British India* (1858); C. Fawcett, *First Century of British Justice in India* (1934); George Rankin, *Background to India Law* (1946); J.D.M. Derrett, *Religion, Law and the State in India* 274 (1968). (Chapter 9 entitled The Administration of Hindu Law by the British.)
2. By Section 27 of the Regulation of 17th April, 1780, it was enacted "that in all suits regarding inheritance, marriage, and caste, and other religious usages or institutions, the laws of the Koran with respect to Mahomedans, and those of the Shaster with respect to Gentoos, shall be invariably adhered to." See Morley, supra note 1, at 178.

3. The Hindu Widows' Remarriage Act, 1856 (Act, XV of 1856).
4. The Dissolution of Muslim Marriage Act, 1939, Sec. 2.
5. See the Hindu Marriage Act, 1955 (Act, 25 of 1955).
6. See Tahir Mahmood, *Progressive Codification of Muslim Personal Law in Islamic Law in Modern India* 80 (T. Mahmood ed. 1972). Nawaz, *Some Reflections on Modernization of Islamic Law,* Ibid. at 59. Sivaramayya, *Equality of Sexes as a Human and Constitutional Right and the Muslim Law.* Ibid. at 69. Faridi, *Islamic Personal Law in India : Scope and Methodology of Reform.* Ibid. at 123.
7. See J.D. Mayne, *Hindu Law and Usage* 174-76 (11th ed. 1953).
8. Madras Hindu (Bigamy Prevention and Divorce) Act, 1949.
9. Bombay Hindu Divorce Act, 1947.
10. Saurashtra Hindu Divorce Act, 1952.
11. See for example, Srinivasa Iyanger, *Hindu Law Reform,* M.L.J. 8 (1941) (Golden Jubilee number); Asirvathan, *State and Social Legislation in India* M.L.J. 239 (1941).
12. For the history of the Hindu Code see U.S. Sarkar, *Epochs in Hindu Legal History* 392-394 (1958); J.D.M. Derrett, *Hindu Law Past and Present* 55 (1957).
13. Hindu Marriage Act, 1955, Sec. 13(1)(i).
14. Ibid. Sec. 13(1)(ii).
15. Ibid. Sec. 13(1)(iii).
16. Ibid. Sec. 13(1)(iv).
17. Ibid. Sec. 13(1)(v).
18. Ibid. Sec. 13(1)(vi).
19. Ibid. Sec. 13(1)(vii).
20. Sec. 13(1-A)(i) as amended by the Hindu Marriage Amendment Act (44 of 1964).
21. Ibid. Sec. 13(1-A)(ii).
22. Sec. 13(2)(i) of the Hindu Marriage Act, 1955. In *Smt. Venkatamma* v. *Venkataswami,* A.I.R. Mys. 118 (1963), the wife was able to successfully resist the husband's petition for restitution of conjugal rights under this provision.
23. Hindu Marriage Act, 1955, Sec. 10(1)(a) and (b). In the State of Uttar Pradesh desertion and cruelty are grounds for divorce, cf. Sec. 2 of the Hindu Marriage (Uttar Pradesh Sanshodhan) Adhiniyam, (No. XIII of 1962). It may be mentioned that the Law Commission had recommended that cruelty and desertion be made grounds for divorce, see the Report of the Law Commission of India on Hindu Marriage Act, 1955 and Special Marriage Act, 1954 para 5.2 and 7.15 at 56 and 68 (Fifty-ninth Report, March 1974). Cruelty and desertion are now grounds for divorce.
24. For a discussion on the subject see Ch. VII, Section A at pp. 179-188. The period has now been reduced to one year.
25. The Indian Penal Code, 1860, Sec. 497.
26. Sec. 10(1)(f) of the Hindu Marriage Act, 1955.

. *Rajani* v. *Prabhakar,* A.I.R. Bom. 264 (1958).

28. See. Mulla, *Hindu Law* 671 (13th ed. 1966).
29. *Chandra Mohini* v. *Avinash Prasad*, A.I.R. S.C. 581 (1967).
30. *Mahalingum Pillai* v. *Amsawalli*, 2 M.L.J. 289 (1956).
31. *Subbarama* v. *Saraswathi*, A.I.R. Mad. 85 (1967). For a detailed account of the law relating to adultery, see P.K. Virdi, *The Grounds for Divorce in Hindu and English Law* 51 (1972).
32. Hindu Marriage Act, 1955, Sec. 23(1)(a).
33. See Mul!a, supra note 28, at 617, 618; S.V. Gupte, *Hundu Law of Marriage* 154 (1961) ; For a detail account of the law relating to cruelty see Virdi, supra note 31, at 118 et seq.
34. *Russell* v. *Russell*, [1895] A.C. 315.
35. See sec. 10(1)(b) of the Hindu Marriage Act, 1955.
36. *Kamala Devi* v. *Amar Nath*, A.I.R. J & K 33 (1961).
37. *Shyamsunder* v. *Shantamani*, A.I.R. Orissa 50 (1962).
38. See for example, *Siddagangiah* v. *Lakshamma*,A.I.R. Mys. 115 (1968); *Kusum Lata* v. *Kamta Prasad*, A.I.R. All. 280 (1965); *Chander Parakash* v. *Sudesh Kumari*, A.I.R. Delhi 208 (1971); *Smt. Putul Devi* v. *Gopi Mandal*, A.I.R. Pat. 93 (1963); *Smt. Mango* v. *Premchand*, A.I.R. All. 447 (1962).
39. *P.L. Sayal* v. *Sarla Rani*, A.I.R. Punj. 125 (1961).
40. *Bhagwat* v. *Bhagwat*, A.I.R. Bom. 80 (1967).
41. *Williams* v. *Williams*, [1963] 2 All E.R. 992.
42. See Mulla, supra note 28, at 648. Virdi, supra note 31, at 71.
43. 12 Halsbury's Laws of England, para 453, 454 at pp. 240-41 (3rd ed. 1955).
44. *Bipinchander Shah* v. *Prabhavati*, A.I.R. S.C. 176 (1957).
45. *Leela Devi* v. *Manoherlal*, A.I.R. Madh. Pra. 349 (1959).
46. *Narayan Prasad* v. *Prabhadevi*, A.I.R. Madh. Pra. 28 (1964).
47. *Lang* v. *Lang*, [1954] 3 All E. R. 571; [1955] A.C. 402.
48. See sec. 13(1)(vi) of the Hindu Marriage Act, 1955.
49. The following books were consulted while writing this section: J.D. Mayne, *Hindu Law and Usage* 175 (11 ed. 1953); Steele, *Law and Custom of Hindu Castes* (1868); S. Roy, *Custom and Customary Law in British India* (1911); Jolly, *Hindu Law and Custom* (1928); See also Derrett, *Divorce by Caste Custom*, 65 Bom.L.R. 161 (1963).
50. *Collector of Madura* v. *Mootooramlingiah*, 12 M.I.A. 397 at 436 (1868).
51. *Sankerlingam* v. *Subban*, 17 I.L.R. Mad. 479 (1894).
52. Sec. 29(2) of the Hindu Marriage Act, 1955.
53. *Smt. Premanbai* v. *Channoolal*, A.I.R. Madh. Pra. 57 (1963).
54. *Gurjit Singh* v. *Mst. Angrez Kaur*, A.I.R. S.C. 142 (1968).
55. *Madho Prasad* v. *Shakuntala*, A.I.R. All. 119 (1972).
56. *Keshav Hargovan* v. *Bai Gandi*, A.I.R. Bom. 107 (1915); 29 I.C. 952 (1915).
57. See Mayne, supra note 7, at 175-76.
58. "*Talak* in its primitive sense, means dismission; in law it signifies the dissolution of a marriage, or the annulment of its legality, by certain words". See *Al-Marghinani*. The *Hedaya* or Guide 72

(Hamilton Trans. 2nd ed. 1870); Neil B.E. Baillie, *A Digest of Muhammedan Law* 204 (Third Impression 1957).

59. Abdur Rahim, *Muhammadan Jurisprudence* 340 (1911).
60. Ibid. at 336.
61. Ameer Ali, *Mohummadan Law* 530 (4th ed. 1917).
62. Sec. 2 of the Muslim Personal Law (Shariat) Application Act, 1937.
63. See Mulla, *Principles of Mahomedan Law* 293, Sec. 307 (17th ed. 1972); K.P. Saksena, *Muslim Law as Administered in India and Pakistan* 260 (4th ed. 1963); B.R. Verma, *Muslim Marriage and Dissolution* 139 (1971); A.A. Fyzee, *Outlines of Muhammadan Law* 126 (2nd ed. 1955). This and the following Sections are based on the books referred to above.
64. See Fyzee, Ibid, at 129.
65. Dissolution of Muslim Marriages Act, 1939, Sec. 2(vii).
66. *Gulam Sakena* v. *Falak Sher Allah Bakhsh*, A.I.R. Lahore 45 (1950).
67. *Abdul Karim* v. *Aminabai*, A.I.R. Bom. 308 (1935).
68. For example, *Nizamuddin* v. *Huseni*, A.I.R. Madh. Pra. 212 (1960).
69. For example, *Sk. Sahib Ali* v. *Jinnatan Nahar*, A.I.R. 64 C.W.N. 756 (1960).
70. Dissolution of Muslim Marriages Act, 1939, Sec. 2(ii).
71. *Naniman Nissa Begum* v. *Serajuddin*, A.I.R. Pat. 467 (1946).
72. 2 Baillie, *Digest of Mohammadan Law* 87-98 (1869).
73. *Badrulnisa Bibi* v. *Mohammnd Yusuf*, A.I.R. All. 23 (1944).
74. *Jamila Khatun* v. *Kasim Ali*, A.I.R. Nag. 375 (1951).
75. *Mobiya Khatun* v. *Shaikh Anwar*, A.I.R. Cal. 218 (1971).
76. *Bai Fatma* v. *Munna Miranji Haji*, A.I.R. Bom. 107 (1957).
77. *Mt. Khatijan* v. *Abdulla*, A.I.R. Sind. 65 (1943).
78. *Noor Bibi* v. *Pir Bux*, A.I.R. Sind. 8 (1950). It may be mentioned that there is a difference of opinion on the point among the Pakistani Courts. Some Courts have held that if the wife refuses herself to the husband without lawful cause and deserts her husband, she has no right to claim maintenance; while other Courts have held that a wife would be entitled to dissolve the marriage upon proof of her husband's failure to maintain her. See Mulla, supra note 63, at 309-10.
79. *A. Yousuf* v. *Sowramma*, A.I.R. Ker. 261 (1971).
80. Ibid. at 264.

Concept of "breakdown of marriage" in Indian Law 7

IT IS the purpose of this chapter to examine the extent to which the breakdown theory has been recognized in the matrimonial law in India.

HINDU LAW

The remedy of divorce is based upon the concept of matrimonial guilt under the Hindu Marriage Act, 1955. Therefore, under its scheme an innocent party alone can obtain divorce by proving the commission of a wrong by the respondent. Under the provisions, divorce can also be had if there has been no resumption of cohabitation for a certain period after the passing of the decree of judicial separation or on the ground of non-compliance of the decree of restitution of conjugal rights after the passing of such a decree. Until 1964 the relevant provisions read :[1]

> Sec. 13(1) Any marriage solemnized, whether before or after the commencement of this Act, may, on a petition presented by either the husband or the wife, be dissolved by a decree of divorce on the ground that the other party,
>
> (viii) has not resumed cohabitation for a period of two years or upwards after the passing of a decree for judicial separation against that party; or
>
> (ix) has failed to comply with the decree of restitution of conjugal rights for a period of two years or upwards after the passing of the decree.

The above provisions were so interpreted by the courts as to debar the party against whom the decree of judicial separation or restitution was granted from obtaining divorce. In other words, the guilty party was not entitled to obtain divorce.

In order to remedy the situation an amendment was made in 1964. The amendment now reads :[2]

> Sec. 13 (1A) *Either party to a marriage*, whether solemnized before or after the commencement of this Act, may also present a petition for dissolution of the marriage by a decree of divorce on the ground—
>
> (i) that there has been no resumption of cohabitation *as between the parties* to the marriage for a period of two years or upwards after the passing of the decree for judicial separation in a proceeding to which they were parties; or
>
> (ii) that there has been no restitution of conjugal rights *as between the parties* to the marriage for a period of two years or upwards after the passing of the decree for restitution of conjugal rights in a proceedings to which they were parties.

It may be pointed out that under section 23 of the Hindu Marriage Act[3] the court must be satisfied before granting a relief (whether the relief is by way of divorce, nullity of marriage or judicial separation or restitution) that the petitioner is not in any way taking advantage of his or her own wrong. Thus, it is apparent that there is a clash of principles under the amended section and section 23. Under the former even a guilty party can sue and obtain divorce; under the latter, granting of relief to such a party would amount to rewarding his own wrong. This situation has given rise to a difference of opinion among the various courts. In *Chaman Lal* v. *Mohinder Devi*,[4] a decree of restitution of conjugal rights was obtained by the wife. The husband did not comply with the decree. When, on the expiry of the period of two years since the decree of restitution was passed, the husband applied for divorce under the amended section. the court relying on section 23(1)(a), rejected his petition. Pandit, J., conceded that by virtue of the amendment of 1964 either party can petition for divorce:[5]

> . . . but under section 23(1)(a), the court before granting the relief to the petitioner had to be satisfied that he was not in any way taking advantage of his own wrong for the purpose of such relief. The moment the court was satisfied that he was taking advantage, the petition had to be dismissed.

In *Syal* v. *Syal*[6] and *Someswara* v. *Leelavati*[7], both the Punjab and the Mysore High Courts came to similar conclusions on identical facts. The Bombay High Court was also confronted with the same question, namely, whether in granting relief under the amended section the court has to take into consideration section 23(1)(a) of the Hindu Marriage Act, 1955. In *Laxmibai* v. *Laxmichand*[8], the wife obtained a decree of restitution of conjugal rights. Later, the husband petitioned for divorce under section 13(1A) of the Act alleging that after the passing of the decree of restitutions of conjugal rights a period of more than two years had elapsed. The lower court granted the decree of dissolution. The wife appealed. There was evidence that the husband did not make any efforts to comply with the decree of restitution of conjugal rights granted in favor of the wife. The appellate court, therefore, took into consideration section 23(1)(a) of the Act and held that the husband was taking advantage of his own wrong. The decree of divorce was denied.

Again, in *Madhukar Bhaskar* v. *Saral*,[9] the Bombay High Court was called upon to construe the same provisions. In this case, the wife had obtained a decree of judicial separation alleging cruelty and desertion by her husband. Thereafter, the husband filed a petition for divorce under section 13(1A)(i) of the Act. He alleged that a period of two years or upwards had elapsed after passing of the decree of judicial separation. The lower court dismissed the petition. The court was of the view that the husband was taking advantage of his wrong in the sense that he did not assure the wife (in whose favor the decree of judicial separation was granted) of his good conduct nor tried to effect a reunion. Aggrieved by this decision the husband appealed. The appellate court reversed the decision of the lower court and granted the decree of dissolution. The court admitted that regard must be had to section 23(1)(a) of the Hindu Marriage Act before granting relief under section 13(1A), but was unable to agree with the decision of the lower court that in a case, such as this, there was any obligation on the part of the husband to assure the wife of his good conduct in future. The court said :[10]

> If there is no such obligation on him, there is no question of his being in the wrong by not carrying out such obligation such as to disentitle him to the relief of divorce.

Similarly, in *Jethabai* v. *Manabai*,[11] the same court held that a husband, against whom the decree of judicial separation was granted on the ground of desertion, did not remain under an obligation to cohabit with the other spouse. Therefore, if the respondent did not make any efforts to resume cohabitation, he did not commit a wrong under section 23(1)(a) of the Act and was entitled to a decree of divorce under section 13(1A)(i).

The last two cases mentioned above were cases involving the petitioners (respondents to the judicial separation proceedings) seeking the relief of divorce. In those cases, it was held that a decree of judicial separation imposed no obligations on the respondent to take any steps toward reconciliation. Therefore, in seeking the relief of divorce under section 13(1A)(i) of the Act, the petitioners were not taking advantage of their wrong. But the question whether or not a petitioner is taking advantage of his wrong will arise only in cases of restitution. For, a decree of restitution of conjugal rights imposes an obligation on the respondent to comply with the decree. If the petitioner (respondent to the decree of restitution) does not make efforts toward reconciliation and asks for the decree of divorce under section 13(1A)(ii) of the Act, his petition can be dismissed by virtue of section 23(1)(a). This, in fact, was the view taken by the courts in the cases we have examined above. However, it could be established that the petitioner, who was a respondent in a restitution proceedings, is not taking advantage of his wrong then, he could obtain divorce despite section

23(1)(a). A ruling to this effect is given by the Delhi High Court in *Ram Kali* v. *Gopal Das*.[12]

The wife, in this case, had obtained a decree of restitution of conjugal rights against her husband in 1961. The husband filed a petition for divorce in 1965 under section 13(1A)(ii) on the ground that after the passing of the decree of restitution of conjugal rights there had been no resumption of cohabitation for a period of two years and more. It was argued on behalf of the wife that the husband had failed to comply with the decree of restitution of conjugal rights and that he was seeking to take advantage of his wrong by applying for the dissolution of the marriage. The husband pleaded that his wife had instituted separate suits for maintenance and for the recovery of dowry against him and his relatives. He alleged that he had asked the wife towith draw the cases against him and then approach for a compromise. The husband contended that under these circumstances, he could not be expected to effect a reunion. The court while discussing the amended section observed :[13]

> But the failure to perform the decree of restitution of conjugal rights, *per se*, without more, will not disentitle the spouse to the relief. To hold otherwise will, in most cases, defeat the purpose of the amendment, made in section 13, by the Hindu Marriage (Amendment) Act, 1964. . . .

The court stated that the question whether a spouse who has failed to comply with the decree of restitution of conjugal rights is disentitled under section 23(1)(a) of the Act from obtaining divorce will depend upon the facts and circumstances of each case. In the instant case, the demand of the husband to withdraw the cases against him before he could comply with the court's order was considered as reasonable. His failure, therefore, to comply with the decree of restitution of conjugal rights did not, in the opinion of the court, amount to "taking advantage of his own wrong". Accordingly, a decree of divorce was granted to the husband.

Some writers such as Paras Diwan[14] and Dolia[15] have taken a view that under the amended section the guilty spouse is entitled to obtain divorce. This, in their view, accords with the objects for which amendment was made.

Justice Deshpande[16] has, in a recent article, tried to reconcile section 13(1A) and section 23(1). According to the learned judge, the conduct of the party after the decree of separation or restitution has been passed should be taken into account and seen in the light of section 23(1) whether the guilty spouse in an earlier proceedings is or is not taking advantage of his own wrong by filing a suit for divorce under section 13(1A). In other words, the conduct of the guilty spouse prior to such decrees should be dispensed with. He says :[17]

> The specific and limited effect of sub-sec. (1A) of sec. 13 is to preclude the Court from taking into account that portion of the conduct of the parties which has already been considered by the Court in the proceedings leading to the decrees for judicial separation and restitution of conjugal rights. The intention of the Legislature in giving both the judgment-debtor and the decree-holder the right to make an application for divorce was to eliminate the consideration of such conduct.

Derrett,[18] writing in 1968 on the subject had advocated for a similar approach for reconciliation between the two sections. He stated :[19]

> . . . so long as it is open to the formerly "guilty" party to show that a different set of facts obtains, and that his (or her) claim to a divorce rests upon another footing—that in fact he does not take advantage of his own "wrong"—a divorce can be obtained under the Act of 1955 as amended in 1964, notwithstanding that it was against him that the decree for separation or restitution was passed.

Courts too, have taken a view that for the purpose of granting the relief of divorce under the amended section, the "wrong" contemplated under section 23(1)(a) should refer to the conduct of the petitioner (respondent in original proceedings) subsequent to the passing of the decree of restitution of conjugal rights. It may be mentioned that the rule laid down by the courts applies to the cases of restitution and not to the cases of judicial separation. This judicial construction may be considered as giving rise to an anomaly, namely, that it distinguishes the cases of judicial separation from those of restitution. But, it could be argued in support of the judicial interpretation that the legal consequences that flow from these two decrees are different. A decree of judicial separation does not impose any obligation on the respondent to resume cohabitation, whereas a decree of restitution of conjugal rights does impose an obligation on the respondent to comply with the decree. Therefore, the conduct of the petitioner (i.e., respondent to a decree of judicial separation) seeking divorce under section 13(1A)(i) becomes irrelevant under section 23(1)(a), whereas his conduct subsequent to the passing of the decree of restitution of conjugal rights may be considered under section 23(1)(a).

Though considerable controversy exists among the writers on the subject which has not so far been raised in the Supreme Court, the fact remains that the breakdown concept has been recognized in the Hindu Marriage Act after its amendment in 1964.

Continuous absence of consortium has been accepted as a marital failure for which remedy is provided. This is evident from the statement of objects and reasons laid down in the bill of the Amendment Act XLIV of 1964 which read :[20]

> The right to apply for divorce on the ground that cohabitation has not been resumed for a period of two years or more after the passing of the decree for judicial separation, or on the ground that conjugal life has not been restored after the expiry of two years or more from the date of decree, for restitution of conjugal rights should be available to both the husband and wife, as in such cases it is clear that the marriage has proved a complete failure. There is, therefore, no justification for making the right available only to the party who has obtained the decree in each case.

In so far as other grounds are concerned the divorce law is based on the concept of guilt. But under the two situations contemplated by the amended section it must be conceded that the breakdown theory has found its way in India.

We may recall that the Court of Appeal of New York was confronted with a similar proposition in the *Gleason* case as did the courts in India. But in the *Gleason* case the rule of "clean hands" was invoked as a common law doctrine; whereas the same concept has been statutorily incorporated under section 23(1)(a) of the Hindu Marriage Act. It was perhaps easier for the New York Court to have abandoned the common law principle without much difficulty. On the other hand, some of the courts in India, it seems, found it difficult to ignore the principle as it has been statutorily recognized under the Hindu Marriage Act. For the same reason, sound judicial construction limits the power of the court to overcome the difficulty. Perhaps to clarify matters an amendment to section 23(1)(a) is necessary.

CONCEPT OF "BREAKDOWN" IN ISLAMIC LAW

We have seen above that in Islamic law the husband has an absolute right to divorce his wife by pronouncing *talaq* without assigning any reasons. We also noticed that the corresponding right given to the wife in a limited way was to terminate the marriage by *talaq-i-tawfeez* (delegated divorce) or by mutual consent called *Khul*. But what if the wife has not been given the delegated power nor does the husband agree to dissolve the marriage by mutual consent? Of course, the wife can look to the Muslim Dissolution of Marriages Act, 1939 which allows divorce on various grounds. But suppose none of the grounds are available to the wife under the Act. The question is, can she still dissolve her marriage if there are irreconcilable differences, incompatibility of temperament, or there is a serious marital discord !

It was held in a very early case of *Mst. Umar Bibi* v. *Mohammed Din*[21] that Islamic law does not recognize divorce on incompatibility of temperament, dislike or ill-will between the spouses. This has been generally followed by the courts.

It must be pointed out in this context that there are some verses in the *Quran* and some supporting traditions of the Prophet (*Sunna*) which allow the dissolution of marriage if reconciliation is not possible between the spouses and if the "limits of God cannot be observed". The significant verse in the *Quran* lays down :[22]

> And if ye fear a breach between husband and wife send a judge out of his family and a judge out of her family: if they are desirous of agreement God will effect a reconciliation between them; for God is knowing and appraised of all.

Again, Prophet Mohammed is reported to have said:[23]

> If a woman is prejudiced by a marriage, let it be broken off.

Many commentators of great authority have interpreted the verse in the light of the tradition that in cases of mutual discord and when reconciliation fails, the marriage can be dissolved by the *Kazi* (judge). Maulana Mohummad Ali has explained the above Quranic verse thus :[24]

> This verse lays down the procedure to be adopted when a case of divorce arises. It is not for the husband to put away his wife: it is the business of the judge to decide the case. Nor should divorce cases be made public. The judge is required to appoint two arbiters, one belonging to the wife and the other to the husband. These two arbiters will find out the facts, but their objective must be to effect reconciliation between the parties. If all hopes of reconciliation fail, a divorce is allowed, but the final decision for divorce rests with the judge who is legally entitled to pronounce a divorce. Cases were decided in accordance with the directions contained in this verse in the early days of Islam.

He further points out that the principle of divorce spoken of in the *Quran*, which includes among other things, is the decision to no longer live together as husband and wife.[25] A disagreement between the parties to live as husband and wife is called *Shiqaq*. A "breach between the two" referred to in the *Quranic* verse imply that either the husband or the wife want to break off the marriage relationship.[26] A breach of marriage relationship (i.e., *Shiqaq*) may arise from the conduct of either party. For instance, it may arise due to matrimonial misconduct or due to incompatibility of temperament. In all such cases where one of the parties finds it impossible to live together, divorce will follow. Of course, every disagreement will not entitle the parties to dissolve their marriage unless all possibilities of reconciliation have been exhausted.

The above verse of the *Quran*, the tradition and the commentary were pressed into service in *Aboobacker* v. *Mamu Koya*.[27] The facts of the case briefly stated were as follows :

The matrimonial muddle of the unfortunate couples found its way into the court, each spouse filing a suit: the husband for restitution of conjugal rights, the wife for divorce. The parties after their marriage lived together for sometimes when a son was born to them. The wife left with her son for her father's house. She did not return for about two years. The wife was an orthodox Muslim and the husband was of modern persuasion. There were obviously some serious differences between them. The lower court granted the relief to the husband and dismissed the petition of the wife seeking divorce. The wife appealed. She grounded the petition for divorce on three counts: cruelty, failure to provide maintenance and "irreparable breakdown of the matrimony". The Dissolution of Muslim Marriages Act, entitles a wife to obtain divorce on the ground of cruelty and failure to provide maintenance. The Act after listing the various other grounds proceeds to lay down that divorce can be granted "on any other ground which is recognized as valid for the dissolution of marriages under Muslim law".[28]

The contention of the wife respecting cruelty and failure to provide maintenance was not proved. The question thus hinged on the "ground recognized as valid for the dissolution of marriages under Muslim law".

Citing *Quran*, the traditions, and drawing ample authority from the commentaries, Justice Iyer come to the conclusion that when an intolerable situation has been reached, the partners living separate and apart for a substantial time, an inference may be drawn that the marriage has broken down in fact and so should be ended in law. He declared :[29]

> The Islamic ethos accepts irreconcilable breach as a ground for dissolution. In the plaint the wife alleges that for reasons of neglect and cruelty etcetera life with the husband has become insufferable and so she does not intend to co-habit with him at all and desires a divorce. These facts approximate to what has been recognized under Muslim law as a ground for divorce, preserved by section 2(ix) of the Act.

The whole gamut of Islamic law of divorce as applied in modern India can be summed up in his words thus :[30]

> Daily, trivial differences get dissolved in the course of time and may be treated as the teething troubles of early matrimonial adjustment. While the stream of life, lived in married mutuality, may wash away smaller pebbles, what is to happen if intransigent incompatibility of minds breaks up the flow of the stream? In such a situation, we have a *breakdown of the marriage* itself and the only course left open is for law to recognize what is a fact and accord a divorce.

The judgment of Justice Iyer is exemplary in as much as it raises the status of woman to that of the husband in the matter of divorce. This gentle tinkering of the Islamic law has opened a new vista of progressive interpretation. The judgment has brought to light the vitality of the Islamic law to adapt itself to the changing needs of the society. For our purpose, the judgment sheds light on the concept of breakdown of marriage. The concept was imbedded some thirteen hundred years ago in the law of Islam and had found expression in most advanced and civilized countries of today. This realistic and pragmatic approach to divorce has been accepted in the Family Code of the German Republic, in the Divorce Reform Act of England and last but not the least, in some of the American jurisdictions.

NOTES AND REFERENCES

1. Hindu Marriage Act, 1955, Sec. 13 (Act No. XXV) of 1955 (effective 18th May, 1955).
2. Hindu Marriage Amendment Act (Act XLIV of 1964 effective 20th December, 1964). (Emphasis added.) The period has now been reduced to one year. See Marriage Laws (Amendment) ct, 1976.
3 Section 23, Hindu Marriage Act, 1955:
   (1) In any proceeding under this Act, whether defended or not, if the court is satisfied that—
   (2) Any of the grounds for granting relief exists and the petitioner is not in any way taking advantage of his or her wrong or disability for the purpose of such relief. . . .
4. *Chaman Lal* v. *Mohinder Devi*, A.I.R. Punj. & Har. 287 (1968).
5. Ibid. at 288.
6. *Syal* v. *Syal*, A.I.R. Punj. & Har. 489 (1968).
7. *M. Someswara* v. *Leelavati*, A.I.R. Mys. 274 (1968).
8. *Laxmibai* v. *Laxmichand*, A.I.R. Bom. 332 (1968).
9. *Madhukar Bhaskar* v. *Saral*, 74 Bom. L.R. Jl. 496 (1972).
10. Ibid. at 501.
11. *Jethabai* v. *Manabai*, 76 Bom. L.R. 306 (1974).
    For critical comments on this case and other cases on the subject, see Derrett, *Matrimonial Freedom: A Step Forward in Bombay*, 77, Bom. L.R. Jl. 8 (1975).
12. *Smt. Ram Kali* v. *Gopal Dass*, 4 D.L.T. 503 (1968).
13. Ibid. at 507.
14. Paras Diwan, *Modern Hindu Law* 156 (1972).
15. See Dolia, *Hindu Marriage Act (XXV of 1955), Sec. 13(IA)*2 M.L.J. 83 (1968).
16. Deshpande, *Divorce Under Hindu Marriage Act—A Conflict of Principles*, A.I.R. Jl. 113 (1971). See further *S. Garg* v. *K.H. Garg*, A.I.R. Del. 296 (1978).
17. Ibid. at 117.
18. See Derrett, *May a spouse who is in desertion obtain a divorce on the basis of his own wrong*? 70 Bom. L.R. Jl. 117 (1968).
19. Ibid. at 121.
20. Gazette of India, Ext. Part II, Sec. 2, No. 7 at 86 (February 1963).
21. *Umar Bibi* v. *Mohammed Din*. A.I.R. Lah. 51 (1945).
    See further *Mst. Mustafa Begum* v. *Mirza Kasim Raza Khan*, A.I.R. Oudh. 15 (1933).
22. The *Quran*, Ch. IV, Verse 35.
23. Ameer Ali, Vol. 2. *Mohammaden Law* 51 (1911).
24. Mohammad Ali's commentary on the Holy *Quran* cited with approval in *Aboobacker* v. *Mamu Koya*, K.L.T. 663 at 669 (1971).
25. Mohammad Ali, *Divorce in Islam* 4 (The Working Muslim Mission &

Literary Trust, Surrey England). (Date not given).

26. Ibid. at 5-7.
27. *Aboobacker* v. *Mamu Koya*, supra note 24.
28. Dissolution of Muslim Marriages Act, 1939, Sec. 2(ix).
29. *Aboobacker* v. *Mamu Koya*, supra note 24 at 670.
30. Ibid. at 668 (Emphasis added).

Reforms in Islamic Law of Divorce : Problems and Prospects

8

To APPRECIATE fully the difficulties attendant upon the reforms in Islamic law in general and divorce law in particular it is necessary to know in brief the concept of law in Islam which is different from the western conception of law.

We have pointed out earlier that law and religion are blended together in the scheme of personal laws. In the classical theory of Islam, the law of *Quran* (i.e., the law of God) is infallible[1] and unchangeable.[2] It is there for all Muslims for all time and for all places. *Sharia*,[3] i.e., the Islamic law combines both law and religion as do a number of other legal systems of the world. Islamic law in its technical sense is only a part of a complete scheme of *Sharia* which may be treated as a code of life. It is not *lex* but *jus* also.[4] It can be equated with natural law which is universal in its appeal and at the same time consistent with the ideas of the community for which it is intended.

If one looks at *Sharia* through the perspectives of analytical jurisprudence it comes very near to being the same as the command of the Austinian sovereign.[5] In the legal sense *Sharia* in Islamic jurisprudence means only that part of the body of rules of human conduct which adjust the natural rights and obligations of individuals in society. As such it is civil law. But this is not a law which has come by way of a dictate from man to man; instead it is a command of *Allah*, whether expressed in revelation of Mohammed, the prophet, in the shape of Holy *Quran* or in the practices of the prophet himself. Thus, *Sharia* is the source of all laws and to a traditionalist it is the only source of law. It is here where the true opposition comes from the side of modernists because the rules of *Sharia* were, according to the traditionalists, something immutable, unchangeable and eternal.

Before we examine the problems and prospects of reforming Islamic law in India a brief account of how this supposedly rigid and immutable law of *Sharia* has adapted itself to the changing needs of the Arab society will be in order.[6] The basis of reforms and their juristic foundations in Islamic countries will be of immense value when we speak of reforms in Islamic law in India.

It is a well-known fact that the laws relating to marriage and divorce have been modified, rules of *wakfs* (charitable endowments) have been amended, laws of inheritence have been liberalized. To survey changes in all these fields is beyond the scope of this work. Therefore, we would deal only with the law of *talaq* and its reform.

TALAQ AND REFORMS

The public law as developed in various Muslim countries slowly and steadily replaced the corresponding provisions of the *Sharia* whereas the family law retained and even this day retains basically its original form and character notwithstanding that most of the countries were long subjected to alien rule. Thus the growth of Islamic jurisprudence in the sphere of public and family law has been in different directions. While the public law grew more and more receptive to foreign concepts,[7] the family law tended to be less flexible and more conservative remaining true to the *Sharia*. However, the law of *talaq* has been reformed by progressive codification. The reformers knew well that ideas prompted by philanthrophic motives would not be welcomed by the society since the weapon of *talaq* in the hands of a husband was heavily supported by *Quran*. Naturally, therefore, while suggesting reforms they made a cautious approach to the problem. The reformers relied on the authorities on which the conservatives relied, namely, the *Quran* and the traditions. It is ironic that both of them drew their authorities from the same sources. The modernites while introducing innovations in the traditional law of *talaq* supported their arguments with the tradition of the prophet which declared that "of all permitted things the most detestable is divorce in the sight of God";[8] the conservatives protested that it was a right sanctioned in favor of the husband by the *Quran*.

Under Hanafi law all pronouncements of *talaq* by the husband in a heat of passion or under the influence of intoxication is valid.[9] Even a pronouncement uttered by way of jest, oath or threat is valid according to most authoritative commentaries of Hanafi jurists. Relying upon the precept of prophet wherein it was said that for three things, namely, marriage, divorce and manumission jesting is not allowed to dissuade men from trifling with such solemn affairs of life, the Hanafi doctrines carried this by force of analogy in holding that divorce pronounced under such circumstances was valid.[10] However, jurists like Shafi, Malik, Hanbal, Umar Ibn Abdul Aziz and Qadi Shuria held such pronouncements as invalid.[11] The reformers following the opinion of these jurists who held no less authority than the Hanafi jurists, enacted as early as 1915, in the Ottoman Law of Family Rights that repudiation uttered under the influence of intoxication would no longer be given legal effect.[12] The Egyptian Law of 1929 had similar provisions. Taking the cue from these pioneer reformers several countries including Iraq[13], Syria[14], Morocco[15] and Tunisia[16] in their respective codes of personal status have invalidated the formula of *talaq* pronounced in such extenuating circumstances. In India since the Hanafi law as interpreted by the authoritative commentaries is followed, the rigour of the traditional law continues unabated.

Apart from the reforms made with regard to the formula of divorce, the divorce itself has been made dependent on the consent of the court. Tunisia offers the example of the boldest venture in this respect when section 30 of the Code enacts that "Divorce outside a court of law is without legal effect".[17] However, salutary this reform may appear to be, it might give rise to certain amount of difficulty for the courts. As pointed out by Anderson :[18]

> Suppose, for instance, a husband pronounces a thrice-repeated divorce in the privacy of his house, but subsequently tells his wife that he has no intention of seeking a judicial degree and wants to continue the marriage

> relationship; and suppose that she then goes to court and declares that it is against her conscience to live with him any longer. Will the court, in such a case, insists on the husband paying compensation to the wife, as the original offender; or the wife to the husband, as the one who in fact persists in demanding separation; or neither ?

In Pakistan the power of the husband to pronounce an unilateral divorce (irrevocable divorce) has been taken away. Under the Ordinance[19] "a *talaq* unless revoked earlier expressly or otherwise, shall not be effective until the expiration of ninety days from the day on which notice . . . is delivered to the Chairman. . . ." The immediate result of this provision is that the effect of *talaq* even if it be in irrevocable form is delayed.

Reforms and their juristic foundations

The reformers had to justify the reforms not only on religious, moral and social grounds but they had to justify them juristically in order to aid their genuine efforts to ameliorate the conditions of the masses. Therefore, it was imperative for them in order to achieve their objectives to find indirect juristic support for their ideals. This they found in the right of the sovereign in the field of administration of justice and his powers to prescribe forms by which particular disputes were to be resolved.

In the history of development of substantive law adjective law has played a prominent role. *Ubi remedium ibi jus.* If many causes of action could not be satisfied in England in the absence of a proper writ or form of action,[20] naturally in a similar manner, many remedies under a reformed system of Islamic law could not be availed of in Muslim countries in religious courts called the *Sharia* court because of the fact that causes of action had been transferred from one set of courts to another.

Sharia courts were the victim of this device when jurisdiction to take cognizance of particular kinds of cases was narrowed under the pretext of an exercise of the sovereign power of the government. The instances particularly noteworthy concern the land law and laws relating to crimes which the sovereign monopolized and, thus tended to diminish the jurisdiction of the *Sharia* courts. The sovereign, it was contended, had the power to narrow the jurisdiction of a particular set of courts and this gave him competence to redefine the jurisdiction of the *Sharia* courts. Thus in the development of Islamic political theory the power of the sovereign has been treated as supreme.[21]

Another method by which reforms were introduced was to capitalize on the divergent views among the jurists of various schools. Even within the same school the disciples differ from their masters. The reformers took advantage of these divergent opinions and resorted to what may be called a "selective process" moulding the *Sharia* according to the needs of the developing society.[22]

The whole basis from which reforms originated in the Muslim world was by resort to reinterpretation of the original sources independently. It must be pointed out that Islamic law was expounded, interpreted and developed by the jurists who had the authority to do so in the absence of guidance either from *Quran* or traditions of the prophet. In fact the whole corpus of Islamic jurisprudence was built upon the concept of *Ijtehad*, i.e., exerting either individually or collectively to lay down a rule of law not covered either by *Quran* or *Hadis* (tradition). It was accepted that there was to be no further question of exposition of law, the earlier jurists having anticipated every problem and laid down a rule for its solution. This notion leads to what is called "the closure of the gates of *Ijtehad*", by the end of 14th century.[23] From that time onwards every thing that was developed was done by merely following the earlier jurists. This is known in Islamic thought as the doctrine of *Taqlid*. But by the turn of the 19th century the reformers in Egypt as also in other Muslim countries asserted themselves the right of *Ijtehad* and reinterpreted the original sources independently thus paving the way for reforms.[24]

REFORMS IN INDIA

The problem of reforms through judicial interpretation

During the colonial period Muslim personal law remained static not only because of its religious nature but also because of the policy of non-interference by the colonial rulers, which as we have seen, expressly enjoined the legislature to apply Islamic law to the Muslims in India. The judiciary too adopted a cautious approach while applying the principles of Islamic law. This is clearly borne out by the judicial committee of the Privy Council which, time and again, has expressed reluctance to depart from the opinion of traditional jurists while interpreting the texts. In *Aga Mahomed* v. *Koolsom Bibi*, it was observed :[25]

> . . . It would be wrong for the courts on a point of this kind to put their own construction on the *Quran* in opposition to the expressed ruling of commentators of such great antiquity and high authority.

Again, in *Baker Ali* v. *Anjuman Ara Begum*,[26] Sir Arthur Wilson declared that new rules of law were not to be introduced although they seemed to the lawyers of the day to follow logically from ancient texts, specially when the ancient doctors of law had not themselves drawn those conclusions. The attitude adopted by the Privy Council in regard to the traditional law was followed by the courts during the British administration of justice and this legacy is being continued since then.[27] The British Indian courts could resort to the principles of justice, equity and good conscience by progressively interpreting Islamic law in order to meet the changing needs of the Muslim community. But, this they did only in the absence of a clear text or commentary. The need for doing so is greater today than it ever was in view of the changed socio-economic conditions in India after she had gained her independence.

As respect the statutory Islamic law there is larger scope for judicial liberalization than in respect of the traditional law. Deviation from the established principles may pose difficult problems though they may be largely overcome by making use of the diversity of opinion among the jurists themselves. But, in regard to that part of codified law, the courts have more freedom and hence an easier task, since in that case, they are called upon to interpret statutory law which has replaced the traditional law. This judicial relaxation we have noticed earlier while dealing with the judicial interpretation of the Dissolution of Muslim Marriages Act, 1939.

As respect the traditional law of divorce, there has been, however, in some instances, a gentle tinkering in the area by the judiciary. For instance, according to the traditional law, a pronouncement of *talaq* is valid in the absence of the wife and even if it is not communicated to her. But, in *Abdul Khader* v *Azeera*[28] it was held that a *talaq* given in the absence of the wife would be effective only when it became known to her. The ruling in *Chandi* v. *Bandusa*,[29] a decision of the Bombay High Court, is to the same effect.

As regards a *talaq* given in writing, the courts have generally followed the principle of Islamic law that it takes effect from the time of execution of the deed. The law in Pakistan on this point is the same. Islamic law recognizes two forms of writing regarding divorce—customary and non-customary. If the writing is in a customary form, *talaq* takes effect even if it is not communicated to the wife. On the other hand, if the writing is in a non-customary or unusual form *talaq* should be communicated and, further, the intention to divorce must be proved.[30] These principles were applied in *Rasul Baksh* v. *Mst. Bholan*.[31] The husband in this case executed a deed of divorce which was not known or communicated to any person or to the wife. Broadway and Manroe, JJ., declared this deed to be of non-customary form and as the intention to divorce was not proved, it was held that the *talaq* deed was invalid.

The Privy Council had no doubt endeavoured its best to apply and administer the law in a liberal way, but it seems to have hesitated on many occasions with the result that it often failed to appreciate the true spirit of Islamic law. So cautious was its approach that it refused to apply the liberal preachings of sub-schools within the same school, even though there was an authority from Abu Hanifa, the founder of the Hanafi school, to apply the law of any sub-school if the laws propounded by his school caused great hardships. In fact when the Dissolution of Muslim Marriages Act, 1939 was passed entitling a wife to dissolve the marriage, *inter alia*, on the ground of her husband's neglect to maintain her, the statement of objects and reasons[32] clearly said that as there was no provision under the Hanafi law which enabled the wife to obtain divorce on that ground, the Maliki and Shafii law could be followed which recognized that ground as giving a right to the wife to obtain divorce from her husband.

The judiciary in India cannot also resort to *Ijtehad*, i.e., to interpret the original sources independently of the opinion expressed by the ancient doctors and their commentators for, according to Islamic legal theory only Muslims highly learned in *Quran* and master of traditions, expert in Arabic language grammar and rhetoric have the competence to independent exposition of the law.[33] When the *Ulemas* (highly qualified and learned Muslim) in India cannot themselves arrogate this power, it is naive to expect that the judiciary could claim such a power. It is significant to note that in Pakistan the courts have assumed the power to interpret the original texts of Muslim law, independently of the opinion expressed by the ancient doctors. In *Khurshid Jan* v. *Fazal Dad*, Anwarul Huq, J. of the Lahore High Court, observed :[34]

> With great humility I venture to submit that it would not be correct to lay it down as a positive rule of law that the present-day Courts in this country should have no power or authority to interpret the *Quran* in a way different from that adopted by the earlier jurists and Imams. The adoption of such a view is likely to endanger the dynamic and universal character of the religion and laws of Islam.

The Indian judiciary may not adopt a similar attitude but it is surely possible for it to apply the principles of Islamic law in a liberal manner without claiming the powers of *Ijtehad* (reinterpretation of texts). Such a progressive judicial approach to, and a liberal interpretation of, the texts of Islamic law was strongly advocated by M.C. Chagla as early as 1946. He stated :[35]

> Now there is no doubt that these ancient Muslim texts must be considered with the utmost respect. But it must also be remembered at the same time that Muslim jurisprudence is not a static jurisprudence. It is a jurisprudence which has grown and developed with the times and the quotations from Muslim texts should be so applied as

> to suit modern circumstances and conditions. It is also dangerous to pick out illustrations wrenched from their context and apply them literally. Illustration merely illustrate a principle and what the Court should try and do is to deduce the principle which underlies the illustrations.

The judiciary can, it is submitted, play an important role in bringing the traditional Islamic law of marriage and divorce more in conformity with the changing needs of the community. Further, such a process of judicial reform is likely to attract lesser hostility than an attempt to reform the Islamic law by direct legislation.

Progressive codification of Islamic law

We have seen that progressive codification of Islamic law in conformity with the social and religious needs of the Arab society has been achieved, first, by a happy blending of traditional law with contemporary thought, secondly, by the process of selection of principles and opinions from the various schools of Islamic law and thirdly, by reinterpretation of the original sources. The same methods and procedures may be adopted with great advantage in India to codify Islamic law. The best and the most progressive principles from various sub-schools within the same school can be drawn and a code enacted in tune with the socio-religious needs of the Muslim community. Also there is ample scope for *Ijtehad* in the field of family law and particularly in the traditional law of *talaq*.

Many writers, thinkers and social reformers such as Abdur Rahim Iqbal and Sir Syed have advocated that the Muslim community has always the right for collective deliberation in matters of law and religion.[36] Sir Syed said :[37]

> We cannot neglect or ignore the stupendous work done by the early jurists but we cannot be bound by it; we must go back to the original sources, the *Quran* and the *Sunna.*

The effective and the easy way to reform Islamic law is of course by direct legislation. Reforms by this method could be achieved in Muslim countries; but in India reforms by direct legislation is beset with great difficulties as the Constitution guarantees to all its citizens the right to profess and propagate and practice their own religion. It is a fundamental right. The Muslim community would thwart any such step as amounting to an encroachment upon their religion. They may also contend that reforms would violate Article 29(1) of the Constitution which guarantees the right to conserve culture.

To tide over the difficulty of reforming this branch of personal law, the government must appoint a commission consisting of lawyers, *Ulemas* and social reformers to prepare a list of those problems of Muslim personal law including the Islamic law of divorce which stand in need of revision due to the change in socio-economic conditions. The commission then could recommend to the Parliament its suggestions and this would meet the approval of the Muslims as under this circumstances there will be less opposition from the orthodox Muslims. In other words, reforms must come from the Muslim themselves.

But before such an uphill task is undertaken reforms in a limited way could be achieved by regulatory and administrative processes. Such a technique was adopted in many Muslim countries before modern codes of Personal Status appeared on the scene altering and modifying the *Shariat* law. The state may as a regulatory or administrative measure provide that all divorces pronounced by *talaq* must be registered and that no *talaq* should be valid unless efforts at reconciliation have been made and proved futile. But then the problem of those persons divorced under the religious law remains if without registration *talaq* is declared legally invalid. Such instances are not unknown in India. For instance Muslims who marry under the Special Marriage Act, 1954 are governed with regard to divorce according to the provisions of the Act and not by traditional law. If the parties who strictly adhere to the Islamic law of *talaq* consider themselves divorced, they are at perfect liberty to do so, but such a pronouncement will have no legal consequence.

Similar regulatory and procedural measures could be followed in order to check the proclivity of the husband to pronounce a unilateral divorce. The state may provide compensation to the wife in addition to her dower if her husband has without her fault, pronounced an unilateral divorce. How far will such measures be regarded as an encroachment on the religious freedom by the state is debatable.

CONSTITUTIONAL LIMITATIONS AND REFORMS

It is axiomatic that the state should not interfere in the religious beliefs of an individual. Most civilized nations of the free world regard this as a cardinal principle in the constitutional structures. The Constitution of the United States enjoins the states to ensure the free exercise of religious belief and prohibits, in a peculiar historical cirumstances in which the nation was born, the establishment of a state religion. The legislatures and the courts have in the interest of inter-communal harmony in a pluralistic society, engrafted upon this freedom of religion a variety of restrictions in consonance with public order, morality and health.

The propagation, profession and practice of religion had repercussions in the society. And the society was recognized to have a right to so order the practices of one religion as not to interfere, insult or prevent the propagation, profession or practice of other religions. Nor should it jeopardise public order, morality and health.

The Indian Constitution similarly guarantees under Articles 25 and 26 the freedom of conscience and religion.[37a] In a pluralistic society with innumerable religious and cultural diver sities the state had a very delicate path to tread. Historically, the Muslims had come to India as conquerors and had ended up as, it is sometimes alleged, second rate citizens in independent India. Any effort by the state through its legislatures or the courts is, therefore, liable to be tricky and touchy.

Despite this, the state through the said instrumentalities, had succeeded in eroding a certain amount of dogmatic orthodoxy and harmonized the exercise of an alien religion with the religious mores of the indigenous people. It is interesting to see how this has been achieved and to note further impediments in the perfect solution to the problem.

The Constitution of India guarantees to its citizens freedom in matters of religion. It also protects the right to conserve cultural rights. The relevant articles are :

Article 25.

(1) Subject to public order, morality and health and to the other provisions of this Part, all persons are equally entitled to freedom of conscience and the right freely to profess, practise and propagate religion.

(2) Nothing in this article shall effect the operation of any existing law or prevent the State from making any law—

(a) regulating or restricting any economic, financial, political or other secular activity which may be associated with religious practice;

(b) providing for social welfare and reform or the throwing open of Hindu religious institutions of a public character to all classes and sections of Hindus.

Article 26.

Subject to public order, morality and health, every religious denomination or any section thereof shall have the right—

(a) to establish and maintain institutions for religious and charitable purpose;

(b) to manage its own affairs in matters of religion.

It may be noted at once that restrictions by the state upon the free exercise of religion are allowed under the Constitution on grounds of public order, morality and health. Article 25(2)(a) reserved the right of the State to regulate or restrict any economic, financial, political and other secular activities which may be associated with religious practice and under Article 25(2)(b) the State could legislate for social welfare and reform even though by so doing it might interfere with religious practices.[38] A question then arises whether modifications or reforms of personal laws are in consonance with the constitutional provisions.

When the Hindu law was modified by codification abolishing polygamy, a number of petitions challenging the validity of such a law were instituted. It was argued in the Madras[39] and Bombay[40] High Courts that legislation enforcing monogamy infringed the religious freedom guaranteed by the Constitution. In *Srinivasa Aiyer* v. *Saraswati Ammal*[41] the Madras High Court followed the American precedent of *Reynolds* v. *U.S.*[42] which distinguished religious belief from practice. It was held that the state could regulate and restrict a practice if it thought that in the interest of social welfare and reform it was necessary to do so. Similarly, the Allahabad High Court in *Ram Prasad* v. *State of UP*[43] upheld the abolition of polygamy by the Hindu Marriage Act, 1955 on the same reasoning. The Court said that the Hindu religion did not sanction polygamy as an essential religious practice and that even if it did, abolition of polygamy was a measure of social reform. The distinction drawn by the High Courts and the American case referred to between religious belief and practice was rejected by the Supreme Court in *Lakshmindra's* case.[44] It was observed by Mukherjea, J. :[45]

> The guarantee under our Constitution not only protects the freedom of religious opinion but it protects acts done in pursuance of a religion and this is made clear by the use of the expression "practice of religion" in Article 25.

It must be noted that the Indian Constitution does not make any distinction between the profession of religion and the propagation and practice thereof. The restrictions in the interest of public policy, morality, etc., have also been made for understandable reasons drawing upon the experience of other nations. But in the multi-communal and cultural society like that of India the courts would find it extremely difficult to sift essential and integral parts of a religious practice from the extraneous and unessential accretions to religion itself. The Supreme Court of India was confronted by such an unenviable task on many occasions. For example, in *Durgah Committee Ajmer & Another* v. *Syed Hussain Ali & Others*,[46] the respondents who were the Khadims (servants) of the tomb of a Muslim spiritual leader challenged the validity of an Act contending that certain provisions interfered with their religious freedom guaranteed under the Constitution. It was urged that the provisions which gave power to the committee to determine the privileges as well as the functions and powers of the Khadims in the management of *Durgah* (religious institution) infringed their freedom to practice their religion according to custom and according to their concept. It was held that the Act was intended to regulate the functions and duties of the Khadims and that "the impugned provisions merely provide for the regulation of the discharge of the duties by the Khadims and nothing more, and so the plea that the freedom to practice religion guaranteed by Art. 25(1) has been violated does not appear to be well founded".[47]

In *The Commissioner, Hindu Religious Endowments, Madras* v. *Lakshmindra*,[48] the petitioner who was the trustee of a religious trust challenged the validity of the Madras Religious and Charitable Endowments Act, 1951 as it violated the fundamental right guaranteed under the Constitution in matters of religion. The said Act was passed to ensure proper administration and control of the religious trust. Under the Act enormous powers were given to the commissioner respecting the administration of the trust property. He was empowered to enter the religious institution and the place of worship. He could put restrictions on the power of the trustee over personal gifts. He could require the trustee to have a manager appointed for the administration of the affairs of the institution and in case of default, the commissioner could make the appointment himself. It was also provided in the Act that a scheme could be framed for the administration of the trust property. In short, as the Supreme Court stated, one of the provisions crippled the authority of the *mohant* (head of the religious institution) and reduced his position to that of an ordinary priest or a paid servant.

The question that was called for decision was whether the practices of the *mohant* could be regarded as essential and integral part of the religion so as to claim protection under the Constitution. A further question would be: What criteria should be adopted to judge or determine the essentiality of a practice connected with the religion. The Supreme Court ruled :[49]

> . . . what constitutes an essential part of the religion is primarily to be ascertained with reference to the doctrines of that religion itself. If the tenets of any religious sect of the Hindus prescribe that offerings of food should be given to the idol at particular hours of the day, that periodical ceremonies should be performed in a certain way at certain periods of the year or that there should be daily recital of sacred texts or oblations to the sacred fire, all these would be regarded as parts of religion . . .

The above formulation by the court is not as simplistic as it sounds. For, in certain circumstances what constitutes an essential part of religious practice may not be all to clear. The distinction between religious belief and a particular practice might be too thin to be distinguished. For example, Muslims believe that sacrificing an animal on a special religious occasion is an essential part of religion since it is commanded by *Quran*. The court was called upon to adjudge the essentiality of cow slaughter to the practice of Muslim religion in *Mohd. Hanif Quareshi* v. *State of Bihar*.[50] The facts of the case briefly stated were as follows:

The Bihar State enacted laws banning cow slaughter to improve agricultural and animal husbandry. The petitioner contended that it violated the fundamental rights under Article 25 of the Constitution inasmuch as on the occasion of *Baker Id* day, it was the religious practice of the community to sacrifice a cow. The poor members of the community usually sacrifice a cow for every seven members whereas an alternate practice would require one sheep or goat for each member which would entail considerable expense. Therefore, a total ban imposed by the state would prevent the petitioner from sacrificing a cow. The holy *Quran* commanded the people to pray unto the Lord and make sacrifice. *Hedaya*,[51] the most authoritative commentary followed by the courts in India, spells out the modes of sacrifice as one goat per person or a cow or camel per seven persons. The court stated that "the very fact on an option seems to run counter to the notion of an obligatory duty". Therefore, the court concluded it was not obligatory for a person to sacrifice a cow. It found supporting evidence to the proposition in the history of the religious practices of Muslims in India where cow slaughter was prohibited.[52]

The court's logic that since the religious duty of a Muslim to make a sacrifice does not confine him to sacrifice a cow inasmuch as the injunction brooks of an option to sacrifice a goat or a camel instead, is not entirely convincing. A person might be enjoined to do either A or B or C. The fact that he has the option to perform anyone of these does not take away the obligatory character of the duty itself. The economic assumption of the option is clear; it would be cheaper for seven persons to sacrifice one bigger animal rather than one person to sacrifice even a small animal. By taking away the individual's right to cooperate with others for a less expensive method of performing his duty the state is striking at the very root of the obligation itself. In any event, this case demonstrate that where religious injunctions are less clear about the essentiality or otherwise of a particular practice the court may substitute its own judgment.

Howsoever logical this substitution might appear to be, it could lead to trouble. For instance, a court called to distinguish between essential and non-essential religious practices might be tempted to differentiate the rational from the irrational, the secular from the religious. In fact this happened in *Tilkayat Shri Govindlalji* v. *The State of Rajasthan*,[53] Gajendragadkar, J., interpreting Articles 25(1) and 26(b) stated that if a matter was obviously secular and not religious, a court would be justified in rejecting its claim to be a religious practice as based on irrational considerations. As rightly pointed out by Seervai,[54] the real question is whether religious denomination looks upon it as an essential part of religion, and however irrational it may appear to persons who do not share that religious belief; the view of the denomination must prevail, for, it is not open to a court to describe as irrational that which is an essential part of a denomination's religion.

A challenge to Muslim law reform could be grounded squarely on religious scriptures or a more sophisticated strategy might be adopted as an alternative. In the latter case, a constitutional attack may be launched against the reforms by relying upon American precedents where the term "religion" was given a wider and more comprehensive meaning. Let us first discuss the traditional scripture-based argument.

The objector to Muslim law reform invariably contends that his right, *inter alia*, to divorce unilaterally or to enter into plural marriage is sanctioned by *Quran* and it is a right guaranteed under the Constitution. A closer look, however, would reveal that these rights even according to religious law are not absolute rights. While the *Quran* sanctions polygamy it lays down certain conditions which have to be satisfied before such a right could be exercised. The verse[55] permitting polygamy is "marry of a woman who seem good to you, two, three, or four : and if ye fear that ye cannot do justice (to so many) then one (only) or (the captives) that your right hands possess. Thus, it is more likely that ye will not do injustice". Taking the proviso "if ye fear that ye cannot do justice then only one . . ." as a positive injunction and not merely a declaratory order, all the Arab countries[56] have restricted polygamy. The verse permitting polygamy was revealed to prophet at a time when, due to holy wars many women became widows and children orphans. In order to protect them the *Quran* gave permission to marry more than one wife in the interest of the widows and orphans. Judging from the circumstances under which the verse was revealed and the conditions which enjoins upon a person before he can have more than one wife, it can safely be concluded that the right to plural marriages is not a privilege nor an absolute right.

Also, the right to divorce the wife unilaterally was never meant to be an absolute right. Muhammad Ali[57] points out that the impression that a Muslim husband may put away his wife at his caprice is a grave distortion of the Islamic institution of divorce. While the *Quran* sanctions divorce being pronounced by the husband, certain limitations are placed upon the exercise of this right. As stated earlier,[58] the *Quran* lays down specific procedure to be followed before the parties can obtain divorce. The disputes between the husband and the wife are to be referred to judges from the respective people of the two parties. The judges are required to effect reconciliation between the spouses. If reconciliation is not possible then divorce can be obtained.

There are several other restraints placed upon the power of the husband to pronounce divorce.[59] For example, when the wife is divorced irrevocably, the husband cannot marry her unless the wife has been married to a third person and is divorced by him after having sexual connection with her. This is called *halala*. Further, the delegated divorce (*talaq altawfid*) provides that the wife can, at the time of entering into a marriage-contract, stipulate for the right of divorce from the husband in the event of his marrying a second wife or upon the happening of a specified event. Thus commenting upon the nature of the Muslim husband's right to pronounce divorce (*talaq*) Abdur Rahim observes :[60]

> If the exercise of a particular right is likely to lead to abuses, the law would guard against such a contingency by imposing conditions and limitations. There are certain limitations imposed by the law upon the right of the husband to dissolve the marriage.

The Indian courts have never been faced with such a challenge based on religious scriptures. Nevertheless, should reforms be introduced in future, the courts might be confronted with a more sophisticated argument pleaded successfully by the "conscientious objectors" in the American courts.

While the Indian courts are still wrestling with the problem of distinguishing the extraneous and unessential from the essential and integral parts of the religion, the American courts have been faced with the challenging task of freeing the religious belief from orthodox or parochial dogmas. A brief reference to some of these cases may help us in appreciating the further nuances and subtleties that the Indian courts might be called upon to decide in the future. Inasmuch as the Indian courts have frequently drawn inspiration from the American judiciary in the past, it is not unlikely that in the context of Muslim law reform the Indian courts might seek assistance from American pronouncements and redefine the concept of religious belief itself.

In a series of decisions[61] handed down by the United State's Supreme Court over conscientious objection petitions involving the question of refusal to participation in war, it had occasion to interpret section 6(j) of the Military Training Act that exempts from military service persons who by reason of "religious training and belief" are conscientiously opposed to war in any form, that term being defined as "belief in relation to a Supreme Being involving duties superior to those arising from human relations but not including essentially political, sociological or philosophical views or a merely personal code". In *U.S.* v. *Seeger*,[62] and *Welsh* v. *United States*[63] the court refused to confine that term to "orthodox and parochial religious beliefs". The conscientious objector's "sincere and meaningful belief which occupies in the life of its possessor a place parallel to that filled by God" would be sufficient. The court in fact went further to add that the sincerity of the belief must be determined by reference to the registrant's "own scheme of things". In other words, the court must judge whether the belief plays the role of religion and functions as a religion in the registrant's life.

The Indian courts might be faced with what one might call "a conscientious objector" to Muslim law reform. That is, the objector might challenge progressive legislation denying him the scripturally upheld right of polygamy and unilateral divorce on the ground that his sincerely held belief which parallels belief in God, in his "own scheme of things" militates against the said change. The court, in such a situation might have to draw a line between a liberal interpretation in the interest of expanding individual religious freedom that prejudices law reform and a restrictive interpretation that sanctions the reform.[64]

It is not difficult to predict what stand the Supreme Court would take if Muslim law reforms are objected to on grounds similar to that advanced in the American law. For, the Supreme Court has already rejected the definition of religion given by the American Supreme Court in *Davies* v. *Beason*.[65] In that case it was held that "the term 'religion' has reference to one's views of his Creator and the obligations they impose of reverence for His Being and character and of obedience to His will". While refusing to follow this definition the Supreme Court observed :[66]

We do not think that the above definition can be regarded

> as precise or adequate . . . We have great doubt whether a definition of "religion" given above could have been in the minds of our Constitution-makers when they framed the Constitution . . . A religion undoubtedly has its basis in a system of beliefs or doctrines which are regarded by those who profess that religion as conducive to their well being, but it would not be correct to say that religion is nothing else but a doctrine or belief.

Thus the Indian courts are not likely to be influenced by a broader definition of religion[67] adopted by the American Judiciary. This, it is submitted, would support Muslim law reforms.

Another possible, albeit not very forceful, argument that may be raised against reform of Islamic law in India is that such an effort by the legislature will infringe the cultural rights guaranteed by the Constitution. Article 29(1) of the Constitution provides:

> Any section of the citizens residing in the territory of India or any part thereof having a distinct language, script or culture of its own shall have the right to conserve the same.

The argument, it seems, is put forward by mistakenly identifying the practices of polygamy and the right of unilateral divorce exclusively with Muslim culture. The question whether reform of Muslim personal law violates the constitutional provision depends on whether the cultural identity of Muslims in India depends solely or partly upon their religious law. It may be pointed out that Muslims in India are not a unicultural community. Their cultural symbols and practices widely differ according to their regional location, historical background and social status. The attack on reforms on the ground of cultural identity is based on the unfounded assumption and misguided premise that ignore these wide cultural variations among Muslims. A large section of Muslim males is too sophisticated to exercise polygamy, and still a larger section is economically too poor to afford this luxury ! In fact, exercise of polygamy by a Muslim individual is viewed and accepted by Muslim society rather critically and almost disapprovingly. Being an exception in its recurrence and regarded as of doubtful social moral quality, polygamy is not a communally shared cultural value of Muslim community. As rightly argued by Mohammad Ghouse,[69] neither polygamy nor unilateral right to divorce can be identified with Muslim culture. Therefore, reform of Islamic law in India will not be unconstitutional.

NOTES AND REFERENCES

1. For the theory of infallibility of *Sunna* see Schacht, *Origins of Muhammadan Jurisprudence* 23 (1950).
2. According to western notions also there is the immutable theory of natural law, Cicero says:

   There is indeed a true law (lex), right reason, agreeing with nature, diffused among all men, unchanging, everlasting. . . the same law, everlasting and unchangeable, will bind all nations at all times. . . Cicero, DeRepublica, III, 22-23 as quoted in Salmond, *Jurisprudence* 16, N. (v) (12th ed. 1966).
3. The word *Sharia* originally meant the path or track by which camels were taken to water, and so by transfer the path ordained of God by which men may achieve salvation. See Fitzgerald, *Nature and Sources of the Sharia*, 1 Law in the Middle East 85, 86 (1955).
4. Gibb, *Modern Trends in Islam*, 87 (1947).
5. 1 Austin *Lectures on Jurisprudence* 90-91 (1879). See further W. Jethro Brown, *Austinian Theory of Law* 4-7 (1906).
6. For a detailed account of reforms in major Muslim countries see Anderson, *Islamic Law in the Modern World* (1959); see further the following by the same author : *The Significance of Islamic law in the world today*, 9 Am. J. Com. L. 187 (1960); *Reforms in Family Law in Morocco, 2 Jl. of African Law* 145 (1958) ; see also Tahir Mahmood, *Family Law Reform in the Muslim World* (1972).
7. Saba Habachy says :

   Hence, a body of positive legislation has grown up in every Moslem country side by side with the sacred law. And since *Umayyad* Dynasty came into power in 40 A.H. (661 A.D.), the rules of the Islamic community have pursued a *Siassa Madina* or secular policy as opposed to the *Siassa Sharia* or policy of divine origin. Since that date the Islamic theocracy has existed only in theory as an ideal, a city of God, to use the expression of St. Thomas. Habachy, *Islam: Factors of Stability and Change*, 54 Columbia L. Rev. 710 at 717-18 (1954).
8. Abdur Rahim, *Principles of Muhammadan Jurisprudence* 336 (1911).

9. Tyabji, *Muslim Law*, Sec. 130 (4th ed. 1968). According to *Shafai* law, *talaq* pronounced in the state of intoxication is not valid.
10. Abdur Rahim, supra note 8 at 337.
11. Ibid. at 337.
12. See Anderson, *Islamic Law in the Modern World* 56 (1959).
13. See the Code of Personal Status, 1959 Art. 35(I) in Anderson, *A Law of Personal Status for Iraq*, 9 Int. & Comp. L.Q. 542, 553 (1960).
14. See the Syrian Law of Personal Status, 1953, Arts. 89(1) in Anderson, *Islamic Law in the Modern World* 39 (1959).
15. See the Moroccan Code of Personal Status 1958, Arts. 49 & 89(I) in Anderson, supra note above at 56.
16. See the Tunisian Code of Personal Status 1957 in Anderson, *The Tunisian Law of Personal Status*, 7 Int. & Comp. L.Q. 262 (1958).
17. Anderson, supra note above at 271.
18. Ibid. at 272.
19. Sec. 7(3)(5) of The Muslim Family Laws Ordinance, 1961.
20. See Maitland, *Equity* 3 (2d rev. ed. 1949).
21. See Coulson, *A History of Islamic Law*, 185 (1964).
22. *Tachyyur* is the Arabic term for the process of selection. See Coulson, Ibid. at 185.
23. See Fyzee, *Outlines of Muhammadan Law* 35 (1964): For the doctrine of *Taqlid* and its related questions see Abdur Rahim, *Muhammadan Jurisprudence* 171-172 (Reprint 1958).
24. As regards Egypt, the movement of reform was initiated as early as in 1898 by the great jurist Muhummad Abduh. Again in 1915 a committee composed both of *Ulema* and practising lawyers was set up under the chairmanship of Mustaffa'l Maraghi. It was only in 1917 that reforms in family law were actually promulgated. See generally Anderson, *Islamic law in the Modern World* (1959).
25. *Aga Mahomed* v. *Koolsoom Bee Bee*, 24 I.A. 196 (1897).
26. *Baker Ali* v. *Anjuman Ara Begun*, 30 I.A. 94 (1903).
27. See the observation of Govinda Menon and Ramaswami Gounder, JJ. in *K. Veerankutty* v. *P. Umma*, A.I.R. Mad. 515, 516 (1956). See also *Amad Giri* v. *Mst. Begha*, A.I.R. J. & K. I (1955).
28. *Abdul Khader* v. *Azzeera*, A.I.R. Mad., 27 (1944).
29. *Chandi* v. *Bandesha*, A.I.R. Bom., 131 (1961).
30. Mulla, *Principles of Mohammedan Law* 260-61 (1968), B.R. Verma, *Muslim Marriage and Dissolution* 162-63 (1971).
31. *Rasul Baksh* v. *Mst. Bholan*, A.I.R. Lah. 498 (1932).
32. See Government of India, Gazette Part V at 36 (1938).
33. See Abdur Rahim supra note 23 at 170.
34. *Khurshid Jan* v. *Fazal Dad*, P.L.D. Lah. 558 at 608-609 (1964).
35. *Ashrafalli Cassamalli* v. *Mahomedalli*, 48 Bom. L.R. 642 at 652 (1946).
36. See Daniel Latifi, *Change and the Muslim Law in Islamic Law in Modern India* 104-105 (Tahir Mahmood. ed. 1972).

37. Sir Syed, *Tahzib-al-Akhlaq* 120 as quoted in Daniel Latifi, Ibid. at 105.
37a. For a thorough analysis of the relationship between Articles 25 and 26, see P.K. Tripathi, Secularism : Constitutional Provisions and Judicial Review in *Secularim : Its Implications for law and life in India* p. 165, G.S. Sharma (ed.) *1961*.
38. See Seervai, *Constitutional Law of India* 480 (1967).
39. *Srinivasa Aiyer* v. *Saraswathi Amal*, A.I.R. Mad. 193 (1952).
40 *The State of Bombay* v. *Narasu Appa*, A.I.R. Bom. 85 (1952).
41. *Srinivasa Aiyer* v. *Saraswathi Ammal* supra note 39.
42. *Reynold* v. *U.S.* 98 U.S. 145 (1879).
43. *Ram Prasad* v. *State of U.P.*, A.I.R. All. 411 (1957).
44. *Commissioner of Hindu Religious Endowments* v. *Lakshmindra*, S.C.R. 1005 (1954).
45. Ibid. at 1024.
46. *Durgah Committee, Ajmer & Another* v. *Syed Hussain Ali & Others*, 1 S.C.R. 383 (1962).
47. Ibid. at 418.
48. *Lakshmindra's* case supra note 44.
49. Ibid. at 1025.
50. *Mohd. Hanif Quareshi* v. *The State of Bihar*, S.C.R. 629 (1959).
51. *Al-Marghinani*, The *Hedaya* or Guide 592 (Grady ed. 1870).
52. See supra note 50, at 651.
53. *Tilkayat Shri Govindlalji* v. *The State of Rajasthan*, 1 S.C.R. 561 (1966).
54. See Seervai, supra note 38, at 487.
55. The *Quran* Ch. IV. Verse 3.
56. For a thorough account of the reforms in the Arab Countries see Tahir Mahmood, *Family Law Reform in the Muslim World* (1972).
57. Maulana Muhammad Ali, *Divorce in Islam* 3 (the working Muslim Mission & Literary Trust, Surrey, England).
58. See Ch. 7, pp. 175-76
59. See Zafar, *Unilateral Divorce in Muslim Personal Law in Islamic Law in Modern India* 167, 169-173 (Tahir Mahmood ed. 1972).
60. Abdur Rahim, *Muhammadan Jurisprudence* 333 (1968).
61. See for example *United States* v. *Seeger* 380 U.S. 163 (1965); *Welsh* v. *United States* 398 U.S. 333 (1969).
62. *United States* v. *Seeger*, supra note above.
63. *Welsh* v. *United States*, supra note 61.
64. In deciding whether or not a restriction on particular religious practice is justified on grounds of public order, morality and health or for promoting social reforms, the task of the courts is to balance freedom of religion on the one hand and the social interest on the other. See Mohammed Imam, *The Indian Supreme Court and the Constitution* 171 (1968).

65. *Davies* v. *Beason*, 133 U.S. 333 (1890).
66. See *Lakshmindra's* case supra note 44, at 1023.
67. On the question whether broader view of religion should be taken, in the context of personal law reform, Ambedkar said:

    The religious conceptions in this country are so vast that they cover every aspect of life, from birth to death. There is nothing which is not religion and if personal law is to be saved, I am sure about it that in social matters we will come to a stand still. . . I personally do not understand why religion should be given this vast expansive jurisdiction so as to cover the whole of life and to prevent the legislature from encroaching upon that field. See 7 Constituent Assembly Debates 781 (1968).

68. See Mohammad Ghouse, *Personal Laws and the Constitution in India* in *Islamic Law in Modern India* 50, 55 (Tahir Mahmood ed. 1972).

Conclusion 9

APPLICATION OF ANGLO-AMERICAN EXPERIENCE TO INDIAN CONDITIONS

IN EMBARKING upon an enquiry as to the applicability of Anglo-American experience to Indian conditions, certain questions ought to be raised and answered. The questions to which we must address ourselves are these: has the divorce law in India passed or is it passing through the same evolutionary stages in its legal development as did the Anglo-American law ? Do the same causes of a revolutionized concept of divorce in the United States and England obtain in India today ? Along what lines did reform proceed in the Anglo-American system? Should India adopt similar reforms and if she does, must she borrow them bag and baggage, heart and soul from the West ?

In order to answer these questions it is necessary to make a brief digression into the course of level development of divorce law in the United States and England. The English law of divorce is a product of centuries of development within the common law traditions. The strong influence and the dominance of church over matrimonial matters did not facilitate the liberalization of divorce in England. One might have expected an earlier modernization of the idea of divorce in America than is witnessed in England, for the matrimonial law in America was not entrenched in the ecclesiastical moorings. Nevertheless, the impact of the colonial rule and the influence of the common law upon the institutions of the United States have been long lasting.[1] Naturally, therefore, divorce in America followed the same zigzag path of development which its counterpart followed in England.

This is not true in the Indian context, where the policy of the British was motivated by different considerations. They did not desire to cause any upheaval in the social conditions then prevailing in India. Their object was to facilitate trade and they had no desire to encroach upon the religious susceptibilities of their subjects. Thus, the impact of the British rule upon family institutions was minimal. Nevertheless, some laws were passed to meet the demands of the society. But the efforts, as stated by the Law Commission[2] for changes in personal law, were never positively encouraged and the steps taken in that direction were slow, halting and reluctant.

The Hindu law of divorce developed on similar lines as those in England. The doctrine of marriage, as propounded by the Canonical theory, did not recognize divorce for a long period of time in England. Similarly, according to the Hindu notions, marriage was regarded as a *Samskara*[3] (sacrament) and hence considered indissoluble. Divorce was not allowed by the traditional Hindu law. Law has always found some justification to dissolve the marriage. And, that justification was found by the ecclesiastical law in the "matrimonial wrong" committed by one spouse against the other. Just as the remedy of divorce was made available later and the grounds expanded in England, so also under the Hindu law, the remedy of divorce was recognized in some of the states[4] during the British administration of justice in India. Later, the grounds of divorce were expanded and the remedy made available to all Hindus when the Hindu Marriage Act was passed in 1955. The law of divorce, with some modification, was virtually lifted from the Matrimonial Causes Act, 1950 of England and engrafted onto the Hindu Marriage Act of 1955, in the same manner as the Protestant law of divorce was implanted into American soil. Thus, both in the Anglo-American system and the Indian system, divorce was historically based on the concept of "matrimonial wrong".

Then comes the second stage in the story of the legal development. It was realized both in England and America that there was a gap between the law as enacted and the actual practice. The grounds on which divorce was sought were regarded as "symptoms" and not the "real causes". This state of unrealistic law caused dissatisfaction among the people. The hypocrisy and the perjury revealed in divorce proceeding gave further stimuli to modernizing the law. Although, in the United States, the two non-fault grounds, namely, living separate and apart, and incompatibility, were recognized in the framework of fault-oriented divorce law, they proved to be inadequate due to changes in the social conditions. The necessity to alter the very basis upon which dissolution of marriage should take place became apparent. A more realistic approach to solving marital problems was adopted. Thus the concept of breakdown was received in American law.

Both in England and the United States public opinion has greatly influenced civil legislation. The advocacy of reformers, such as Bentham[5] and Milton[6], opened the doors for secularizing of divorce. Also, in India, great reformers such as Mahamohapadaya, Iswar Chander and Ganganath Jha advocated comprehensive reforms.[7] When the British rule came to an end, the Indian leaders soon became aware of the demands of a modern and democratic society. Codification of Hindu law was achieved.[8]

Revision of laws is an indispensable process in any dynamic society. The Law Commission has recently observed :[9]

> With the changing times, notions of fairness and justice assume newer and wider dimensions, and customs and beliefs of the people change. These, in turn, demand changes in the structure of law; every progressive society must make a rational effort to meet these demands. Between the letter of law and the prevailing customs and the dictates of the current value-system accepted by the community, there should not be an unduly long gap.

The Hindu Marriage Act, 1955 has been in operation for about twenty five years now. It has become clear from the reported cases that married couples have often invented false grounds for divorce in order to circumvent the stringency of the law. Many of the reported cases supply us with ample evidence of the manner in which litigation is brought to the court. A few illustrations would be sufficient to appreciate how far law is removed from social realities.[10]

In *S. Chatterjee* v. *Nilima Chatterjee*,[11] the husband filed a petition for divorce alleging adultery of the wife with different persons on diverse occasions. The facts of the case, briefly stated, were as follows. The parties were married for more than twenty-five years and were in their early fifties. They had several grown up children. The wife charged the husband with having illicit relations with several women. She had written a filthy letter to the husband while he was in England for higher studies in medicine. On the other hand, the husband alleged that the wife was a nymphomaniac and he had been putting up for a long time with her sexual lapses. The husband threatened to sue for divorce. The relations between them became seriously estranged. Subsequently, one of the daughters brought a suit against her father (petitioner in the divorce suit) alleging rape on her. The father was acquitted in due course. The petitioner alleged that the wife was instrumental in bringing the suit against him for such a serious offence with a view to forestalling his action for divorce. However, it was found by the court that the four direct acts of adultery the petitioner charged his wife with were false. The petition for divorce was, therefore, dismissed. The husband in this case, as stated by the court, filed the petition to take revenge upon his wife. He was desperately trying to get rid of the wife and the wife was bent upon continuing the marriage relationship. It is difficult to see how in a situation like the one presented by this case, the court could have reacted in a different manner. For, the law requires the petitioner to prove the "guilt" of the respondent and when—and only when—he could prove the "guilt" that a court is authorized to dissolve the marriage. This has been the sad story of many a matrimonial litigation in India where, despite the fact of marriage-breakdown, the law sanctions the continuance of conjugal life.

In *Bejoy* v. *Aloka*,[12] the husband filed a petition for restitution of conjugal rights against his wife who was living with her parents. Earlier, he had filed a petition for judicial separation alleging desertion on the part of the wife. The suit was subsequently withdrawn. The husband sent letters one after another asking the wife to return the ornaments and other articles given to her by his people. He threatened her with dire consequences if his demands were not met. On one occasion he went to the wife's place and assaulted her brother. He made wild allegations of adultery of the wife and referred to her as a prostitute. Before proceeding with the petition, the court called the parties to effect a reconciliation. The husband was willing to reconcile but the wife was adamant. She expressed a fear, because of the husband's past conduct, that he would bring a divorce petition based on false allegations and that she did not trust the husband's word. The efforts at reconciliation failed. The court entered into the merits of the case with the following observation :[13]

> If Aloka is within her right to refuse to return to the matrimonial home, Bejoy is equally within his right not to go further than he has gone.

It was decided that the wife had reasonable cause[14] to withdraw from the society of the husband and hence the petition for restitution failed. The real cause which prompted the husband, as evidenced by the report, was that the husband did not get the dowry as promised to him. By filing a petition for restitution he was preparing to obtain a divorce in due course.

In *Narayan Ganesh* v. *Sucheta Narayan*,[15] the parties were married in 1957 and two daughters were subsequently born in 1957 and 1959. Just before the third daughter was born, relations between the parties became estranged and they lived separately from each other from March 1961. The husband filed a petition in 1962, praying in the first instance, for a declaration to annul the marriage on the ground of fraud.[16] It was alleged that the respondent was suffering from schizophrenia and was treated in a mental hospital. These facts were suppressed from the petitioner before he gave his consent to marry the respondent. In the alternative, the husband prayed for a decree of divorce on the ground that his wife was of unsound mind for a continuous period prescribed by the Act.[17] Finally, the husband asked for a decree of judicial separation[18] on the ground of his wife's cruelty. The wife denied all the charges. The trial court refused the decree of nullity and divorce but granted the decree of judicial separation. The wife appealed against this decree. The husband too appealed against the decree which denied annulment of the marriage and divorce. The appellate court allowed the wife's appeal and set aside the decree of judicial separation granted in favor of the husband by the trial court.

The husband appealed to the High Court against this order. It was found that the allegation made against the wife that she was suffering from schizophrenia was baseless. The evidence also disclosed that the husband was more particular about getting a divorce than to prove cruelty and obtain a decree of judicial separation. The real cause for this matrimonial litigation was incompatibility of temperament between the parties. The husband, a highly placed government officer, expected his wife to "yield to the norms set up by him in his household". The wife, who was also a science graduate, tried her best to come up to the "meticulous standards" set by the husband. The litigation lasted for almost six to seven years. The courts tried to effect reconciliation between the parties but their efforts were of no avail. The marriage had utterly broken; yet it was allowed to continue because the petitioner could not prove the grounds which could have entitled him to obtain a divorce.

A peculiar feature of Indian society is that most wives, after their marriage, have to live with the parents of the husband and his near relatives such as brothers and sisters. Living in a joint family often creates tentions and give rise to quarrels between the wife and the husband's relations. There are numerous cases where the wives had to leave the matrimonial home due to family feuds.[19] Husbands, too, drive away the wives and file a petition for restitution of conjugal rights with an ulterior motive to obtain divorce.[20] In *Sadhu Singh* v. *Jagdish Kaur*,[21] the wife was given "obnoxious, intolerable and inhuman" treatment by her in-laws. She was turned out from the matrimonial home. The husband's conduct was also blameworthy. He made wild allegation against the wife of perverse sex relations with a woman who was a close friend of the wife. The husband filed a petition for restitution of conjugal rights with a view to obtaining divorce. His petition was dismissed.

In a number of cases the remedy of restitution of conjugal rights has been used by the husbands as a defense to escape the liability of maintaining their wives.[22] For example, in *Teja Singh* v. *Sarjit Kaur*,[23] the wife left her husband's house and lived with her parents for about 6 to 7 years. During that period, the husband did not provide her maintenance nor cared to bring her back. When the wife obtained an order from the court for maintenance, the husband instituted the petition for restitution to avoid the liability imposed by the decree. Similarly, in *Gurcharan Singh* v. *Smt. Waryam Kaur,*[24] the wife left the matrimonial home due to the husband's ill-treatment. The husband neglected her and did not ask his wife to return. The wife applied for maintenance against her husband. The very next day she was confronted by the petition for restitution of conjugal rights.

These are but few illustrations of the extent to which the provisions of the Hindu Marriage Act, 1955 have been abused. Clash of personalities, incompatibility of temperament, irreconcilable differences and marital discord are the real causes which have led the spouses to invoke, in vain, the provisions of the law in an effort to terminate their marital tie. Since they could not prove the existence of the specific ground, as in most cases it was faked;[25] they could not succeed in dissolving the marriage. Courts too cannot be blamed for refusing to dissolve the marriage, for, what they are called upon to administer is a divorce law which is mainly based upon the commission of a particular matrimonial wrong and not upon the breakdown theory.

Factual separation in both English and the American systems has been regarded as a good indication that a marriage is not viable. This is particularly true when the period of separation is long enough and when the prospects of reconciliation between the parties are remote. The phenomenon of separation and marriage breakdown seems to be universal. India is no exception to this. There are innumerable cases of desertion and separation. The parties simply live separate and apart without any intention of continuing cohabitation. What most wives are interested in, is to merely obtain maintenance from their husbands and continue their marital status. In all these cases there is obviously a breakdown of marriage. Divorce on the ground of separation will certainly be a great disadvantage to the Indian wives. Apart from the economic hardships involved in the dissolution of marriage, a divorced woman in India, even if shebe young or comparatively beautiful, has little or practically no chance of remarriage.[26] But the question is : should economic hardship or the remoteness of the possibility of remarriage be a sufficient justification to continue dead marriges ?

The problem as pointed out by Rheinstein[27] is not of divorce but of marriage breakdown. True, law cannot control the causes of separation nor cure the evils of marriage breakdown. But, it must recognize social realities. The law should concern itself with the phenomenon of breakdown of marriage rather than deal with problem of legal divorce. Continuance of broken marriages which have failed to achieve their objectives will do more harm than good to the society. Thus, seen in the context of "breakdown" the significance of marriage, as observed by Lord Walker:[28]

> . . . is life-long cohabitation in the home for the family. But when the prospect of continuing cohabitation has ceased the true view as to the significance of marriage seems to require that the legal tie should be dissolved. Each empty tie—as empty ties accumulate—adds increasing harm to the community and injury to the ideal of marriage.

It is for the reasons stated above that the present writer finds a justification for the adoption of breakdown standard as the basis for a new divorce law in India.

When we choose this approach, the immediate question that confronts us is as to how to inject the principle of breakdown into the Indian divorce law. Should breakdown be added as an additional ground to the existing fault grounds as has been done in Canada or under some of the jurisdictions in the United States ? Or, should breakdown become the sole ground for divorce? Should we follow the English model or adopt the approach of the Uniform Marriage and Divorce Act ?

As respects the question whether the ground of breakdown should exist alongside the conventional grounds, it must be emphasized that our preference to adopt the breakdown approach was to eliminate hostility and perjury from divorce law and to dissolve the marriage when it has ceased to function. By retaining the fault-oriented grounds we will not achieve these objectives. Further, the old doctrine, which allows divorce only to the innocent party and denies the same to the guilty, existing side by side with the doctrine which allows divorce irrespective of the guilt of either party, will result in an anomaly. When the same question arose in the context of the English law reforms it was observed by the Archbishop's Group:[29]

> The existing law is almost entirely based on the assumption that divorce ought to be seen as just relief for an innocent spouse against whom an offence has been committed by the other spouse. If then there were inserted into this law an additional clause enabling a guilty spouse to petition successfully against the will of an innocent, the whole context would proclaim the addition unjust. Conversely, if the legislature came to the conclusion that it was right and proper to grant divorce, on the petition of either party and without proof of any specific offence, when—and only when—a marriage was shown to have broken down irreparably, how could it justify retaining grounds which depended on the commission of specific offences, on which only injured party might petition, and which required no evidence of breakdown at all ?

Indian law is in no way different from the earlier English law in this regard. The grant of a divorce is seen as a just relief for an innocent spouse against whom an offence has been committed by the other spouse. Therefore, the logical inconsistency pointed out by the Archbishop Group applies with equal strength to Indian law. One might, as a tactical move, suggest mere addition of the non-fault grounds of breakdown to the existing law in order to satisfy conservative opinion. But the real progress toward reforms which we are contemplating will not be achieved by adopting such a procedure.

The next question would be: whether to follow the English model or adopt the American approach to breakdown. In the former, as we noticed earlier, breakdown is introduced by means of certain facts closely resembling the prior fault grounds. To reduce the principle of breakdown with reference to a set of specific circumstances would rob the doctrine of its flexibility. The courts would tend to establish breakdown within the characteristic verbal formula and try to see whether the case fits into it rather than investigate whether in fact there has been a breakdown of the marriage. Particularly if we adopt the first two guidelines provided under the Divorce Reform Act, 1969, administration of divorce will tend to become highly technical. It is for these reasons that we must discard the technique adopted by the English statute. Instead, we may follow the Uniform Marriage and Divorce Act. Breakdown should be defined with reference to a "living apart" period and a general rule. To obtain further proof of breakdown, a clause as enacted under the Uniform Marriage and Divorce Act[30] which provides that "A finding of irretrievable breakdown is a determination that there is no reasonable prospect of reconciliation" may be included. A combination of the "living separate and apart" provision with a general rule supported by the proof of non-reconciliation between the parties is perhaps the best approach to introducing the breakdown principle into the Indian divorce law.

When we advocate the adoption of a breakdown standard we must not forget the fact that under its scheme divorce could be forced upon an unwilling party. To guard against the eventuality and protect the weaker party—the innocent wife—we must incorporate ample safeguards. If fault were to be eliminated as the basis for granting divorce, lack of fault must be raised to the level of legitimate consideration in granting alimony and making property awards.[31] This is of utmost importance particularly from the Indian standpoint, as a majority of Indian wives are economically dependent upon their husbands unlike their counterparts in England or America.

We have several alternatives for the protection of economic interest of the affected party. One way to deal straight with the problem is to make the decree of divorce conditional upon the petitioner satisfying reasonable financial obligations toward the other party. The other alternative is to incorporate a financial hardship clause as has been done in England. The financial hardship clause should not operate as an absolute bar. Instead, it should operate only as a discretionary bar. For in the majority of the cases involving divorce petitions the defense of grave financial hardship would be available to the wives. By enacting an absolute bar much of the reform we would have achieved would be watered down.

One of the most difficult problems involved in a no-fault divorce proceedings is, therefore, the adjustment of economic rights to protect the spouse against whom a divorce is granted. Let us look at the Uniform Marriage and Divorce Act and see how this problem has been handled.

Under the Act[32] all property acquired by either spouse in any manner is regarded as "marital property". The court is first directed to divide the community property, without regard to marital misconduct, in just proportions after considering all the relevant factors including the contributions of each spouse, the value of the property set apart to each spouse, the duration of the marriage and the economic circumstances of each spouse.[33] The other factors that the court is required to take into account are the contribution of a spouse as homemaker and the desirability of awarding the spouse having the custody of the children, the family home or the right to live therein for a reasonable period. Under the Act, each party is entitled to his or her separate property.

After assigning the marital property, the court is then required to grant a maintenance for either spouse only if it finds that the spouse seeking maintenance: [34]

(1) lacks sufficient property to provide for his reasonable needs; and
(2) is unable to support himself through appropriate employment or is the custodian of a child whose conditions or circumstances make it appropriate that the custodian not be required to seek employment outside the home.

When the abovementioned conditions are satisfied, the court grants the maintenance as it deems just after considering all relevant factors. Here too, the court will consider factors such as the financial resources, the duration of the marriage, the standard of living established during the marriage and the time necessary to acquire sufficient education or training to enable the party seeking maintenance to find appropriate employment.

It may be pointed out that under the Act the power of the

court to deal with the separate property of the spouses is eliminated while making property dispositions. The court is directed to deal with the community property only. The elimination of the traditional discretionary power of the court has been criticised: First, because the UMDA tries to impose the community property concept upon the non-community property states. Secondly, because it is considered as unfair to the spouse who enters the marriage with little property and established a standard of living based upon that property.[35] The Family Law Section of the American Bar Association[36] has strongly objected to the provision which calls the court to deal with the marital property only. Instead, it proposes that the court be given wide discretionary power to make equitable and just division between the spouses of their joint and separate estates.

In India, courts are left without any concrete guidelines in the task of evolving meaningful property and financial settlement when a marriage has reached its terminal stage.[37] The community property concept does not exist in Indian law. Therefore, judging from the social conditons prevalent at the present time, the principle laid down by the UMDA cannot be followed in India. Instead, the principle envisaged under the proposed draft of the Family Law Section would suit the Indian conditions. By providing suitable guidelines and authorizing the court to deal with the separate as well as other property, howsoever acquired by the spouses, the court would be in a better position to adjust the economic rights of the parties in a more equitable and just way. After all, the financial settlement between the parties cannot be made with mathematical precision. What the court is called upon to do is to effect a fair and equitable disposition of the property so far as it is possible in a particular situation.

In order to secure maintenance and alimony under the existing law a spouse must initiate a separate suit under the general law. Particularly, wives have found it extremely difficult to get the maintenance decrees executed against defaulting husbands. The procedural delays cause extreme hardships for most wives and should be altered. We may adopt a more effective procedure for payment of support and maintenance through the use of officer of the court and for enforcement of the court's decrees by the appropriate prosecuting attorney. We may follow the Uniform Marriage and Divorce Act model[38] which can usefully serve Indian needs. Under that scheme, the court is made a trustee for the person entitled to receive payment. The court can order that the maintenance allowance or alimony be paid to an officer of the court, who will record the payments made or arrears due from the judgment-debtor. In a case of default, the officer would serve the defaulter a registered notice demanding payment and in case of non-compliance, would notify the prosecuting attorney. Thereupon, the prosecuting attorney shall initiate contempt proceedings against the defaulter. The prosecuting attorney shall assist the court on behalf of the spouse entitled to receive maintenance to enforce compliance of the decrees.

As an additional safegurad, provision may be made authorizing a court to order the person obligated to pay maintenance and alimony to make an assignment of a part of his earning to the party entitled to payment. The court may also insist, if necessary, that the obligor may provide a suitable security for discharging his financial obligations.

All financial matters could be settled before the grant of the decree of dissolution. The issue of custody of the children could also be decided beforehand. Since more and more women are taking employment and have begun to earn, the possibility of introducing, a "community property" concept may be investigated. The idea of marriage insurance or divorce insurance, call it by whether name, must be considered. The scheme, broadly speaking, may operate somewhat on the following lines. The law can provide for a compulsory insurance at the time parties are married. In the event of divorce the benefits under the policy may be sanctioned in favor of the respondent. This may act as a deterrent or check on the petitioning spouse. Detailed mechanics can be worked out in cases where the parties have contributed towards the premiums of the insurance policy.

There have been two reform movements in the area of divorce in United States and England. First, the recognition of the breakdown of marriage as a basis for dissolution; secondly, the establishment of Family courts[39] and the provision of reconciliation services. When we import the concept of breakdown from the Anglo-American law, we must also make suitable alternative arrangements in the procedural law. Suggesting changes in the substantive law without a corresponding change in the procedure would be like enacting Hamlet without the Prince of Denmark. As stated by Llewellyn,[40] "technique without ideals is a menace . . . ideals without technique are amass".

When a marital relationship has to be terminated on the principle of breakdown, reconciliation and counseling processes have to be strengthened. Under the existing law a duty is cast upon the judges in every case where it is possible to do so consistently with the nature and circumstances of the case to make every endeavour to bring about a reconciliation between the parties.[41] At present the judges have to hear both civil and criminal litigation. They are so burdened with the pressure of work that it could hardly be expected of them to discharge this additional onerous duty.[42]

It has been the experience in the United States that many divorce actions are dropped before trial.[43] This is often due to the counseling efforts and the waiting period provided under the law before a final decree of divorce is granted. One of the important procedural changes that must be effected under the no-fault divorce law in India is to provide for such a procedure allowing the parties to consider, before obtaining a final divorce, what lies ahead of them and their childern. As we have seen, such waiting period has been provided in almost all the no-fault divorce statutes in the United States.

Under such a scheme the court, at the instance of the parties or on its own motion, refers the parties to counseling services. If within a certain period the parties have reconciled, the court will dismiss the petition. Otherwise, the parties may return to the court, ask for final relief. Under these circumstances, the court is more confident that the discord between the parties is serious enough to warrant a decree of divorce. Such a mechanism in the Indian no-fault divorce system will go a long way in furthering the true interests of the parties themselves and of the society at large.

In India, not only marriage counselling services are generally unavailable, there are not even Family courts[44] with special expertise to resolve family disputes. If we adopt the no-fault divorce law, it is imperative that we also establish Family courts. These courts must be provided with a small staff of social workers and experienced and trained counselors. In addition to this, the court should exploit the community resources. Quite often the estranged couple can be reconciled by the intervention of friends and relatives. The judges themselves can play an effective role in the reconciliation process given the time and necessary assistance.

Attorneys too can be of immense help. They should, with the cooperation of the court's staff or with the assistance of relatives and friends, try to effect a reconciliation between the parties. Because of the thorough knowledge of the facts and experience in public relations, the attorneys are well equipped to diagnose the real causes for which the parties want to separate and they can advise accordingly. Particularly, when children would be affected by the dissolution of the marriage, the attorneys can make the parties realize the seriousness of the consequences of divorce. Thus, in a no-fault system of divorce, attorneys would have to play a significant role in helping the parties adjust their relations.

The question whether provision for conciliation and counseling should be made compulsory or voluntary is rather a controversial one. The general opinion in the United States is that conciliation should not be made mandatory. It is because of this that the Uniform Marriage and Divorce Act does not provide for a mandatory conciliation. But proponents of compulsory conciliation seem to believe that if one out of 1,000 marriages could be saved its existence in a divorce statute would be justified. We may provide for mandatory conciliation to start with in India and see how it works in actual practice. In the light of experience we can either continue this procedure or make conciliation optional.

Provision may also be made, as has been done in the English statute,[45] requiring the advocate acting for the petitioner for divorce to certify to the court whether he has discussed with the petitioner the possibility of a reconciliation between the parties. To protect the interests of the minor children provision should be made, as has been done in the Uniform Marriage and Divorce Act,[46] authorizing the court to appoint an attorney to represent such children in a proceeding for dissolution of marriage. The appointment may be made by the court on its own motion or at the request of the parties. One further point in connection with the safeguards may be made. Under the existing law, no petition for divorce can be presented within one year of the solemnization of the marriage.[47] However, leave may be obtained to file the petition within one year if the case involves exceptional hardships to the petitioner or depravity on the part of the respondent. This rule which gives a fair trial to a marriage must continue. With the safeguards mentioned above, we can, without hesitation, adopt the breakdown approach to the marital dissolution.

Divorce by mutual consent has been incorporated in the Hindu Marriage Act, 1955 (Sec. 13B. Marriage Laws Amendment Act, 1976). As has been mentioned, mutual consent is a ground of divorce under the Special Marriage Act, 1954.[48] It is also a ground recognised under Islamic law. Custom permitting divorce by mutual consent is in vogue and valid under the Hindu Marriage Act.[49] Therefore, breakdown of marriage as a ground for divorce can exist alongside with this ground under Hindu law.

Article 44 of the Indian Constitution directs that the State shall enact a Uniform Civil Code for its citizens.[50] A uniform divorce law based on the concept of breakdown applicable to all the communities will, at least partly, contribute to further the cause of the Civil Code. At the same time, the absolute and unilateral power of the Muslim husband would be taken away. Also, the spurious customs of the Hindus to dissolve the marriage by setting up all kinds of customs of doubtful validity and the difficulty of proving its existence would be precluded under the proposed scheme.

But the crucial question is : how to bring about a change in the existing law. What steps ought to be taken in order to convince the reformers or the public of the beneficial effects of a no-fault divorce system? We have examined in the preceding chapter the obstacles that come in the way of reforms of personal laws relating to the two dominant communities in India—Hindus and Muslims. At least, the difficult and the complex problems that are attendant upon the reform of Muslim personal law do not seem to be present in respect of Hindu law reforms. For, both the Hindu law and the Hindu society have shown a remarkable tendency to adjust and adapt to the changing needs of time. This is evident from the fact that the customary law and practices of the Hindu community have been altered, modified and abrogated either by legislative interference or by judicial legislation from time to time.

While usage and customary practices of the Hindus which do not run counter to the general spirit of traditional law, were given full play during the British administration of justice, customary practices of the Muslim community which were at variance with Islamic law (*Shariat*) were abrogated by the *Shariat* Act, 1937.[51] As a result, Muslim law developed strictly as it ought to be, within the confines of Islam. The courts could not exercise the freedom of reinterpreting the original sources of *Sharia* (Islamic law). Whereas Hindu law progressed, though haltingly, adapting itself to the demands of the Hindu community. When India became independent, the reformers were able to achieve a great success in removing inequities and injustice from which the traditional Hindu law suffered in the area of family relations. But the same could not be done in respect of Muslim community. Muslims are a minority community and the Government could not take such liberty in altering their traditional law. Instead, it thought it best to leave to Muslims themselves the task of initiating the movement for reform. Accordingly, whereas, in the majority of the Muslim countries Islamic law has been altered to bring it in conformity with the changing needs of their societies, the same could not be done in India.

If one examines the development of Hindu law from this historical standpoint, it becomes clear that reforms in Hindu law are easier to effect than in Muslim law. Therefore, it is conceivable that changes in the divorce law of the Hindus are bound to occur. It is only a matter of time.

Be that as it may, a thorough empirical study of the law and practice of the divorce in the society should be undertaken as a first step toward reforms. It is not known what effect the decree of judicial separation has upon the separated spouses. The cases of desertion are assuming enormous propositions. How the spouses who have deserted or the spouses who have been deserted are adjusting to the circumstances is not known. Some light is thrown on the problem by reported cases that have arisen under the Hindu law. It is seen that husbands who have deserted their wives have either tried to contract a second marriage or have formed irregular unions.[52] There may be many more cases of bigamy which have not reached the courts. How many petitions for divorce or judicial separation are filed and in how many cases was the relief given or refused must be obtained. Such an empirical study can help us understand the undesirable effects of existing divorce laws and provide necessary insight for proposing further reforms.

India is passing through the same stages of industrial and economic development as the West had witnessed once. She is making great strides toward social advancement. Growing literacy among women has opened new avenues as well as challenges. Their role in a modern society is fast changing. These changes will naturally have far reaching effects on matrimonial relations. The Islamic law of divorce which entitles a Muslim husband to repudiate his wife unilaterally is against the *Quranic* injunctions and tradition (*Sunna*). Courts too have, of late, not hesitated to demonstrate their judicial fury against this law. For example, Khalid, J., has boldly declared:[53]

> Should Muslim wives suffer this tyranny for all times? Should their personal law remain so cruel towards these unfortunate wives? Can it not be amended suitably to alleviate their suffering? My judicial conscience is disturbed at this monstrosity. The question is whether the conscience of the leaders of public opinion of the community will also be disturbed.

The manner in which the provisions of the Hindu Marriage Act have been abused is an eloquent testimony to the distance between the law in the books and the law in action. In short, the divorce law in India has failed to cope with social realities. It is better for the courts under the existing circumstances to investigate the true causes of marital breakdown rather than ask the petitioner to prove adultery or desertion "beyond reasonable doubt".

In the final analysis the breakdown approach seems to be a better alternative to the problem of divorce. Its adoption into the divorce law in India has to be canvassed not because it is the panacea for divorce, but because its acceptance would entail a lesser evil.

NOTES AND REFERENCES

1. See generally Lawrence M. Friedman, *A History of American Law* (1973).
2. Law Commission of India, Fifty-Ninth Report on Hindu Marriage Act, 1955 and Special Marriage Act, 1954, para 1.14 at 9 (March 1974).
3. Kane, *History of Dharmasastra*, 2, part 1, 427, 620 (1941); Mayne, *Hindu Law* 101 (11th ed. 1953); *Sundrabai* v. *Shivnarayana*, 32 Bom. 81 (1908); *Krishna Chandra* v. *Emperor*, A.I.R. Cal. 214 at 217 (1937); *Gopala Krishna* v. *Venkatarasa*, 37 Mad. 273 (F.B.) (1914).
4. For example, Bombay Hindu Divorce Act, 1947; Madras Hindu (Bigamy Prevention and Divorce) Act, 1949.
5. Bentham, *Theory of Legislation* 387 (1931).
6. Milton, *Doctrine and Decipline of Divorce* (*Tetrachordon*) at 33-34 (1945).
7. See Derrett, *Religion, Law and the State in India* 327 (1968).
8. For a detailed account of the codification of Hindu Law, see Derrett, Ibid. at 321 et seq.
9. Supra note 2 para, 1.16 at 10.
10. It is not intended here to survey the plethora of cases that reveal the sad state of matrimonial litigation. An excellent account of the manner in which spouses have litigated for their matrimonial rights and remedies may be found in Derrett, supra note 7 (chapter entitled Aspects of Matrimonial Causes under the Hindu Code) at 352. See further by the same author, *Critique of Modern Hindu Law* 324, 436 (1970).
11. *S. Chatterjee* v. *Nilima Chatterjee*, 74 C.W.N. 168 (1969).
12. *Bejoy* v. *Aloka*, A.I.R. Cal. 477 (1969).
13. Ibid. at 478.
14. The Hindu Marriage Act, 1955 provides: Sec. 9.
    (1) When either the husband or the wife has, without reasonable excuse, withdrawn from the society of the other, the aggrieved party may apply, by petition to the district court, for restitution of conjugal rights and the court, on being satisfied of the truth of the statements made in such petition and that there is no legal ground why the application should not be granted, may decree restitution of conjugal rights accordingly.
15. *Narayan Ganesh* v. *Sucheta Narayan*, 71 Bom. L.R. 569 (1969).
16. The Hindu Marriage Act, 1955 provides *inter alia*: Section 12.
    (1) Any marriage solemnized, whether before or after the commencement of this Act, shall be voidable and may be annulled by a decree of nullity on any of the following grounds, namely:—
    * * * (a) and (b) omitted.
    (c) that the consent of the petitioner, or where the consent of the guardian in marriage of the petitioner is required under

Section 5, the consent of such guardian was obtained by force or fraud.

17. A marriage may be dissolved by a decree of divorce on the ground that the other party has been incurably of unsound mind for a continuous period of not less than three years immediately preceding the presentation of the petition. See section 13(1)(iii) of the Hindu Marriage Act, 1955.
18. Sec. 10(1)(b) of the Hindu Marriage Act, 1955.
19. See for example, *Gurucharan Singh* v. *Waryam Kaur*, A.I.R. Punj. 422 (1960); *Smt. Putul Devi* v. *Gopi Mandal*, A.I.R. Pat. 93 (1963); *Smt. Mango* v. *Premchand*, A.I.R. All. 447 (1962).
20. *Joginder* v. *Pushpa*, A.I.R. P. & H. 397 (F.B.) (1969); *Sayal* v. *S.*, A.I.R. Punj. 489 (1968). If there has been no resumption of cohabitation between the spouses after the passing of the decree of restitution of conjugal rights for a period of two years or upwards, it is made a ground for divorce under Section 13(1A)(ii) of the Hindu Marriage Act, 1955.
21. *Sadhu Singh* v. *Jagdish Kaur*, A.I.R. Punj. 139 (1969).
22. For a good discussion on the subject, see Rajkumari Agarwala, *Restitution of Conjugal Rights Under Hindu Law : A Plea for the Abolition of the Remedy*, 12 J.I.L.I. 257 (1970). See further Derrett, supra note 7, at 371.
23. *Teja Singh* v. *Sarjit Kaur*, A.I.R. Punj. 195 (1962).
24. See *Gurucharan* case supra note 19.
25. See *Harbhajan Singh* v. *Brij Balab Kaur*, A.I.R. Punj. 359 (1964).
26. See Rajkumari Agarwala, *Changing Basis of Divorce and the Hindu Law*, 14 J.I.L.I. 431.441 (1973). While she admits, as it seems, that divorce on the ground of separation evidencing breakdown of marriage could replace the existing law, she seems to be hesitant to advocate for its adoption at the present time. She says: "Forced hurry in the matter may not be conducive because divorce has been recently introduced in Hindu law. Society ought to be given time to get accustomed and adjusted to new relief". Ibid. at 440.
27. See Rheinstein, *Marriage Stability, Divorce and the Law* 266 (1972).

    The law can preclude divorce but it cannot prevent factual marriage breakdown. The Law can deny freedom of remarriage, but it cannot thereby prevent a man and woman from living together in a union which may be called irregular but which may resemble matrimony in every respect except the absence of legal bond. All the divorce law can do is to prevent the transformation of the factual relationship of concubine into a legitimate marriage. Rheinstein, Ibid. at 277. See also Kahn-Freund, *Divorce Law Reform*? 19 M.L.R. 573, 576-77 (1956).
28. See Royal Commission on Marriage and Divorce, Cmnd. 9678, at 341 (1956).
29. Putting asunder, A Divorce Law for Contemporary Society, para 69 at 57 (S.P.C.K. 1966).

30. Sec. 305(c) of the Uniform Marriage and Divorce Act (hereinafter cited as the UMDA).
31. See Baer and Davis, *Merit in No Fault Divorce*, 60 Ill.B.J. 766 at 768 (1972).
32. UMDA, Sec. 307.
33. Ibid.
34. Ibid. Sec. 308(a)(1) and (2).
35. See Podell, *The Case for Revision of the Uniform Marriage and Divorce Act*, 18 S.D.L. Rev. 601, 607 (1973). See further note, *Property Maintenance and Child Support Decrees under the Uniform Marriage and Divorce Act*, 18 S.D.L. Rev. 559, 564 (1973).
36. See Sec. 307 of the Proposed Draft of the Family Law Section in 18 S.D.L. Rev. 700 (1973).
37. For a good discussion of the law on the subject see Ram Singh, *Matrimonial Property Law Among Hindus*, 6 J. Fam. L. 129, 149 (1966).
38. UMDA, Sec. 311.
39. For a detailed account of the system, structure and the working of the Family Courts in the United States, see Dyson and Dyson, *Family Courts in the United States*, 8 J. Fam. L. 507 (1968).
40. Llewellyn, *The Adventures of Rollo*, 2 U. Chi. The Law School Record, 3 at 23 (1952).
41. Hindu Marriage Act, 1955, Sec. 23(2).
42. Courts have no doubt tried to effect reconciliation but in almost all the cases their efforts have proved futile. This illustrates that marriages are usually broken down without any possibility of future reconciliation by the time the parties come to the court.
43. See Hansen, *The Role of Trial Judge in Reconciling Parties Headed for Divorce in Therapeutic Family Law* 272 (Nester C. Kohut ed. 1968).
44. In its recent report the Law Commission of India has recommended for the establishment of Family Courts in various states. See The Law Commission of India, Fifty-Ninth Report on Hindu Marriage Act, 1955 and Special Marriage Act, 1954, para 1.21 at pp. 12-13 (March 1974). The Commission has also suggested that the court may adjourn the divorce proceedings for a reasonable period not exceeding fifteen days and refer the parties to seek counseling. The court, on its own motion, can appoint persons to effect reconciliation between the parties. Based on the report of the counselors the court could dispose of the petition accordingly. Ibid. para, 8.24 at 82.
45. Divorce Reform Act, 1969, Sec. 3(1).
46. UMDA, Sec. 310.
47. Sections 14 and 29 of the Hindu Marriage Act, 1955 and Special Marriage Act, 1954, respectively.
48. Special Marriage Act, 1954, Sec. 28.
49. Hindu Marriage Act, 1955, Sec. 29(2).
50. For critical comments on the constitutional directive and the reforms

of Muslim Personal law, see, U. Baxi, Muslims law Reform, Uniform Civil Code and Crisis of Common Sense in *Family Law and Social Change*, (ed. Tahir Mohmood) (1975) see further for an excellent discussion on the subject Tahir Mohmood, Islamic law and the Debate on an Indian Civil Code in *Islamic and Comparative Law Quarterly*, Vol. I, 21 (1981).

51. The Muslim Personal Law (Shariat) Act, 1937 provides: Sec. 2. Notwithstanding any custom or usage to the contrary, in all questions . . . regarding interstate succession, special property of females . . . marriage, dissolution of marriage, including *talaq*, *ila*, *zihar*, *lian*, *khula*, and *mubaraat*, maintenance . . . the rule of decision in cases where parties are Muslims shall be the Muslim Personal Law (*Shariat*).

52. See for example, *Bhaurao Shanker* v. *The State of Maharashtra*, 67 Bom. L.R. S.C. 423 (1965); *Kanwal Ram* v. *H.P. Administration*, A.I.R. S.C. 614 (1966); *Rajula Vai* v. *Suka*, A.I.R. Madh. Pra. 57 (1972).

53. *Haneefa* v. *Pathummal Beevi*, K.L.T. 512 at 514 (1972).

Epilogue 10

RECENT DEVELOPMENT

THE LAW Commission in its seventy-first Report has recommended the adoption of irretrievable breakdown of marriage as a ground for divorce.[1] But unlike the English law which envisages marriage breakdown on the proving of any of the five facts, the Commission refers to only one fact for proving the breakdown of marriage, namely, that the parties have lived apart for a period of three years or more immediately preceding the presentation of the petition. While in England the "fault theory" has been replaced by the "breakdown theory" in the matter of divorce, the Law Commission recommends merely the adding of the irretrievable breakdown to the existing grounds under the Hindu Marriage Act, 1955.

According to the Law Commission there is "no inherent contradiction or fallacy in having both the new and the old grounds". It is stated that since no proof of irretrievable breakdown as a result of adultery, cruelty or desertion is required under its scheme the retention of the grounds based on "fault notion" would be in order. Furthermore, the Law Commission is of the view that since fault grounds have to be proved in order to get a decree of divorce, any additional proof of irretrievable breakdown would be improper. This, the Commission stated, would make the present provision more stringent.[2]

We have discussed and commented upon the question of retaining the "fault grounds" alongside with the breakdown ground in divorce law in American jurisdiction.[3] The rationale for not retaining the "fault-oriented" grounds in the U.S. or in Canada apply with equal force to Indian divorce law. The Law Commission disapproves of the divorce law based on "fault theory". It states that "because of the matrimonial offense, judges and lawyers are sometimes reduced to the role of scavengers. It is desirable to get rid of the public washing of dirty linen which takes place in long-drawn out cruelty cases or in cases based on fault".[4] But at the same time it retains the law based on matrimonial guilt. This, it is submitted with respect, defeats the object for which an amendment is recommended.

While introducing the "breakdown theory" into the divorce law, the Commission has rightly taken note of the necessity to protect the interest of the parties involved. It recommends that the court shall not pass a decree of divorce unless adequate provision for the maintenance of the children has been made. The recommendation also safeguards the interest of the wife. The wife is given the right to oppose the grant of a decree of divorce on the ground that dissolution would result in grave financial hardships to her.

In English law under the Divorce Reform Act, 1969 (which is embodied in the Matrimonial Causes Act, 1973) such a "hardship" clause exists. In that law as we have noticed, the wife is entitled to oppose the grant of divorce on two grounds: (1) grave financial hardships and (2) other hardships. But the Law Commission of India has discarded the second ground. The report states that the grant of the right to the wife to oppose divorce on the ground of "other hardships" would open the way for all kinds of pleas which might render divorce on marriage breakdown illusory in a large number of cases.[5]

It may be pointed out that even the right given to the wife to oppose divorce on the ground of grave financial hardships runs counter to the philosophy or ideal of marriage breakdown. It would be better to dissolve the marriage conditional upon the husband fulfilling his financial obligation towards the wife. The writer is in agreement with Kusum when she says that a better solution would be to make more effective provision for maintenance and security for the wife but in no case should the marriage which has broken down be compelled to linger on.[6]

At the time of going to press, a Bill has been introduced in the Lok Sabha to further amend the Hindu Marriage Act, 1955 incorporating irretrievable breakdown of marriage as a ground for divorce in add tion to the already existing grounds under the Act.[7]

The statement of objects and reasons of the Bill states that there has been a demand "from various quarters" for making breakdown of marriage as a ground for divorce. It mentions the recommendation made by the Law Commission in support of the inclusion of irretrievable breakdown of marriage as a cause for divorce. The Bill adopts *in toto* the recommendations of the Law Commission mentioned above.

There has not been any change in the substantive law of divorce in England since this work was completed. Nor is there any significant interpretation of the law relating to the breakdown of marriage. Most of the divorce petitions relate only to financial settlements and custody of children.

In the United States almost all the States except Illinois and South Dakota have either adopted the breakdown of marriage as a principal ground for divorce or have added this ground to the existing divorce law.

NOTES AND REFERENCES

1. See Law Commission of India, Seventy-first Report, 1978.
2. Ibid, at pp. 22-23.
3. See supra at pp. 113-114 and pp. 234-235.
4. Law Commission Report supra note 1 at pp. 14-15.
5. Ibid, at p. 38.
6. Kusum, *Irretrievable Breakdown of Marriage* 20, J.I.L.I. 188 at 302 (1978).
7. Lok Sabha Bill No. 23 of 1981 (Introduced on 27th February, 1981). The Bill also seeks to amend the Special Marriage Act, 1954 incorporating irretrievable breakdown of marriage as an additional ground for divorce. It may be pointed out that the Hindu Marriage Act was amended in 1976 adding two more grounds for divorce, i.e., divorce by mutual consent and in the case of a wife that the marriage was solemnized before she attained the age of 15 and she had repudiated the marriage after attaining the age of 15 and before 18 years. See the Marriage Laws (Amendment) Act, 1976, Sec. 13(1A)(2)(iv) and Sec. 13B.

Bibliography

Agarwala, Rajkumari, *Changing Basis of Divorce and Hindu Law*, 14 J.I.L.I. 431 (1973)

Agarwala, Rajkumari, *Restitution of Conjugal Rights Under Hindu Law : A Plea for the Abolition of the Remedy*, 12 J.I.L.I. 257 (1970)

Alexander, *Family Life Conference Suggested New Judicial Procedures and Attitudes Toward Marriage and Divorce* 32. J. Am. Jud. Society, 38 (1948)

Ali Ameer, *Mohammadan Law* (1917)

Ali Mohammed, *Divorce in Islam* (The Working Muslim Mission and Literary Trust, Survey England)

Al-Marghinani, *The Hedaya or Guide* (Hamilton Trons 2nd ed. 1870)

Al-Marghinani, *The Hedaya or Guide* (Grady ed. 1870)

America and English Encyclopaedia of Law 747 (1968)

Anderson, *Islamic Law in the Modern World* (1959)

Anderson, *A Law of Personal Status for Iraq*, 9 Int. and Comp. L.Q. 542 (1960)

Anderson, *The Tunisian Law of Personal Status* 7 Int. and Comp. L.Q. 262 (1958)

Anderson, *The Significance of Islamic Law in the World today*, 9 Am. J. Com. L. 187 (1960)

Asirvatham, *State and Social Legislation in India*, M.L.J. 239 (1941)

A Survey of Mental Cruelty as a ground for Divorce, 15 DePaul L. Rev. 159 (1965)

Baillie, Neil B.E., *A Digest of Muhammedan Law* (1957)

Barton, *Questions on the Divorce Reform Act, 1969*, 86 L.Q.R. 348 (1970)

Bates, *Divorce Reform in England*, 3 Tasmania Ul. Rev. 343 (1970)

Beamer, *The Doctrine of Recrimination in Divorce Proceedings*, 10 Kansas (City) L.Rev. 213 (1942)

Bear and Davis, *Merit in No Fault Divorce* 60 Ill. B.J. 766 (1972)
Bentham, *Theory of Legislation* (1931)
Biggs, *The Concept of Matrimonial Cruelty* (1962)
Bishop, J.P., *Marriage, Divorce and Separation* (1891)
Blake, N., *The Road to Reno* (1962)
Bodenheimer, *Reflections on the Future of Grounds for Divorce*, 8 J. Jam. L. 179 (1968)
Bodenheimer, *The New Canadian Divorce Law*, 2 Jam.L.Q. 213, (1968)
Bradway, *The Myth of the Innocent Spouse*, II Tulane. L. Rev. 377 (1927)
Brody, *California's Divorce Reform: Its Sociological Implications*, 1 Pac. L.J. 223 (1970)
Bromley, *Family Law* (1971)
Brown, W., Jethro, *Austinian Theory of Law* (1906)
Brown, Necille, *Cruelty without Calpability and Divorce without Fault*, 26 M.L. Rev. 625 (1963)
Brown, *The Act of 1969—The First Year*, 122 New L.H. 528 (1972)
Clark, *Divorce Policy and Divorce Reform*, 42 Colo.L. Rev. 403 (1971)
Clerk, H., *Law of Domestic Relations* (1968)
Cantor, *The Right of Divorce*, Atlantic Monthly, 67 (November 1966)
Cheshire, *The International Validity of Divorces* 61 Law Quarterly Rev. 352 (1945)
Cohen, *Divorce Reform—Another Point of View*, 47 Conn. B.J. 88 (1973)
Connell, Fredrick P.O., *Marriage, Divorce and the Uniform Marriage and Divorce Act*, 17 N.Y.L.F. 983 (1971)
Couch, *Toward a More Realistic Divorce Law*, 43 Jul. L.Rev. 43 (1969)
Coulson, *A History of Islamic Law* (1964)
Derrett, *Critique of Modern Hindu Law* (1970)
Derrett, *Divorce by Caste Custom*, 65 Bom. L.R.161 (1963)
Derrett, *Hindu Law Past and Present* (1957)
Derrett, *May a Spouse who is in Desertion obtain a divorce on the basis of his own wrong*? 70 Bom. L.R.H.117 (1968)
Derrett, *Matrimonial Freedom: A Step Toward in Bombay*, 77 Bom L.R.H. 8 (1975)

Derrett, J.D.M., *Religion, Law and the State in India* (1968)
Dicey, *Law Public Opinion in England During the Nineteenth Century* (1920)
Diwan Paras, *Modern Hindu Law* (1972)
Doppler, *American Needs Total Divorce Reform Now* (1973)
Dyson, *Family Courts in the United States*, 8 J. Jam. L., 507 (1968)
Fawcett, C., *First Century of British Justice in India* (1934)
Fellows, Alfred, *The Case Against the English Divorce Law* (1932)
Fitzgerlad, *Nature and Sources of the Sharia Law in the Middle East* (1955)
Flood, Don, *The Dissolution of Marriage* (1962)
Foote, Levy and Sander, *Cases and Materials on Family Law* (1971)
Foster and Freed, *The Divorce Reform Law* (1970)
Foster, *Divorce Reform and the Uniform Act*, 18 S.D.L. Rev. 572
Foster and Freed, *Divorce Reform: Brakes on Breakdown*, 13 H. of Jam. L. 443 (f.n. 30) (1974)
Foster and Freed, *Family Law Cases and Materials* (1972)
Freeman, *Adultery and Intolerability*, 35 M.L.R. 100 (1972)
Freeman, *The Search For a Rational Divorce Law*, 24 Cur. L. Prob. 178 (1971)
Freund, Kahn, *Divorce Law Reform*, 219 M.L.R. 573 (1956)
Friedman, M., *A History of American Law* (1973)
Fyzee, *Outlines of Muhemmadan Law* (1964)
Gallapher, *No Fault Divorce in Delaware*, A.B.A.J. 873 (1973)
Ghoeese, Mohammad, *Personal Law and the Constitution* in Tahir Mohmood (ed.), *Islamic Law in Modern India* 50 (1972).
Gibb, *Modern Trend in Islam* (1947)
Giesen, *Divorce Reform in Germany*, 7. Fam L.Q. 351 (1973)
Goddard, *A Report on California's New Divorce Law: Progress and Problems*, 6 Fam. L.Q. 405 (1972)
Goldsteen and Gitter, *On Abolition of Grounds for Divorce: A Model Statute and Commentary*, 3 Fam. L.Q. 75 (1969)
Goodhart, *Cruelty, Desertion and Insanity in Matrimonial Law*, 79 L.Q. Rev. 98 (1963)
Gorecki, Jan, *Divorce in Poland* (1970)
Graveson, R.H., *The Background of the Century in a Century*

of Family Law (1957)

Gupte, S.V., *Hindu Law of Marriage* (1961)

Habachy, *Islam: Factors of Stability and Change*, 54 Columbia L. Rev. 710 (1954)

Hall, *Matrimonial Cruelty and Mens Rea*, 104 Cambridge Law Journal 104 (1963)

Hansen, *The Role of Trial Judge in Reconciling Parties Headed for Divorce in Therapeutic Family Law* 272 (1968)

Hartley, C. Gasguoine, Divorce (Today and Tomorrow) (1957)

Hogoboom, *The California Family Law Act of 1970; 18 Months Experience*, 27 Mo. B.J. 584 (1971)

Holdsworth, I.W., *A History of English Law* (1936)

Honigman, *What No-Fault Means to Divorce Law*, 51 Mich. S.B.J. 16 (1972)

Howard, G.E., *History of Matrimonial Institutions* (1904)

Imam Mohammad, *The Indian Supreme Court and the Constitution* (1968)

Ingram and Ballard, *The Business of Migratory Divorce in Nevada*, 2 Law and Centem. Prob. 302 (1935)

Irreconcilable Differences; California Courts Respond to No-Fault Dissolutions, 7 Loyolo of Los Angles L. Rev. 453, (1974)

Iyanger, Srinivasa, *Hindu Law Reform*, M.L.J. 8 (1941)

Jacobson, Paul H., *American Marriage and Divorce* (1959)

Jackson, J., *The Formation and Annulment of Marriage* (1969)

Jolly, *Hindu Law and Custom* (1928)

Kane, L., *History of Dharmasastra* (1941)

King, *Marriage, Divorce and Custody Reform in South Dakota*, 18 S.D.L. Rev. 654 (1973)

Kitchin, B., *A History of Divorce* (1912)

Krom, *California's Divorce Law Reform : A Historical Analysis* 1 Pac. L.J. 156 (1970)

Lasch, *Divorce American Style*, N.Y. Rev. 3 (1966)

Law Commission, *Reform of the Grounds of Divorce : The Field of Choice*, Omnd. 3123, 16 (1966)

Latifi, Daniel, *Change and the Muslim Law in Tahir Mahmood* (ed.), I *Islamic Law in Modern India* 104 (1972)

Lecin, *The Divorce Reform Act, 1969*, 33 M.L.R. 632 (1970)

Lecin, *Marital Cruelty : New Wine in Old Bottles* 2 Fam. L.Q. 296 (1968)

Lee, B.H., *Divorce Law Reform in England* (1974)

Leo, Oregon, *No-Fault Marriage Dissolution Act*, 51 Ore. L. Rev. 715 (1972)

Levy, R., *Uniform Marriage and Divorce Legislation : A Preliminary Analysis* (1968)

Mackenna, *Divorce by Consent and Divorce for Breakdown of Marriage*, 30 M.L.R. 121 (1967)

Manchester, *Divorce and Grave Financial or Other Hardship*, 118 Sol. J. 193 (1974)

Mayne, J.D., *Hindu Law and Usage* (1953)

McAnerney and Schoonmaker, *Connecticut's New Approach to Marriage Dissolution*, 47 Conn. B.J. 475 (1973)

McCurdy, *Divorce : A Suggested Approach with Particular Reference to Dissolution for Living Separate and Apart*, 9 V. and L. Rev. 685 (1956)

McGregor, O.R., *Divorce in England* (1957)

Merll, H., *Section 305 : Genesis and Effect*, 18 S.D.L. Rev. 358 (1973)

Merrivale, Lord, *Marriage and Divorce* (1936)

Migratory Divorce : The Alabama Experience, 75 Harv. L. Rev. 568 (1962)

Milton, *Doctrine and Decipline of Divorce* (1945)

Mohmood Tahir, *Family Law Reform in Muslim World* (1972)

Moore, *An examination of the Recrimination Doctrine*, 20 S.C.L Rev. 685 (1968)

Moore, *A Critique of the Recrimination Doctrine*, 68 Dic. L. Rev. 157 (1964)

Moran, *Divorce for Incompatibility of Temperament*, 9 Duke B.A.J. 49 (1941)

Morley, W.H., *Administration of Justice in British India* (1958)

Morris, David, *The End of Marriage* (1979)

Moskin, Robert J., *Morality in America* (1966)

Mulla, *Principle of Mohemedan Law* (1972)

Neill, William L.W., *Divorce in the Progressive Era* (1967)

1971 Midyear Report and Recommendation of the Family Law Section to the ABA House of Delegates on the Uniform Marriage and Divorce Act, 5 Fam. L.Q. 133 (1971)

Orfield, *Divorce for Temperamental Incompatibility*, 52 Mich. L. Rev. 659 (1954)

Paulson and Walter Wadlington, Monrad G., *Statutory*

Materials on Family Law (1974)

Paulson, *Migratory Divorce* : Chapter III and IV, 24 Ind. L.J. 25 (1948)

Peters, *Towards Reforms of Marriage Termination*, 20 Drake L. Rev. 211 (1979)

Ploscowe, Morris, *A Modern Divorce and Judicial Separation Act for New York*, 30 Alabany L. Rev. 1 (1966)

Podell, Ralph J., *The Case for the Revision of Uniform Marriage and Divorce Act*, 18 S.D.L. Rev. 601 (1973)

Pollock, F. and Maitland, F., *The Law of Divorce* (1853)

Property Maintenance and Child Support Decrees Under the Uniform Marriage and Divorce Act, 18 S.D.L. Rev. 559 (1973)

Rahim, Abdur, *Mohammadan Jurisprudence* (1968)

Rankin, George, *Background to India Law* (1946)

Reforms of Family Law in Morrocco 2 Jl. of African Law 145 (1958)

Renton, A. Wood, and Phillimore, G., *The Comparative Law of Marriage and Divorce* (1910)

Rheinstein, *Divorce Around the World, in* Bohannan (ed.), *Divorce and After* 140 (1979)

Rheinstein, *Divorce Around the World*, in Bohannan, (ed.), *Divorce and After* 143 (1971)

Rheinstein, *Trends in Marriage and Divorce Law of Western Countries* 16 Law and Contem. Prob. 3 (1953)

Rosentaum, *Divorce Reform in England : The Decline of the Matrimonial Offense*, 12 J. Fam. L. 365 (1972-73)

Ricke, *The Dissolution Act of 1973 : From Status to Contract*, 49 Wash L. Rev. 375 (1914)

Rosenau, *Those "Quickie" Alabama Divorces*, 18 Ala. Lawyer, 37 (1957)

Ruskin and Katz, *The Dying Doctrine of Recrimination in the United States of America*, 35 Can. B. Rev. 1046 (1957)

Rutman, *Departure from Fault* 181, I.J. Fam. L. 183 (1961)

Saksena, K.P., *Muslim Law as Administered in India and Pakistan* (1963)

Sarkar, U.S., *Epochs in Hindu Legal History* (1958)

Sass, *The Iowa No-Fault Dissolution of Marriage Law in Action*, 18 South Dakota L. Rev. 629 (1973)

Saul, *Proof of a No-Fault Divorce Case*, Los Angeles B. Bull. 99 (1970)

Sayre, *Divorce for the Unworthy : Specific Grounds for Divorce* 18 Law and Contem. Prob. 98 (1953)

Sehacht, *Grigins of Muhammadan Jurisprudence* (1950)

Sehoenlaunt,. *No-Fault Divorce : A Practical Approach to the Problem of Marital Failure*, 27 Mo. B.J. 579 (1971)

Schulman, *Incompatibility : A "New Approach" to the Dissolution of Marriage*, 20 U. Kansas L. Rev. 227 (1972)

Seervai, *Constitutional Law of India* (1967)

Singh, Ram, *Matrimonial Property Law Among Hindus*, 6 J. Fam. L. 129.

Staff, *Reconciliation and the Uniform Marriage and Divorce Act*, 18 S.D.L. Rev. 611 (1973)

Steele, *Law and Custom and Customary Law in British India* (1911)

Suckman and Fose, *Ferment in Divorce Legislation*, 12 Fam. L. 515 (1973)

The End of Innocence : Elimination of Fault in California Divorce Law, U.C.L. A.L. Rev. 1806 (1970)

The No Fault Concept : Is this the Final Stage in the Evolution of Divorce ? 47 Notre Dame Lawyer, 959 (1972)

Traynor, *Law and Social Change in a Democratic Society*, U. Ill. L.F. 230 (1967)

Turner, *Retreat From Fault—An English Lawer's View*, 46 Neb. L. Rev. 66 (1967)

Tyalji, *Muslim Law* (1968)

Untying the Knot : The Course and Patterns of Divorce Reform, 57 Cornell L. Rev. 649 (1972)

Uniform Marriage and Divorce Act, 9 ULA 455 (Master ed. 1973)

Vernier, L.. American Family Laws (1932).

Verma, B.R., *Muslim Marriage and Dissolution* (1971)

Virdi, P.K., *The Grounds for Divorce in Hindu and English Law* (1972)

Wadlington, *Divoree Without Fault Without Perjury* 52 Va. Rev. 32 (1966)

Walker, *Disarming the Litigius Man : A Glance at Fault and California's New Divorce Legislation*, 1 Pac. L.J. 182 (1970)

Wels, *New York : The Poor Mens' Reno*, 35 (1950)

Wordswarth, *A History of English Law*, 621 (1956)

Zafar, Unilateral Divorce in Muslim Personal Law in Tahir Mohmood, (ed.) *Islamic Law in Modern India* 167 (1972)

Index